"This book makes an important contribution to intelligence and military history while telling the exciting story of the courageous exploits of Gilbert Insall and his attempts, ultimately successful, to escape from German prison camps during the First World War. It reveals fascinating new details of the ingenuity displayed both by individuals and by intelligence organisations still taking early shape in providing information and practical help to prisoners and their families."

GILL BENNETT, INTELLIGENCE HISTORIAN

"This is not just a fascinating account of an extraordinarily brave man and his determination to return to active duty; it is a groundbreaking account of prisoner of war escapes during the First World War."

MICHAEL SMITH, AUTHOR OF THE SECRETS OF STATION X

"Tony Insall's masterful and eminently readable book is more than a historical account; it offers us all a source of inspiration."

AIR MARSHAL SIR CHRISTOPHER HARPER, FORMER DIRECTOR GENERAL OF THE NATO INTERNATIONAL MILITARY STAFF

THE EXCEPTIONAL ACHIEVEMENTS
OF GILBERT INSALL

THE MADNESS
OF COURAGE

TONY INSALL

FOREWORD BY AIR MARSHAL SIR CHRISTOPHER HARPER

Biteback Publishing

First published in Great Britain in 2025 by
Biteback Publishing Ltd, London
Copyright © Tony Insall 2025

Tony Insall has asserted his right under the Copyright, Designs and Patents Act 1988 to be identified as the author of this work.

ISBN 978-1-78590-868-2

10 9 8 7 6 5 4 3 2 1

A CIP catalogue record for this book is available from the British Library.

Set in Adobe Caslon Pro and Futura

Printed and bound in Great Britain by
CPI Group (UK) Ltd, Croydon CR0 4YY

To my grandfather Jack,
a respected historian of early aviation,
whose work inspired me to write this book

CONTENTS

MAP OF GERMANY IN 1914

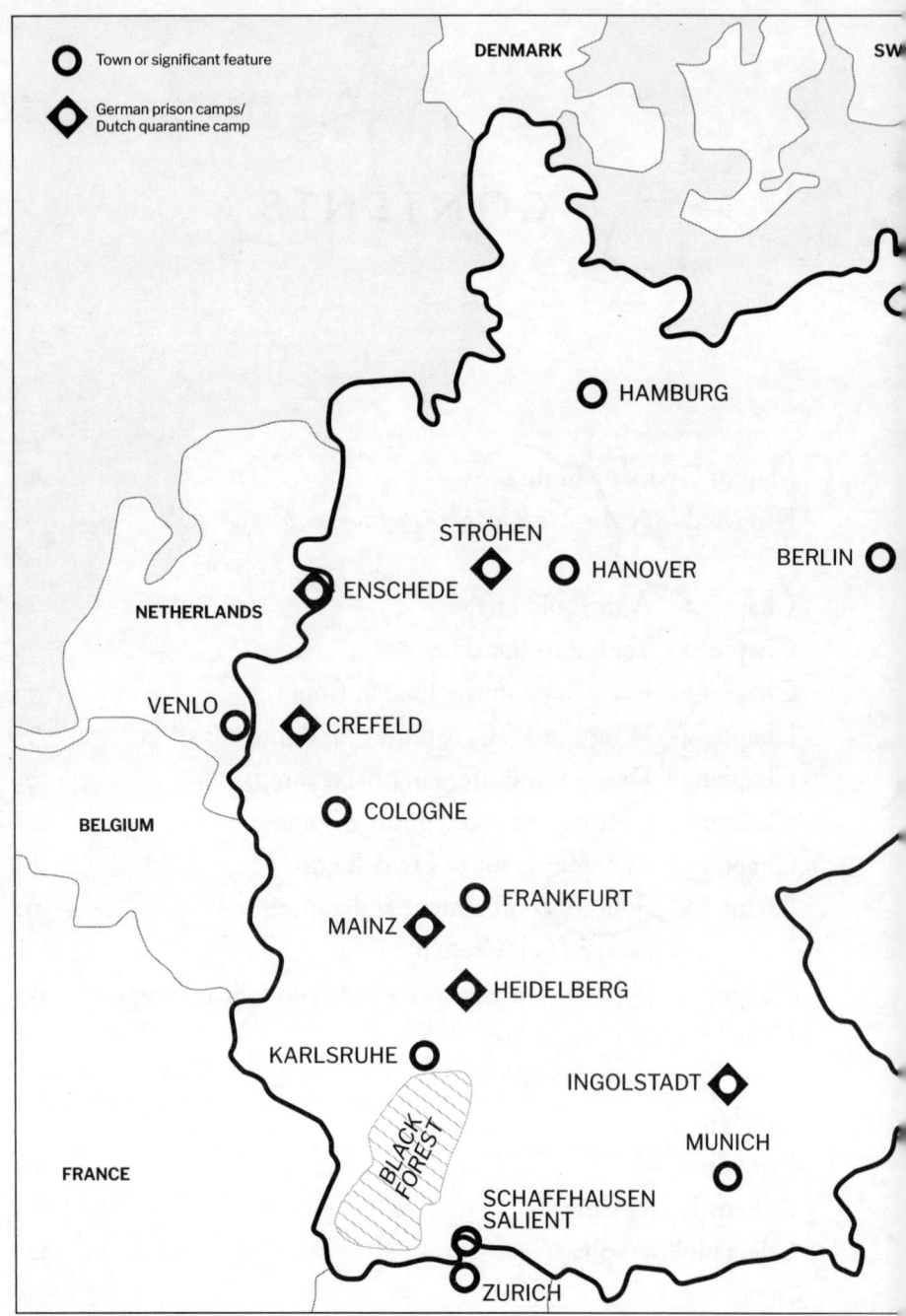

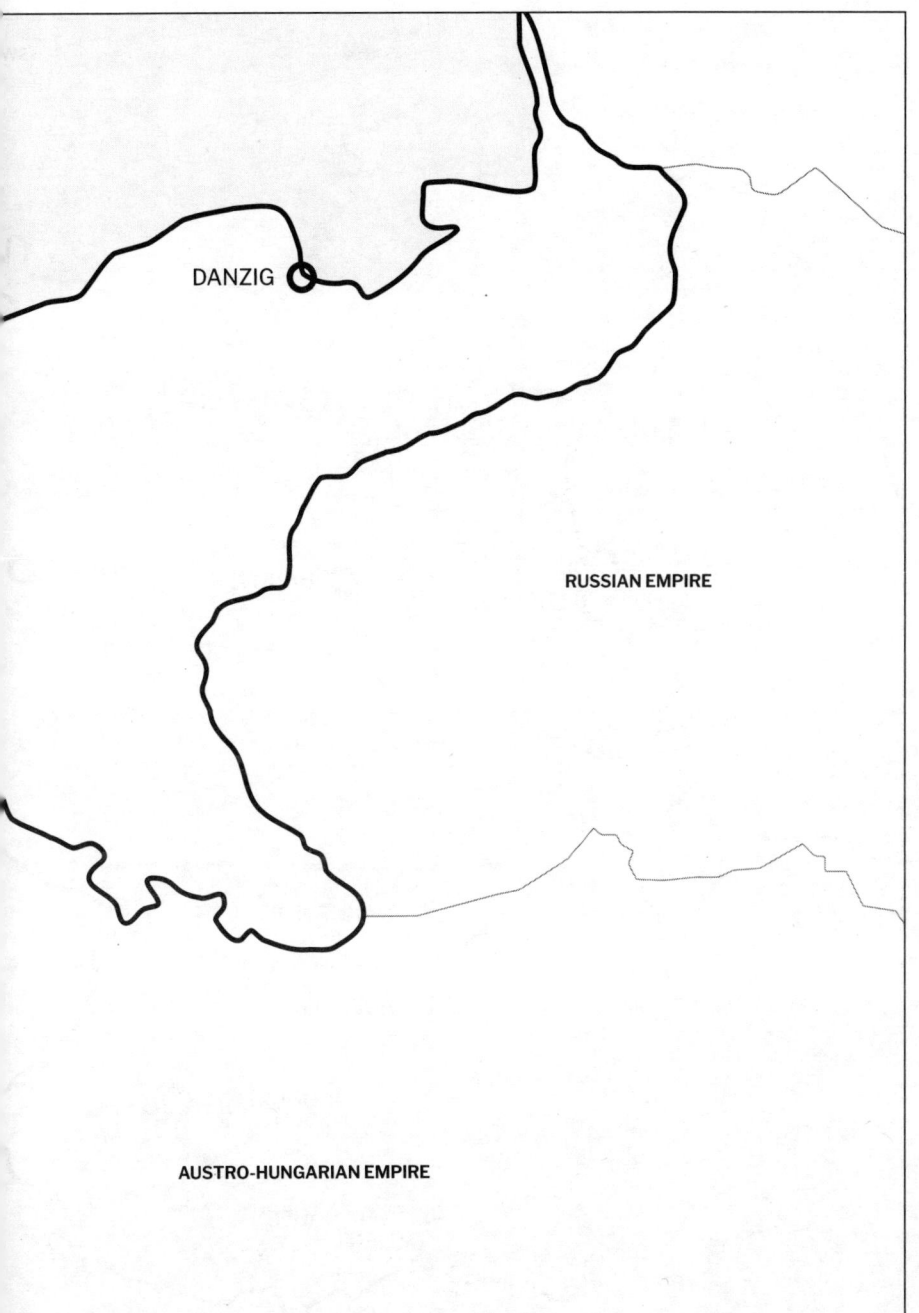

DANZIG

RUSSIAN EMPIRE

AUSTRO-HUNGARIAN EMPIRE

FOREWORD

It is my distinct honour to introduce Tony Insall's book about his great-uncle, Group Captain Gilbert Stuart Martin Insall VC MC. This is a story of unparalleled bravery, talent and seemingly indefatigable determination, and it serves as a timeless inspiration to us all.

Those who have ever had the privilege of serving in the military will know that we still strive to build on the foundations laid by pioneers like Insall. The challenges faced by today's service members have evolved considerably, and the technology associated with warfighting would probably be unrecognisable to him. However, the core values of courage, integrity and excellence associated with military service remain unchanged.

Insall's journey began in the nascent days of aviation, a period marked by both innovation and peril. His actions during the First World War, particularly on that remarkable day in November 1915, exemplify incredible levels of bravery and determination. He engaged an enemy aircraft, forced it down and then, with his own machine damaged and out of fuel, landed between trenches on the front line. Enduring constant bombardment, he supervised the repair of his aircraft under the cover of darkness so that he could fly it home the following day. This is not just a tale of derring-do; the heroism demonstrated by Insall earned him the Victoria Cross (VC), the United Kingdom's highest military decoration awarded for valour in the face of the enemy.

But Insall's bravery did not end there. Captured later in the war, he was held as a prisoner of war in a succession of prison camps. He tunnelled out of Heidelberg, and then concealed himself on a horse-drawn cart to get away from Crefeld. After concealing himself in a cramped space under a washroom floor, his daring escape from Ströhen on his third attempt in August 1917 and subsequent return to service further underscored his resilience and unwavering commitment to duty. For his persistent efforts to escape, he was awarded the Military Cross (MC). Remaining in the Royal Air Force and rising to the rank of group captain, Insall's career spanned both World Wars. As you will read, his legacy is not just in the medals he earned but in the example that his life story sets for future generations.

I would also contend that Insall's VC and MC each represent a different aspect of valour. Pursuing and shooting down an enemy aircraft, in the most challenging of conditions, is arguably 'hot-blooded' courage; it demands skill and immediate, decisive action while under fire. Planning and executing an escape from a prisoner of war camp, on the other hand, requires patience, ingenuity, guile and an unwavering will to overcome prolonged adversity. Both forms of bravery are, however, rooted in the same fundamental qualities: mettle, grit, resilience and steadfast commitment to duty. The title of this book is *The Madness of Courage*. Mischievously, I cannot help but wonder whether some form of 'madness' is, indeed, also a prerequisite?

During my own career, I had the privilege of commanding No. 41(F) Squadron, flying the Jaguar aircraft; later I also commanded the Jaguar force at RAF Coltishall, and No. 1 Group. I participated in active operations over Bosnia–Herzegovina and northern Iraq and served in senior NATO appointments, including as the UK Military Representative to NATO and Director General of NATO's International Military Staff. These experiences certainly reinforced my belief in the enduring values of honesty, integrity and excellence that Gilbert Insall so vividly embodied.

That said, while flying a Jaguar on operations over northern Iraq, I experienced being shot at – but not hit – by hostile anti-aircraft artillery. Without making light of the encounter, I cannot imagine that seeing soundless expanding black cotton wool balls within 100 metres of a pressurised, air-conditioned cockpit was anything like the sensation of being under fire while in the freezing cold environment of an open-cockpit Vickers Gunbus. Nonetheless, modern-day acts of valour, such as those displayed daily by our military personnel in current conflicts, do echo the bravery of Insall and his contemporaries. Whether it is flying missions over hostile territory, coordinating evacuations in genuinely perilous circumstances, conducting rescue missions on land or at sea or delivering humanitarian aid to conflict zones, we should all be grateful that their spirit of patriotism, service and sacrifice stays constant.

Quite rightly, a full account of the actions that led to Gilbert Insall's being awarded the Victoria Cross is displayed on a history board in the entrance to No. XI(F) Squadron – which now flies Typhoon aircraft – at RAF Coningsby in Lincolnshire. But this story now deserves to be told far more widely. Tony Insall's masterful and eminently readable book is more than a historical account; it offers us all a source of inspiration. It reminds us that the qualities that mark out greatness – bravery, skill, determination and a relentless pursuit of excellence – are timeless. As you read about Gilbert Insall's remarkable accomplishments, I hope that you will be inspired to reach new heights in your own endeavours, in whatever course of life you have chosen.

Sir Christopher Harper KBE MA FRAeS
Air Marshal (Ret'd)

CHAPTER 1

A MAD OLD BUGGER

Group Captain Gilbert Insall, my great-uncle, holds a unique record. He is the only person to have both won a Victoria Cross and escaped successfully from a German prisoner of war camp during the First World War.* Gilbert trained as a pilot and was posted to 11 Squadron in the Royal Flying Corps (RFC), in which my grandfather Jack also served as an observer. Gilbert won his VC in November 1915. He was involved in combat with a German fighter, which he shot down. After descending to a low level to drop a bomb and ensure its destruction, his own engine was damaged and he was obliged to make a forced landing just behind the French front line. Ignoring intensive German shelling, he oversaw repairs to his aircraft overnight and took off – again

---

* Though there were a couple of others who came near to qualifying. Corporal Charles Garforth VC was taken prisoner in October 1914. He escaped three times, once getting almost to the Dutch border before he was recaptured. And if we expand the parameters to include the civilian equivalent of the VC awarded to someone in the First World War but who got away in the Second, then Group Captain Harry 'Wings' Day, well known for his involvement in the Great Escape from Stalag Luft 3 in March 1944 during the Second World War, also deserves a mention. He was awarded the then civilian equivalent of the VC, the Albert Medal, for saving lives on HMS *Britannia* after it had been torpedoed in November 1918, shortly before the end of the war. (He exchanged this for a George Cross in 1971.) Following his recapture after the Great Escape, he was sent to several concentration camps at Sachsenhausen, Flossenburg and then Dachau. In April 1945, he was moved over the Brenner Pass in South Tyrol to Villabassa. He escaped again from there as the Americans approached and this time reached the Allied lines. So his success, like his earlier medal, came right at the end of another war.

under heavy fire – and returned to base the following morning. A few weeks later, after an encounter with another German aircraft in which he was quite badly wounded by anti-aircraft shrapnel, he was shot down and captured.

After three months in hospital, he was sent to a series of prison camps. Once he had recovered from his injury and, later in September 1916, from an operation for acute peritonitis performed without anaesthetic (he was told that this was due to the scarcity of drugs in Germany, which precluded their use for prisoners[1]), he began to plan an escape. All of his attempts required at least some temporary confinement in unpleasantly constricted areas. His first, at Heidelberg, was through a tunnel more than forty yards long, which required the removal and disposal or concealment of some five tons of earth. For the second, from Crefeld,* near Düsseldorf, he and Captain William Morritt hid in a space which had been created among piles of boxes on a cart transporting prisoners' luggage to storage. It was very cramped and Morritt was obliged to kneel on Gilbert's head for much of the journey, before they slipped unobtrusively off the cart and attempted to get away from the area. After being transferred to Ströhen, Gilbert and several companions concealed themselves in a claustrophobically small space they had excavated under the floor of the bathhouse (which was just outside the camp perimeter) and remained there for seventeen hours, enduring the heat of a summer's day while a fruitless search for them was carried out. They eventually emerged early the following morning and reached Holland a few days later in September 1917.

But this is not just a story about Gilbert, for he could not have

---

* Now known as Krefeld but spelled as Crefeld until 1925. This was the spelling used by prisoners of war at that time.

managed to plan and execute his escapes without assistance from
his family, then based in Paris. In the first years of conflict, the War
Office provided no assistance or advice to servicemen to help them
prepare for the consequences of capture. And, before the beginning
of 1917, there was no British organisation to provide escaping equipment or advice either. So, prisoners wanting to escape had no official
support. Fortunately, in some cases, families were able to provide
help. My family played a significant role and found some clever ways
of helping Gilbert once they managed to work out ways of communicating safely with each other without attracting the attention of
German censors. They were able to provide nearly all the escaping
equipment which he required, mainly maps, files and compasses –
though also, remarkably and with French assistance, a large pair of
wire cutters, which were successfully smuggled in to him. But that
was not all. Gilbert's father (another Gilbert, so hereafter called
Gilbert senior) was also active in lobbying officialdom on his behalf
and in raising public awareness about some of the harsh conditions
in which prisoners were held and how they were being punished.
For example, when Gilbert was sentenced to five months in solitary confinement (in a cell measuring nine feet by six feet, with
restricted light), Gilbert senior drew attention to it by writing to *The
Times*. His complaint attracted plenty of attention and sympathetic
comment. Gilbert senior also arranged for questions to be asked in
Parliament and wrote repeatedly to the Foreign Office Prisoners of
War Department. This encouraged others to do the same. It was
against this background that the government decided to negotiate
with Germany over changes to the treatment of prisoners, leading
to the Hague Agreement of July 1917, whereby such extreme punishments were discontinued. As a result, Gilbert was spared having to

serve most of the five-month sentence in solitary he had received for his escape from Heidelberg. There were a few other improvements too which made life as a prisoner a little more tolerable.

Conditions in German prison camps during the First World War were different from those in the Second, not least because the Geneva Convention had not by then been signed. (Though that certainly did not prevent the harsh treatment of, as well as some serious crimes being committed against, prisoners during the Second World War.) Two Hague Conventions were negotiated in 1899 and 1907, but they were not effective and both sides tended to interpret or violate them as they saw fit – for example, over the use of gas as a chemical weapon. But there's no doubt that conditions in German camps were considerably worse than those in the UK. The American Deputy Red Cross Commissioner to Switzerland, Carl Dennett, wrote of the treatment of Allied prisoners of war (PoWs): 'Germany ... notoriously failed even to provide them with the necessities of life, and it is a fact beyond dispute that the ravages of disease, including tuberculosis, due to malnutrition, and even starvation, have killed tens of thousands of prisoners in the hands of the German military forces.'[2]

Prisoners were given poor and inadequate food, and all but officers were required to work, sometimes in agriculture but also in salt and coal mines and similar places in appalling conditions – and sometimes dangerously close to the front lines. Overall, 11,147 British prisoners are officially listed as having died in captivity, but the real figure is estimated to be significantly more than that.[3] French figures were higher still.

Gradually, towards the end of the war, the War Office began to realise the advantages which could be gained from helping prisoners

to escape – not just in terms of the disruption which escaping prisoners could cause to their German captors but also in securing the
return of trained, skilled fighting manpower. There could also be
propaganda value, too. The main British intelligence organisations
of that period – GHQ1b and MI1c (which later became known as
the Secret Intelligence Service, SIS, or MI6) both began at the end
of 1916 to develop sections which concentrated on helping prisoners
of war. (As will be described in Chapter 8, the French had already
started to do so, with some effect, rather earlier.) MI1a also played
a role, though it was more analytical than operational. My family,
and in particular my grandfather Jack, developed contacts with
these organisations and exchanged information with them about
escaping activities. However, family links with Gilbert were so well
developed that they were in a position to decline an offer of assistance from MI1c in July 1917, a few weeks before Gilbert succeeded
in getting out of Ströhen. They had a very productive relationship
with the French intelligence service as well. Indeed, it was actually
the French who gave them the most practical assistance.

Very little is known about the work of these escape sections.
Few documents have survived. In 1919, the War Office instructed
officers in the Intelligence Corps to burn nearly all their files. The
papers which survived that weeding were mostly destroyed in the
Blitz.[4] However, it has been possible to discover hitherto unpublished material about some of the early activities of these sections,
as well as my family's links with them. The British organisations
were operating on a fairly small scale and, since they only began
their work in the later part of the war, did not have much opportunity to achieve significant results. Nonetheless, some of those
who had been in MI1a or who had successfully escaped played a

significant role[*] when a reconstituted MI1a was in the late autumn of 1939 renamed and turned into what became the much larger, better-known and considerably more effective organisation MI9.[5] It is estimated that some 23,000 prisoners of war, assisted by MI9 and its American counterpart MIS-X, managed to escape successfully during the Second World War. This was admittedly from a much larger number of conflict zones.[6] When attempting a comparison between the two wars, it is difficult to make a reliable estimate of the numbers. However, the War Office calculated that there were some 190,000 British and empire prisoners captured in the First World War – though there were also around another 100,000 who for one reason or another were unregistered. About 570 of them escaped successfully, mainly other ranks, not officers, who were able to abscond from outside working parties relatively easily and thus did not have to solve the problem of how to get out from a well-guarded camp. (Of this total, 420 were British prisoners.) Around fifty of the 570 were officers.[7] Of those, thirty-five – well over half – were from the RFC.[†] How many more might have got out if they had been better supported?[‡]

---

[*] A good example was provided by A. J. Evans, who arranged for maps to be given to prisoners who might be in a position to escape via the Schaffhausen salient on the Swiss–German border, a crossing which he had successfully used himself more than twenty years previously. He had visited it on holiday and confirmed that it could still be used. See Helen Fry, *MI9* (London: Yale University Press, 2020), p. 18. This was, incidentally, the location which Gilbert and his compatriots were aiming for when they escaped from Heidelberg in March 1917.

[†] My grandfather Jack, when working at the Imperial War Museum (IWM) after the First World War, compiled a list of all those RFC, Royal Naval Air Service (RNAS) and RAF officers who escaped successfully, and contacted them to ask whether they would be willing to donate items which they had used during their escapes, to be included in an exhibition he was curating. There were thirty-five names on the list, of whom one (Captain R. J. Tipton) had escaped from Turkey and another (Second Lieutenant G. H. Eastwood) had escaped from Holland, and a third (Captain C. A. Ridley) was really an evader rather than an escaper, for he was never captured, but he provided some material for the exhibition so deserves to be included! (IWM, EN 1/2EXH2/3.) There was at least one other successful escaper whose name was not on the list: Captain Willie Loder-Symonds of the Wiltshire Regiment, who was killed in an accident in May 1916 before the end of the war. So the total was at least thirty-six, of whom thirty-four are known to have escaped from Germany.

[‡] Accurate figures are generally not available for comparison. However, some 2,800 RAF aircrew who failed to return from operational sorties during the Second World War either evaded capture or – more rarely – escaped from captivity. (http://www.rafinfo.org.uk/rafescape/)

There was another consequence of the failure of the War Office to provide guidance to aircrew and troops on dealing with capture, although the extent of the damage it caused is practically impossible to calculate. Files in the French military archives in Vincennes contain reports of valuable intelligence, much of it British, obtained from the interrogations of German aircrew after they had been captured. But it's clear that German interrogations of captured British aircrew were also sometimes remarkably effective. Although many German files did not survive the Second World War, some have been recovered in the course of my research which describe the interrogations of captured British aircrew. These reveal the extent of the information which they divulged, as well as information obtained from documents which they were carrying with them when captured. Some of those reports were obtained from aircrew serving in 11 Squadron, where Gilbert and Jack were posted: they include both Gilbert himself and Thomas Donald, Gilbert's observer. If, overall, the Germans did as well as the British (which the available documents suggest is quite possible), then a lot of information will have been given away. Once escape training began to be provided from early 1917, GHQ1b also started providing briefings and lectures to aircrew on how to behave after capture and what to expect during their interrogation, and we can see that its importance was emphasised even more strongly in MI9 briefings during the Second World War.

What sort of person was my great-uncle Gilbert? I well remember the first time I met him. It was in the mid-1950s, when our lives were more formal and small children were not much included in family gatherings. So I was excited to be allowed for the first time to join the adults when he and my great-aunt Olwen came for lunch. My mother asked how their journey had been from

Yorkshire and Olwen, a rather precise and correct woman, stiffened, looked at Gilbert and said crisply and emphatically, 'Ah, he's a mad old bugger.' She explained that Gilbert preferred to drive in the middle of the road (there were far fewer cars then), liked overtaking and hated being overtaken himself. Gilbert stoically ignored this exchange and just got on with his lunch.

That memory has stayed with me, particularly since I started thinking about researching and writing a book about him. For Olwen's description of Gilbert as a competitive, determined and stubborn driver picks out some of the characteristics necessary for someone to achieve what he did during the war. Two significant achievements which require rather different types of courage. It's a theme which deserves to be considered further. When the Canadian Lieutenant Peter Anderson returned to London after successfully escaping from Germany in October 1915 (thus becoming the only Canadian officer to succeed in getting back to Britain[8]), he was invited to Buckingham Palace to meet George V, who often asked to see such returnees.* The King observed to him that 'he considered the bravery involved in escaping was, if anything, greater than that required on the battlefield, which was usually the product of the heat of the moment'. He added:

> He had heard many interesting experiences related by men who had received the VC but he remarked that nearly all had received this coveted decoration for something they did on the spur of

---

* Not only was Anderson the sole Canadian commissioned officer to have successfully escaped from Germany; he was also, at the age of forty, one of the oldest. (Major Crofton Vandeleur of the Scottish Rifles was actually the oldest at the age of forty-seven.) After the war, Anderson was awarded a bar to his Distinguished Service Order for this escape. The citation stated that it was in recognition of gallant conduct and determination in escaping or attempting to escape from captivity. There were a series of bravery awards, usually an MC, made to escapers, mainly in 1919, though some were backdated as they were not gazetted until 1920. Gilbert was also one of those later awarded an MC for his escape.

the moment; a few minutes, a few hours at the most. But he said, 'You took your life in your hands for days and weeks,' adding, 'I am proud of you.' It was splendid.[9]*

So, to leave the comparative safety of a prison camp and travel through an unknown country where everyone was an enemy, suffering hunger, privation and often extreme physical conditions, demanded not just courage but determination, ingenuity, imagination, guile, good planning and a very large dose of luck. Talking of hunger, when Johnny Evans and Sidney Buckley (both RFC officers) arrived in Switzerland after jumping off a prison train in June 1917, they had both lost three stone on their journey and weighed only seven stone. This was perhaps not surprising: to achieve this, they had walked some 250 miles in eighteen nights.[10] Or of privation: Geoff Greene, a Canadian who spent time in solitary confinement in the cell next to Gilbert's in Crefeld in the spring of 1917, wrote of returning captured prisoners: 'It was sad to see the continuous stream brought back; practically everyone in the last stage of exhaustion from lack of nourishment, cold and lying out night after night in the rain.'[11] Some too were shot, badly beaten or mistreated after their recapture. And as for luck, in October 1917, Lance Wingfield had reached the River Ems, the final barrier to crossing from Germany into Holland, when he was discovered by a sentry. The man was an Alsatian, who hated Germans, and so instead of arresting Wingfield, he took him to a point further down the river and showed him the best crossing site, also providing him with advice on the location of patrols. Wingfield reached Holland

---

* For readers who are interested in pursuing this theme further, I'd recommend *The Anatomy of Courage*, by Lord Moran (London: Robinson, 2007). Moran, who was later Churchill's doctor, served in the trenches with the First Battalion of the Royal Fusiliers from the autumn of 1914 to the spring of 1917. While researching for his book after the war, he also drew on his contacts with pilots in the Royal Air Force.

successfully.[12] And Johnny Evans, whose final and successful escape had included several very close calls where he and Sidney Buckley narrowly avoided being picked up, concluded the account of his various attempts to escape from Germany with the following observation: 'In my opinion, no prisoner of war has ever escaped without more than a fair share of luck, and no one ever will. However hard you try, however skilful you are, luck is an essential element in a successful escape.'[13]

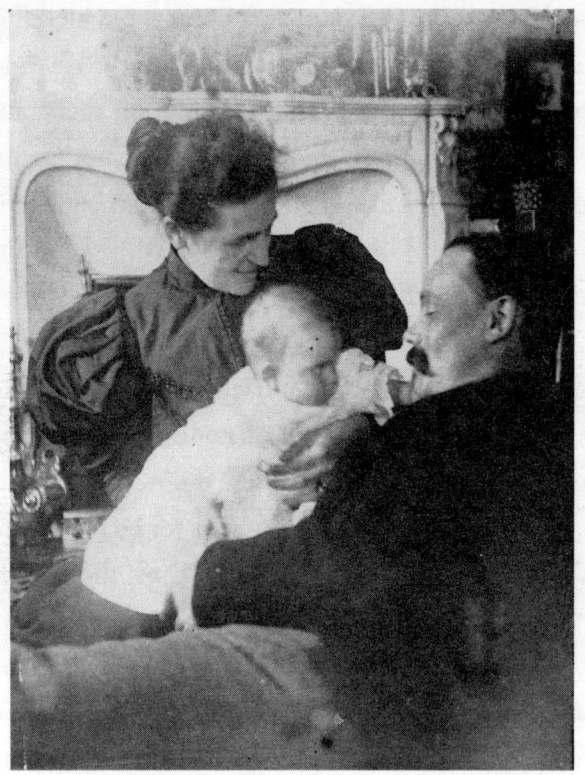

Gilbert aged three months with his father and mother.

Gilbert was born in Paris in June 1894, the eldest son of another Gilbert and Mary. Gilbert senior was a dentist who had been a professor of dentistry at the University of Paris before setting up a successful private practice. Gilbert's younger brother Jack, my grandfather, was born two years later in March 1896. Cecil, the third brother who will also feature in this story, arrived in 1898. Gilbert and Jack both studied at the Anglo-Saxon school in Paris, as did Cecil a little later. All grew up to be bilingual. By a remarkable coincidence, Claude Templer, with whom Gilbert later escaped from Ströhen, was educated there at the same time. (An even more remarkable co-incidence, which happened just after Gilbert had been shot down, will be described in Chapter 4.)

Gilbert (third from right, back row) *and Jack* (seated, extreme right) *at the Anglo-Saxon school in Paris, 1909–10. Claude Templer is believed to be at the back on the extreme left.*

When they were a little older, Gilbert and Jack started to study dentistry, because they had aspirations to take over their father's practice in due course. They were also good at hockey, and in 1913–14, both played for the university in matches against other university teams, in both France and Germany.

Gilbert and Jack were very interested in the early development of aviation, and at weekends used to cycle down to Buc, near Versailles, where Louis Blériot (the first aviator to cross the Channel) and the Farman brothers, Henri and Maurice, were experimenting and developing new machines. Gilbert and Jack helped out, for assistance was usually needed in moving aircraft out of their sheds. They got to know Maurice Farman especially well, and he would sometimes take them up for flights. Both Blériot and the Farman brothers built aircraft which were used by the RFC during the early part of the war. (Some of Gilbert's photographs, taken during these visits, are included in the plate section.)

A rare early photograph of Maurice Farman at the controls of one of his own aircraft, taken by Gilbert, probably in 1912.

In August, when it became apparent that war was about to break out, the Insall family was advised by the British consul to return to England. At that stage, it was not certain whether Britain would fulfil its undertaking to come to the assistance of France if it was attacked. But the situation in France had already started to become volatile. When Germany breached Luxembourg neutrality and invaded it on 2 August 1914, two days before Britain declared war, there were demonstrations in Paris, and Jack and Cecil saw German shops being vandalised. (Though Cecil also commented that there had not been much cordiality shown to Britain either in the period after the Boer War, and that he and his brothers sometimes had stones thrown at them and were abused by young lads when they were on their way to school. That changed following the German invasion of Belgium on 4 August, which led to Britain declaring war the same day. When British troops arrived in France shortly afterwards, they were greeted with a rapturous reception.)

So the family decided to leave. They took a horse-drawn omnibus to the Gare du Nord and caught the last passenger train out of Paris, experiencing chaotic scenes on their journey. By the time they reached Boulogne, a general mobilisation had been declared, so reservists were flocking to join their units, and everyone's papers were being minutely examined. The family eventually boarded the *Maid of Kent* and watched as a ship's officer came up from below, carrying a large blackboard upon which had been chalked a signal just received, stating that as from 11 p.m. the previous day, Britain had been at war with Germany. It was, they heard later, the last non-naval crossing to be made from France to England. After the chaos and disorganisation in Boulogne, they were struck by the contrast, as they approached Folkestone, when they saw holidaymakers strolling up and down the promenade in blazers and flannels, and ladies with their parasols, apparently without a care in the world. This was uncannily similar to an early scene in the film *Oh! What a Lovely War*, which had its premiere just over fifty years later, when the holidaying Smith family are shown entering Brighton's West Pier where General Haig is selling tickets.

The Insall family stayed in Surrey for a few weeks, uncertain what to do next. After the Battle of the Marne in early September, when the German advance towards Paris was halted and turned back, Gilbert senior decided that he would return to Paris to rescue his dental practice as soon as it was practicable. Gilbert and Jack resolved to stay and to enlist in the University and Public Schools Brigade of the Royal Fusiliers. Although it was permitted to sign up at the age of eighteen, you needed to be nineteen to go and fight overseas. This is what Jack wanted to do, as he told the recruiting officer. The latter quietly pointed out that he must therefore have made a mistake on the form which he had just filled out, so he completed another one in which he falsified his age. I sometimes wondered whether this piece of family history was credible, but then I found the evidence in the National Archives – the certificate of attestation which he had completed showed clearly that he was claiming to be just nine months younger than his elder brother, when it should have been twenty-one months![14]

Shortly afterwards, Gilbert and Jack paraded in Hyde Park and were then transported down to Surrey, where they spent the next six months doing a great deal of rather tedious drilling and route-marching. In March 1915, they were informed that the War Office was making an urgent appeal for volunteers to join the Royal Flying Corps and to be trained as pilots. Their platoon commander recalled their involvement in aviation while living in Paris and encouraged them to follow it up, which they did. They applied for an immediate transfer to the military wing of the Royal Flying Corps. Jack described how the adjutant assisted them in completing the form:

Against the heading 'Previous Experience', we wrote the significant entry: 'Close interest in progress of aviation while resident
on the Continent (Paris). Passenger ascents at Buc (Versailles)
with M. Maurice Farman.'

The plural in the word 'ascents' worried me a little, but I gave
way to the considered opinion of our Adjutant, who pointed out
that in effect it was a joint application, and that [with] my brother having two ten-minute flights according to his entry, and I one,
that made three in all and if that was not plural, he didn't know
what was!'[15]

By this time, the RFC had already transferred four squadrons to
France. When Gilbert was subsequently required to complete
further forms in connection with his transfer, he added additional
information to his application, stating that he was fluent in French
and German, that he was accustomed to the use of French maps
and – exaggerating a little further of his experience of aviation –
that he had 'often flown with French pilots around Paris and taken
photographs from machines'.[16]

In the meantime, Gilbert senior returned to Paris with the rest
of his family. Cecil should have gone back to school. However, the
Anglo-Saxon school had been forced to close because many of the
students had left, the English teachers had returned to Britain to
enlist and their French counterparts had also been mobilised. So he
got a job with the Red Cross – first in a hospital which was staffed,
unusually, by a Japanese medical team that had arrived in Paris to
take over its running. He began work there in the mortuary, which,
as a tender sixteen-year-old, he found very difficult. Since he spoke
fluent German, he then acted as an interpreter for his Japanese
colleagues, who knew no other European language. Cecil was later

transferred to the transport section, where he learned to drive and was given much of the responsibility for its organisation. He too had some early aviation experience. He had won a model aeroplane competition in 1911, for which the prize was a flight in a Maurice Farman biplane. He was later also given a ride in a Caudron biplane by a French officer, who subjected him to some fairly violent aerobatics, which he survived without becoming in the least bit airsick.

In the autumn of 1917, when Cecil was just nineteen, the French government suddenly altered the agreement whereby at the age of twenty-one, the sons of foreign nationals who were born in France could adopt either the nationality of their parents or French nationality. The shortage of manpower led them to reduce this age to eighteen and to conscript those foreign nationals who were not already on active service. Unlike the British government, which took a different view, the French declined to recognise the Red Cross as active service, and so Cecil was deprived of his French identity papers and was called up. He wanted to join the British forces, much preferring the RFC for family reasons, but could only enlist in the army while he was in Paris. Fortunately, the now liberated Gilbert was in Paris on leave. It was arranged that Cecil would enlist in Paris and would be escorted back to Britain by Gilbert, who would be able to facilitate his transfer into the RFC. After a spell on kite balloons as an observer, Cecil trained as a pilot on airships and spent time on anti-submarine patrols over the English Channel.[17] He had his fair share of excitement, too, for his balloon was nearly brought down when he was flying at a low level near some Royal Navy (RN) destroyers on the track of a German submarine. One of them saw a loose mine floating in the water and enthusiastically opened fire to sink it, without noticing how close Cecil was. Fortunately, he saw the danger in time and ascended just high enough to avoid serious damage when the mine exploded.[18]

Once they got to France in July 1915, as will be described, Gilbert and Jack were to experience similar risks on an almost daily basis.

CHAPTER 2

TAKING TO THE SKIES

The Royal Flying Corps which Gilbert and Jack joined in March 1915 was still in its infancy, for it had only been founded on 13 April 1912. What was the history of aviation up to this point, and how much had it developed and started to be used for military purposes, both in Britain and elsewhere in Europe?

Remarkably, the concept of using flight in some form for aerial reconnaissance had already been in practice for well over a hundred years. The first recorded use of balloons by military forces came in 1794, when the French Committee of Public Safety created the Corps d'Aérostiers. Their balloons were sporadically used for reconnaissance during the French Revolutionary Wars, being first deployed during the Battles of Charleroi and Fleurus in 1794. They were also used for aerial observation during the American Civil War (1861–65) and the Franco-Prussian War (1870–71). The Royal Engineers began experimenting with the first British balloons in 1878 and by the following year had built and were using five of them. This can reasonably be described as the first use of an air force in the British Empire, and similar balloons were later used in military manoeuvres in 1880 and 1882. Balloon detachments took part in campaigns in Bechuanaland* in 1884 and the Sudan in 1885. They were sufficiently valued that a Balloon Section was created as a distinct unit of the Royal Engineers in 1890, and they were used again during the Boer War (1899–1902).[1] In 1903, the Committee on Military Ballooning concluded that aerial observation was essential in time of war. The subsequent development of powered flight after the Wright brothers' first success in the same year gave further food for thought to far-thinking strategists. Thus, Brigadier General David Henderson† wrote as early as 1907:

> The possibilities of reconnaissance have been greatly enhanced by the invention of aeroplanes and dirigible airships, and in the wars of the future there can be no doubt that the use of aircraft will make the acquisition of information, both strategic and tactical, more certain and more easy than in the past. It may be frankly conceded that aerial reconnaissance is, even now in the early stages of its development, the method by which information of any considerable forces of the enemy can be obtained most rapidly, accurately and completely.[2]

As new aircraft began to be developed which were capable of flying further, faster and higher, thought began to be given to extending the role that might be given to them, which could conceivably go beyond reconnaissance to control of the air. However, in July 1910,

---

* Now Botswana.

† Henderson (later Lieutenant General Sir David Henderson KCB KCVO DSO) enjoyed the distinction of being the oldest army officer to qualify as a pilot. Born in 1862, he earned his wings in 1911, at the age of forty-nine, and so was well placed to use his experience to exercise constructive influence over the development of military aviation. Another mature student was Hugh Trenchard (later Marshal of the Royal Air Force Hugh Trenchard, 1st Viscount Trenchard GCB OM GCVO DSO), who qualified at the age of thirty-nine in 1912. Since he was 6ft 3in., he must have found the cramped and exposed cockpits of those early aircraft to be extremely uncomfortable. Trenchard (nicknamed 'Boom' because of his stentorian voice) was – like Henderson – rapidly promoted and became the commander of the Royal Flying Corps in France from 1915 to 1917. He is known as 'The Father of the Royal Air Force' and served twice as the Chief of the Air Staff.

the General Staff decided that, while it could 'not arrest or retard the perhaps unwelcome progress of aerial navigation', it would be a while before it would be necessary to develop aircraft to defend the island.[3] That negative position did not last long. In February 1911, the Royal Engineer Air Battalion was formed, comprising No. 1 Company (Airships) and No. 2 Company (Aircraft), commanded by Colonel Hugh Sykes. The responsibility was assigned to the army because by then it already had considerable experience in building balloons. Moreover, at that time, there was thought to be little possibility of producing an airship which would be capable of accompanying a naval fleet to sea.* It was not entirely clear what roles balloons might have for the army, but it was generally thought that a balloon could be used:

- As a scout for reconnaissance purposes.
- As an offensive weapon to drop explosives, for example on heavily armed troops.
- For carrying raiding parties.

By this time, there was growing evidence of the advantages which could be gained from developing military aviation, as well as the benefits of having a service commanded by officers who had practical flying experience, in a separate branch of the army. The French, who had founded their air force as the Service Aéronautique in 1909 (it did not become an independent military branch until 1934) had been exercising and experimenting with the use of aircraft to deter and force back hostile aircraft encroaching into their territory on

---

* The Admiralty did nonetheless experiment by producing a large rigid airship capable of naval reconnaissance work. It was designated His Majesty's Airship (HMA) No. 1, more commonly known as the *Mayfly*, but after it was badly damaged in an accident during mooring trials in 1911, the project was abandoned.

reconnaissance missions as early as 1910, when during an exercise a Farman intercepted two 'hostile' aircraft and forced them to return to their own base after being 'attacked'.[4] Moreover, in 1911, Hugh Sykes was invited to observe French aerial manoeuvres and took the opportunity to study the technical aspects of French aeroplanes and their capabilities, as well as the organisation and training of the French service.[5]* He also toured northern France, selecting possible landing grounds, which would prove invaluable during the retreat from Mons.† His visit coincided with a directive from Prime Minister Asquith to the Committee of Imperial Defence (CID) to determine what else needed to be done to secure 'an effective aerial service' for the armed forces. A committee was set up which included both Henderson and Sykes as members. Their report was accepted by a technical subcommittee of the CID in February 1912, and with the support of the Admiralty and the War Office, it led to the creation of the Royal Flying Corps two months later, on 13 April 1912. Sykes was appointed to command its Army Wing. During this period, the French position remained pre-eminent and the report which Sykes had produced after his visit there, entitled 'Notes on Aviation in France', 'could be considered one of the important pre-war organisational influences on British aviation'.[6]

A Naval Wing of the RFC was also formed at the same time.

---

* The French (and the Germans) had made significantly more progress than the British in developing aviation during the period before the outbreak of war, and France was the recognised world leader in flying. For example, by the end of 1911, France had issued more than 500 pilot's certificates, compared with just 110 in Britain. When the RFC was first formed, it had an establishment of fewer than 200 personnel and seventeen aircraft, with a further thirty-six on order – but half of these were to come from France, and all would be powered with French engines – a testament to their greater reliability. At this time, the French service possessed over 100 aircraft, and the Germans had a similar number too. During the financial year 1913/14, the resources allocated to expenditure on military aviation amounted to 1.8 per cent in Britain, compared with 2.6 per cent in France and 2.7 per cent in Germany. In August 1914, the five most important aviation records (which included distance, duration, height and speed) were all held by either France or Germany. (Peter Dye, *The Bridge to Airpower: Logistics Support for Royal Flying Corps Operations on the Western Front, 1914–1918* (Annapolis: Naval Institute Press, 2015), pp. 25–6.)

† See Chapter 3.

The Admiralty did not greatly care to have naval aviation subsumed into what was at that time essentially an army corps. Consequently, it developed its own training centre (at Eastchurch, near Sheerness in Kent) and demonstrated the extent of its independence by announcing the creation of the Royal Naval Air Service (RNAS) shortly afterwards. So powerful was the Admiralty then that this action was never challenged. The RNAS was formally recognised on 1 July 1914 and remained under the Admiralty until it was transferred back into the Royal Air Force on its creation on 1 April 1918.

The Admiralty's rather brazen insouciance did have one very beneficial consequence. There were few resources available then for aircraft design and construction. For reasons of economy, the War Office had directed that all aircraft (military and naval) should be built at Farnborough, where the Balloon Factory had expanded and developed to become the Army Aircraft Factory and where Geoffrey de Havilland was the chief designer.* The Admiralty did not care for this and so turned to private enterprise for what it needed. This provided a stimulus for the growth of private firms. Companies like A. V. Roe, Shorts, Sopwith, Airco, Handley Page and Vickers all flourished. They developed and built new aircraft, many of which later made significant contributions to the growth of effective British air power. 'So [the Admiralty] performed a lasting service by encouraging the emergence of a civilian aeroplane and aeroplane engine industry.'[7]

The RFC only possessed a handful of aircraft when it was created in 1912. However, by the beginning of the war, together with the

---

* De Havilland was an aviation pioneer and aerospace engineer. In his early years at Farnborough, he designed, or participated in the design of, a wide variety of prototypes. He later joined Airco, at Hendon. It flourished during the war, producing many thousands of military aircraft. All of those with the prefix DH were designed by him. The de Havilland Aircraft Company he founded produced the Mosquito, which has been considered the most versatile warplane ever built, and his Comet was the first jet airliner to go into production.

RNAS, its establishment had grown to 270 aircraft and 2,073 personnel – and increased thereafter exponentially. As a result, there were 22,171 aircraft and a total strength of 274,494 personnel serving in the RAF by the end of the war.[8]

Acceptance of the value of military aviation was further assisted by the outcome of some military exercises and manoeuvres in September 1912. These were staged around Cambridge and witnessed by King George V with General Foch, the senior French observer, with two opposing forces commanded by Lieutenant Generals Haig and Grierson. Both generals were equipped with aircraft, but Grierson used his force both more astutely and more extensively. He was able to establish the position of Haig's units through aerial reconnaissance and took care to conceal the subsequent movements of his own into positions of decisive advantage. Consequently, he was able to win a clear victory. This provided a powerful lesson in the value of control of the air.

What were these early aircraft like, and how reliable were they to fly? Jack, describing the pre-war visits which he and Gilbert used to make to the airfields outside Paris (where Blériot and the Farman brothers had started to develop their aircraft before Blériot's first Channel crossing in July 1909*), wrote of the basic methods they saw being used. They would watch while Blériot would attach his aircraft (a monoplane with which he was then experimenting) to a spring-balance (normally used to determine the weight of an object, but in this case a crude means of gauging the power which it was generating), tinker with the engine and then start it up:

---

* These days, we take flying for granted, but the conquest of the Channel by aviation was something of a sensation and provided Blériot with instant fame, celebrated on both sides of the Channel. *The Times* commented presciently: 'The conquest of the air changes the fate of nations as the discovery of the New World changed them. It may give vast new opportunities for some and take away old opportunities from others. It will be a curse or a blessing, according to the use which men will make of it.'

Blériot would run the engine slowly for a moment or two, and then open the throttle, and the dust and gravel would rise in a cloud and hurl themselves against the doors of the shed, and Blériot's long, drooping moustaches would stand away from his face like horizontal black horns, as he twisted in his seat to watch the hand of the spring-balance waver and turn.

And when, as now and then happened, the 'pull' gave a satisfying reading on the dial, he would throttle down to a spluttering tick-over, bellow '*ça va!*' and the mechanic would detach the rope fastening the spring-balance to the machine, and away the latter would go, with its pilot's moustaches back to normal, taxiing erratically far away to the right until it was impossible to distinguish detail, and then turning in a slow semicircle. One would see the plume of smoke and dust rising, and hear the engine's distant clatter, and one would wait until the clatter turned to a sort of tattoo and the dust-devil began to move. And then one would see the machine gather speed, and the tail start to rise. As a rule, this would last for about thirty seconds, and then the tail would sink back while the machine continued to advance. Then the tail would rise once more, the body of the monoplane would become horizontal again and the aeroplane would rise clear off the ground three, four or five feet, perhaps even ten. I don't remember it ever getting higher than that and it never, while we were present, remained airborne for longer than four or five seconds, covering a distance of rather less than thirty yards. But it would have been powered flight and ... his mechanic and any onlookers would throw their hands into the air with joy.[9]

Both Blériot and the Farman brothers provided aircraft for the RFC's use during the early stages of the war, when it did not have enough for its needs. Indeed, a Blériot flown by Captain Philip Joubert de la Ferté carried out one of the first aerial reconnaissances in France on 19 August 1914, a fortnight after the outbreak of war. However, Blériots based at wartime airfields did not perform satisfactorily. They could not be kept in suitable conditions and after several nights out in the open, the fabric covering them started to show signs of flabbiness, affecting their speed, rate of climb and manoeuvring capability.* Farman Longhorns and Shorthorns did not have this problem, and Longhorns in particular were used extensively and over a long period, both in combat squadrons and also for training. Longhorns, incidentally, were so called because of a rather curious front-mounted elevator located some six feet in front of the cockpit nacelle. Shorthorns lacked this superstructure. Both Gilbert and Jack were trained on them. So was Arthur Gould Lee, a pilot who joined the RFC in 1916. He wrote subsequently that all these early aircraft were by modern standards as primitive as bows and arrows. Not only were they fragile in construction, with wooden, wire-braced frameworks and wings, covered with doped fabric, but they were rudimentary in their layout and equipment.[10] The quality of design and building techniques were not always of a high standard either, for there were few well-trained designers and much experimentation as the Air Committee† tried to develop aircraft with better performance. Accidents due to structural failure of the airframe – as well as engine problems – were common.

When did aircraft start to be armed, and what sort of weapons did they carry? Some experiments were carried out in 1913 by a section formed by the RFC to consider the use of arms and bombs, 'though

---

* They did, nonetheless, continue to be used until June 1915, for despite their poor performance, the RFC could not afford to dispense with them before then.
† The Air Committee was established to act as an intermediary between the Admiralty and the War Office in matters relating to aviation.

it was actually the RNAS which initially took a greater interest in this subject, conducting ground-breaking experiments and demonstrating that bombs could be dropped successfully from aircraft'.[11] The section assessed what sort of armaments might be both effective and capable of being carried on aeroplanes – and its creation provides evidence that there was at least some expectation of aerial conflict occurring if war broke out. But machine guns were too heavy, and anyway could not be securely mounted. The Lewis light machine gun was used instead. However, a supply shortage meant that the first RFC aerial combats on 25 August 1914 were conducted by pilots and observers using revolvers and rifles. The first aircraft equipped with Lewis guns did not reach France until a month later.[12]

Lewis guns seem to have been particularly susceptible to jamming, usually because imperfect construction sometimes caused misshapen cartridges which did not fit the breech. This could be – and often was – fatal for a crew if it happened in the middle of combat, because they could not defend themselves against enemy aircraft, which during this period were generally capable of greater speed. The problem cost Jack an eye in 1916, when he was examining a piece of faulty ammunition and the round exploded, hitting him in the face. This prevented him from continuing to fly.

What were conditions like for the pilots in these aircraft? Arthur Gould Lee provided a graphic description:

Every aeroplane of the day had an open cockpit, in which one sat swathed in layers of woollen underclothing, fleece-lined leather greatcoats and sheepskin thigh-boots, with which to resist the perishing cold three or four miles up. There was no heating, no oxygen for high flying, no retractable undercarriage, no engine starter, no radio links with air or ground, no brakes to help with landing and taxiing and, most vital of all, no parachutes. And there were no instruments worth the name. But we did carry a hammer to rectify simple machine-gun stoppages![13]

The crew of an FB5, location unknown, showing quite how exposed their positions were.
Source: 11 Squadron

Pusher aircraft – that is aircraft such as the Farman Shorthorns and Longhorns and the Vickers FB5s,* which were all flown by both Gilbert and Jack – had the engine situated behind the cockpit. Vickers FB5s were nicknamed 'Mossies', because they were thought to be so slow that they accumulated moss in the air. They therefore tended to be colder than tractor aircraft, which had the engine in front. One of the 11 Squadron commanding officers (COs), Lieutenant Colonel T. O'B. Hubbard (perhaps predictably nicknamed 'Mother', with whom Jack frequently flew), reckoned that they were the coldest aircraft which he had ever had to fly. He described it as like sitting in a refrigerator, adding that clothing was inadequate

---

* FB stood for fighting biplane.

and crews often froze and sometimes could not get out of their aircraft after they landed. The records of 11 Squadron highlight that many members of aircrews were severely frostbitten as a result during the winter of 1915–16.[14] 'Sidcot' suits, the result of a fortuitous discovery by Sidney Cotton, were not invented until the winter of 1916.* But despite their lack of speed and their lack of comfort, the FB5s were well regarded and proved effective.

Gilbert dressed in flying gear in front of his FB5 in October 1915. The clothing available in those days did not provide adequate protection for aircrew flying at heights up to 10,000 feet, and they often froze, literally.

---

* Cotton was tuning up his engine, dressed in dirty, begrimed overalls, when he and other pilots were ordered to take off and intercept an enemy aircraft. By the time they returned, all were frozen, except Cotton, who felt warm. He had not had time to change and so was still wearing his filthy overalls. On closer inspection, he found that they were saturated with oil and grease, which he concluded had provided an airtight seal which retained his body heat. He asked for leave, went to London and made up a flying suit to his own specifications. This had separate layers of thin fur, airproof silk and a Burberry material, which were combined in a one-piece overall. The overalls he designed also had some other practical features, such as fur patches at neck and cuffs to retain heat and deep pockets to hold maps and avoid the need for pilots to scrabble for them on the floor of their cockpit. He gave an abbreviation of his name to the product, Sidcot suits, which were still widely used during the Second World War. (Ralph Barker, *The Royal Flying Corps in France: From Mons to the Somme* (London: Constable, 1994), p. 170.)

Training in those early days was organised in a fairly haphazard way. There was no established manual to provide guidance for students. Instruction was provided by more experienced pilots with no particular educational skills. By 1915, there were also instructors who were being given a break from operational service on the front. Sometimes their nerves had been affected and they had no particular interest in or enthusiasm for what they were doing. Other instructors just shouted at and mercilessly hectored their nervous pupils.

Aircraft also varied in how easy they were to fly and the degree of friendliness they offered beginners. Some, like the Farman Longhorns, were solid and dependable, while with some of the others, like the early Caudrons, there was practically no difference between stalling speed and full speed, so they had to be flown at full throttle. Others still needed a sensitive touch on the controls, which would often be beyond an understandably clumsy beginner. The consequences of this were far reaching. Estimates of the number of deaths among aircrew in the First World War have varied wildly, but the most credible show that a total of 6,933 airmen were killed while flying. Of these, the number killed in training accidents between 1914 and 1918 was just over two thousand, almost a third of the total.[15] The situation improved considerably in December 1916, when the estimable Robert Smith-Barry was sent to command the School of Flying at Gosport, where he completely reorganised flying training methods and introduced effective training courses for instructors.[*]

---

[*] It is harder to calculate the casualty figures for the Second World War, but the proportion of training and accidental deaths was significantly lower. There were just over 8,000 deaths in training and accidents among the 55,000 deaths in Bomber Command crews, and over 5,000 deaths from similar causes among aircrew serving on Coastal Command and Fighter Command. In total, over 22,000 RAF, Dominion and Allied personnel were killed in flying accidents in the Second World War, out of a total number of around 102,000, i.e. a little over 20 per cent. (I am grateful to Dr Alastair Noble of the Air Historical Branch for these figures.)

Gilbert (third from left), with Stanley Caws on his left, with fellow flying students at Brooklands in the spring of 1915.
Image via Imperial War Museums

For the initial stages of their flying training, Gilbert and Jack were sent down to Brooklands, near Weybridge, where they arrived at the beginning of March 1915. Brooklands had originally been a motor racing track and was requisitioned by the War Office for flying training. It was not at that stage equipped as a military camp, and so Gilbert and Jack were billeted together with other flying students at the Blue Anchor pub* nearby and enjoyed congenial company and some predictably lively evenings. Gilbert and Jack were very close during this period, providing each other with advice and help. One fellow student, a former Canadian Mountie called Stanley Caws, with whom Jack became extremely friendly, christened them the 'Gold Dust Twins'† because they

---

* It still exists today. The pub enjoyed some notoriety not long after the war when the landlord was murdered by his wife's French lover, a crime for which he was later executed.

† This curious nickname was a reference to an all-purpose cleaning agent which was at that time manufactured in North America and later sold in Canada and Britain. Its advertising campaign featured the 'Gold Dust Twins', 'Goldie' and 'Dustie', and during that period the phrase came to describe two talented individuals working closely together for a common goal.

seemed to be almost inseparable.[16]* Two other students who were also there when they arrived were Robert Hughes-Chamberlain and Hugh de Crespigny. Both subsequently served with Gilbert and Jack in II Squadron, and Jack often flew with de Crespigny, as his observer.

Because the Brooklands circuit was quite large, the area was also big enough to accommodate an airfield suitable for training purposes. Though if for any reason a student pilot had to carry out a forced landing not long after he had taken off, Brooklands was probably not the place to do it. One corner of the site accommodated a sewage farm, which was occasionally visited by unfortunate pilots who had neither the altitude nor the speed to be able to manoeuvre sufficiently to avoid it...

The aircraft used at Brooklands at this time were Farman Longhorns and Shorthorns. The first instructors for Gilbert and Jack were two non-commissioned officers (NCOs), Sergeants Rees and Wyatt. Their initial flights must have been something of an experience. Jack wrote that he had the impression of 'sailing along in a large cage, with a high wind pressing on my exposed upper half to the accompaniment of a busy metallic rattling from behind, where the 70 hp stationary Renault engine spun the huge two-bladed Integral propeller almost within reach of my hand'. He added: 'I suppose that I was awed by the thought of being in due course alone at the controls of this huge laced-in contraption of pale-yellow sticks and piano wire, but there was too much afoot for my mind to dwell on this.'[17]

Sergeants Rees and Wyatt gave Gilbert and Jack a relatively helpful introduction to flying, for they were reasonable and fairly

---

* Caws was later killed in combat with several German Fokker fighters, during a duel with Max Immelmann, on 21 September 1915. (Immelmann's own diary records the incident in some detail.) *The Official History of the Royal Canadian Air Force* records that Caws was the first Canadian airman to have been killed during the First World War. (https://www.iwfbf.co.uk/personal-interest-section/to-the-stars-the-incredible-life-of-stanley-winther-caws)

mild-mannered men – unlike quite a few of the other instructors. Though while they were shown what to do, the students were given no explanation of any of the principles on which flight was based and had to work that out for themselves. Another of Jack's early instructors was Sergeant Porter, a former Guardsman, who had a fine parade ground voice, capable of carrying considerable distances. Jack discovered its power on his first attempted take-off, when he started by sharply moving the throttle from the setting for tick-over right up to its limit. This produced full revs almost immediately, as well as a deafening noise and considerable shuddering. He feared that the engine would tear itself out of its mounting. As he quickly moved the throttle back, Porter shouted in a voice likely to have been heard in Weybridge and Byfleet, 'What the bloody hell are you playing at? Do you want to tear the bleedin' thing out of the [unprintable] machine?'[18] Though the effect which that rebuke could have on a nervous novice can be imagined, it did not happen often to them. Other student pilots had far worse experiences. Arthur Gould Lee describes how when waiting to be given his first flight in a Farman, he was picked out of the waiting group of students by the major in command, who took him up to 300 feet and ordered him to take over:

I was petrified. I had no idea what to do. I gazed at the control, a sort of cycle handlebar with looped ends, known as the spectacles, set on a central column. Below was a rudder bar for my feet. I timidly rested my hands on the loops and let my toes gently touch the rudder. For a moment, the plane kept on a straight course, then the right wing started to drop, the looped bar followed, and she began to slip sideways. I was fascinated, waiting for something to happen.

'Straighten her up, you bloody fool!' came a bellow in my ear. Desperately I pressed the bar down further to the right. The right wing dropped steeper and went on dropping.

'What the f---ing hell are you trying to do, you bleeding idiot?' came the bellow.

In a panic, I pushed the handlebar away from me. The Rumpety* dipped her nose indignantly, shuddered, and banked suddenly over. Then the controls were snatched from my feeble hands, and during a full, unbroken minute of bellowing in my ear, I learned what a wonderful flow of expletives a Flying Corps instructor could possess. Then we turned for home and landing. I at once received a flood of vituperation as I had never known before.

I tried to explain that I'd not been given a single lesson, but he wouldn't listen and threatened to have me sent back to my regiment. Then he stalked off. When he was clear, my fellow pupils rolled off their petrol tin seats with laughter, but I was not much amused … I happened to be desperately keen on flying and would have hated to lose my long-coveted chance to become a pilot.[19]

Arthur Gould Lee persisted, achieved his ambition and was posted to France, where he served for eight months at the front, being shot down three times by ground fire and also completing well over 100 patrols on Sopwith Pups and Camels.

To be able to qualify as a pilot, students needed to show a considerable degree of resolve, determination and imagination.

Both Jack and Gilbert felt that their training was going well. But it will seem remarkable to the modern reader that both were invited to take the first part of the Royal Aero Club certificate,

---

* A nickname for this type of Farman.

which qualified them as pilots, barely a week after they had started their training. In Jack's case, this happened after he had completed just four flights with his instructors, and he was invited to take his test on his first solo flight!

The test which he took required him to take off and ascend to a height of some 500 feet and fly round two successive figures of eight. He was then to land, take off again, climb up to the same sort of height and then switch off the engine and touch down in a small prescribed area, about the size of a tennis court, which was marked out with white cloth. He managed this, but his landing was much too heavy and he cracked one of his undercarriage struts, being fortunate not to do any more serious damage. But this was not taken as a serious problem and he was adjudged to have passed. He was awarded an aviator's certificate, No. 1,109, on 12 March 1915.

Gilbert was ordered to take his test two days later. He had a more difficult problem to overcome than a heavy landing, for at the time of his test, he had not mastered the art of making a right-handed banked turn – and he would need to perform two of these if he was to complete the prescribed figures of eight successfully. As Jack detailed in his book *Observer: Memoirs of the RFC, 1915–18*, Gilbert had successfully performed a left-hand banked turn, but by the time he was in a position to do the right-hand one,

> he found himself approaching the slope of St George's Hill from the side, as it were, with no option but to turn away to the right. Unfortunately, by the time this change of direction had become unavoidable, he found himself nearing down upon the private residence of a local bigwig and heading directly for what he recognised as the bathroom window, wherein stood the figure of a young woman.

'It was, I think,' he subsequently told me, 'the maid doing a bit of cleaning. She certainly looked as scared as I was!' He then told me how he had 'tapped his way round on the rudder', trusting the distance away from his observers on the ground to cover up the flatness of his turn, and how he brushed past the open bathroom window with next to nothing to spare, returning to the centre of the aerodrome, where he had executed a full-blooded left-hand turn, fully banked, to everyone's satisfaction.[20*]

Gilbert in uniform and with his newly acquired pilot's wings, just before he was deployed to France in July 1915.

---

* A word of explanation may be helpful here. When an aircraft makes a banked turn, for example to the left, the upper wing generates more lift and increases the rate of turn. The way to correct this is to apply the opposite rudder (in this case the right) and to keep the nose up to make the turn more even and balanced. This would help to avoid skipping and skidding through the turn, which would be quite uncomfortable for the pilot and his passenger. In a balanced turn, the passenger might not even realise that a turn is being made. By 'tapping the rudder' incrementally, Gilbert would have been able to exercise more control over his turn by making it in small stages, but this would have been a fairly painstaking, slow and laborious way to get round a corner. It is not clear why he found it easy to make turns to the left but not to the right. It might have been the gyroscopic effect of the propeller, or the sensitivity of this particular aircraft. The Farman Longhorn had a very long reach to the tail assembly, so it would have been quite sensitive to the controls.

Gilbert's manoeuvres proved to have been at a sufficient distance to fool the examiner, and he was also awarded his aviator's certificate, in his case No. 1,110, on 14 March 1915. It is tempting to speculate that sibling rivalry might have led his younger brother to have a bit of fun about this at Gilbert's expense...

Two incidents from this period provide good examples of quite how difficult and dangerous flying might be. After he had earned his certificate, Jack took the opportunity to fly solo whenever possible. On one occasion, flying at 600 feet, he saw a bank of evening mist drifting in below him and he tried to fly underneath it and land before it reached the airfield. This did not work, and he suddenly found himself in murk with no visibility. He throttled back but forgot to put the nose down and – everything then happened very quickly – he felt the aircraft slipping sideways and downwards at excessive speed. He struggled with the controls, opened the throttle and just managed to bring the nose up to climb away from the ground, barely avoiding the roof of a hangar as he shot past it. He overcompensated and found himself going back downwards at a greater speed than he had ever previously experienced. He just managed to pull up and climbed away at full throttle, recovering to make a safe landing. He later discovered that the instructor had heard the noise of his aircraft, realised that something was seriously amiss and closed the doors of the hangar in which he was holding a class. He did not wish his students to see the accident which he expected was about to happen. Jack was very lucky. He had not been given any guidance on what to do in those circumstances but was fortunately able to react instinctively in a way that coped with the emergency.

A few days later, he was in the mess having breakfast when he fell into conversation with a senior instructor whom he had not previously met. They had a pleasant discussion about some of Jack's early experiences of aviation in France and his meetings with Blériot and Farman as well as some of the other French aeronautical pioneers. Then his companion got up and said that he had a date with a Blériot monoplane, joking that he hoped it would be able to get off the ground without recourse to a spring-balance. Jack lingered over a coffee but was startled by the arrival of the station sergeant major who burst in, beside himself and clearly very distressed. He was eventually able to explain that the Blériot flown by Jack's breakfast companion had some sort of problem shortly after take-off and had sideslipped into the ground. The pilot had not been able to prevent the accident. 'He hadn't a chance,' the sergeant major added. 'The windscreen took him like this across the forehead [he held his hand edge-on, horizontally above his eyes]. It sliced the top of his head off, like the top of an egg... Bloody Blériots.'[21]

All the students were given extra flying that morning.

Not long after that incident, Gilbert and Jack were among a handful of students from Brooklands who on 13 April 1915 were sent to Netheravon, on Salisbury Plain. There they joined No. 8 Reserve Squadron to continue their training, before transferring to the recently formed 11 Squadron, in preparation for their move to France. It was during this period that King George V visited the Central Flying School at Upavon. Six aircraft from 11 Squadron were flown there for an inspection. They later escorted the King as he drove from there to Bulford. However – in an indication of the engine problems which were going to take some time to resolve – only three aircraft completed the journey. The other three had to return home with engine trouble.[22]

CHAPTER 3

EARLY DAYS ON THE FRENCH FRONT

W hat sort of state was the Royal Flying Corps in by the time that 11 Squadron arrived in France in the summer of 1915?

The RFC, just as much as its German opponents, had faced a steep learning curve. Perhaps understandably, neither side could fully anticipate what might be expected of them when war broke out. Not least, how would they get to the front line, wherever that was, and what should they do there? British planning had been helped by the imaginative Colonel Hugh Sykes, who was the RFC's Chief of Staff in France in 1914–15 and later became the second Chief of the Air Staff. Prompted by the deteriorating political situation in Europe, he held what was referred to as a 'concentration camp' at Netheravon in early June 1914, when he organised a series of logistical exercises to test preparations for both mobilisation and some of the tasks which people might be required to take on if war did break out in Europe. He brought together detachments from those RFC squadrons then in existence – all of 2, 3, 4, 5 and 6 Squadrons and some aircraft and crews from 1 and 7 Squadrons too. Unfortunately, and providing an early harbinger of problems to come, while flying down from Montrose, 2 Squadron lost three aircraft in forced landings and another in thick fog while two crew members were killed in a crash. The exercises which the participants undertook practised a wide range of subjects – reconnaissance of areas to search for transport and troops, photography with hand-held cameras and changing landing grounds, as well as motorised transport movements (this at a time when the army was still generally using horse-drawn transport) – while committee meetings were tasked with working out likely personnel and stores requirements. Other exercises also experimented with gunnery, bombing, wireless communication and maintenance. However, aircraft reliability proved to be a problem, and no more than thirty aircraft from the total complement of over fifty available were ever airworthy at one time.[1] The camp and its rehearsals were quite widely publicised and considered to be quite a propaganda success.

On 6 August 1914, two days after the outbreak of war, the Cabinet decided to send a British Expeditionary Force (BEF) to France, which was initially to consist of four infantry divisions and one cavalry division. Embarkation began on 9 August and the BEF was assembled at its concentration point of Maubeuge, some twenty miles south of Mons, by 20 August. The first RFC aircraft to be ordered to France were those of 2, 3, 4 and 5 Squadrons. Between them, they comprised a substantial proportion of the 63-frontline aircraft which the RFC had at its disposal on the outbreak of war. These four squadrons left between 11 and 13 August, barely a week after war had been declared. They assembled near Dover, and preparations for a potentially hazardous crossing of the Channel included the purchase from local suppliers of tyre inner tubes. These were intended to serve as lifebelts for the crews in the event of engine failure causing a landing in the water. If that happened, then the inner tubes were to be inflated by mouth – which in the circumstances would have been an uncomfortably slow process. A further precaution was to instruct pilots that they were not to attempt a Channel crossing until they had climbed to a height of 3,000 feet, thought to be sufficient to allow them to glide far enough to reach dry land in the event of engine failure. Sykes went down to Dover and saw each aircraft off individually.[2] They were then instructed to make for Amiens airfield, before later moving on to their forward base at Maubeuge, alongside the BEF. Although several aircraft were delayed by engine failures, all arrived safely at Amiens. However, on the final leg to Maubeuge, a BE8 (unreliable and generally unpopular with aircrew) stalled and caught fire shortly after take-off, killing both pilot and observer. Another BE8 crashed on the same journey following a control failure, killing the passenger and seriously injuring Robert Smith-Barry, who suffered two broken legs and a smashed kneecap but fortunately recovered sufficiently to return to frontline duties and later to reorganise flying instruction comprehensively.

The logistical tail for this deployment would have made an impressive sight. The prescribed establishment for each squadron in August 1914 consisted of twenty-six lorries and tenders, as well as six motorcycles and six trailers, to transport personnel, equipment and spare parts. The headquarters staff, commanded by Brigadier General Sir David Henderson, needed plenty of support as well. The vehicles used had not been manufactured to military requirements but were a motley collection of requisitioned vehicles, including some which still carried the logos of their previous owners, such as Peek Frean, Stephens Ink, a very large black and green Carter Paterson haulage vehicle and an equally large and colourful green and white Maple's removals pantechnicon.[3]

Unsurprisingly, this curious and eye-catching mixture of transport prompted humorous comments from post-war historians, as well as observations suggesting that the ragtag selection of transport available to the RFC reflected the low priority which it had been given and that it had been obliged to make do with the remnants of what was available. But that does not do justice to what the RFC achieved, at a time when peacetime resources were very limited, as the following explanation of how the problem of securing military transport from private companies had been resolved makes clear:

> The War Office had introduced a novel scheme in 1911, at the urging of the Treasury, under which participating firms could claim a subsidy equal to half the cost of a lorry. This operated on the basis of a grant (£50 towards purchase and £20 per annum for maintenance to agreed standards) paid on the understanding that in an emergency the vehicle could be purchased by the War Office for full-time use. When war was declared, there were over one thousand vehicles registered under the scheme, many of which were destined for the RFC and subsequently appeared in France still sporting their commercial colours, such as No. 5 Squadron's brilliant scarlet lorry, previously operated by Maple's Store, advertising 'HP Sauce – the World's Appetiser'. Not surprisingly, such incongruous sights fostered a belief that the RFC was woefully underprepared for war. In fact, it was evidence of an innovative and pragmatic solution to that perennial problem – matching limited national resources to limitless military needs. The RFC was, in effect, the first fully motorised organisation in the British Army.[4]

The RFC's first reconnaissance flights were carried out just a few days later, on 19 August, by Philip Joubert de la Ferté of 3 Squadron and Gibb Mapplebeck of 4 Squadron. They were hampered by low cloud and poor visibility, but Mapplebeck was able to provide some useful information which showed that a German cavalry detachment in front of the British line was much smaller than had been calculated. Over the next few days, they began to refine their techniques, sending out more and larger sorties which provided valuable details of German troop movements towards the British front line. Their reports were not always acted upon, because at that time the BEF had no structures capable of accepting and exploiting uncorroborated aerial observations. When the French started to pull back their Fifth Army from Mons, the BEF commander, Sir John French, agreed to remain in an exposed position to cover the first stage of their retreat. However, RFC reconnaissance reports soon showed that the BEF was in danger of being outflanked to the west, while the French retreat to the east was exposing its right flank. To ensure that this information was fully appreciated and acted upon immediately, the RFC commander, David Henderson, took the reports to BEF headquarters in person. Historians have commented that 'the air reconnaissance that came back with this information was probably the most fruitful of the whole war'.[5] Though they performed another perhaps equally valuable service shortly afterwards. Following the British retreat from Mons towards the Marne, contact was lost with the German First Army, commanded by General Alexander von Kluck, against which the BEF had been deployed. This caused considerable concern. RFC reconnaissance helped to establish that the First Army was moving across their front to link up with other German armies, which could enable them to attack the French in strength. This manoeuvre left von Kluck's own right flank exposed. French forces commanded by General Joffre attacked along a 100-mile front during the Battle of the Marne, forcing the Germans to retreat. This great strategic victory marked the end of the German sweep into France, as their fast-moving offensive was curtailed, and removed the threat to Paris. Though, as a result of their initiative, the Germans had succeeded in capturing a large part of the industrial north-east of France, which they retained for the next four years – a serious blow to the French manufacturing capacity and its economy. It also marked the beginning of the trench warfare that was to characterise the rest of the war.

The chaos caused by the speed of the German advance meant that RFC squadrons were forced to move back several times in short order to avoid capture by advancing troops, which was not always easy along roads choked with dispirited retreating troops and transport. Logistics became a problem, not least because sometimes they remained in one location for just a single night, for example being forced to leave St Quentin and moving back to La Fère, fifteen miles to the south. On that occasion, short of fuel and forced to fly low by poor weather and driving rain, pilots of 5 Squadron glimpsed below them in the murk the distinctive sight of their scarlet Maple's Store transport lorry, with its distinctive HP Sauce logo, heading towards their new base...[6]

Once lost ground was recovered after the German retreat, the front began to stabilise quite close to where it had started. The RFC began to adapt to a new existence, with reasonably permanent bases and regular patrols over the same areas, so they could become accustomed to the territory which they were charged with reconnoitring. Consequently, squadrons began to develop increasingly close links with the corps commanders in their area, and in November it was recognised that it made sense for them, initially two at a time, to be formed into Wings. (Later, when 11 Squadron arrived, it became a part of the Third Wing.[7])

On 7 September, Sir John French, when writing a report on the retreat from Mons, acknowledged the contribution which had been made by the RFC. He wrote:

> I wish particularly to bring to your Lordship's notice the admirable work done by the Royal Flying Corps under Sir David Henderson. Their skill, energy and perseverance have been beyond all praise. They have furnished me with the most complete and accurate information which has been of incalculable value in the conduct of operations. Fired at constantly by friend and foe,[*] and not hesitating to fly in every kind of weather, they have remained undaunted throughout. Further, by actually fighting in the air, they have succeeded in destroying five of the enemy's machines.[8]

The first successful RFC action occurred on 25 August and involved 5 Squadron, which was based at Le Cateau. A Taube reconnaissance aircraft was seen approaching the airfield. The squadron CO ordered the crew of an Avro 504, Lieutenants C. W. Wilson and C. E. C. Rabagliati, to drive him off. Rabagliati, the observer, was equipped with a Lee–Enfield .303 rifle. He directed Wilson to fly to a position ahead of and just below the Taube, then opened rapid fire with his rifle. The German aircraft descended to the ground

---

[*] Both French and British ground forces were responsible for shooting down RFC aircraft which they had mistakenly thought were German. The problem was largely caused by the fact that the red cross on Union Jacks, which was painted on aircraft to show that they were friendly, was frequently mistaken by gunners and marksmen as German Maltese Crosses – though sometimes too the troops were simply indiscriminate as to their targets. The French suggested that the British should adopt the same circular marking as they themselves used. An understandable national pride prevented this idea from being accepted, but it led to a solution where a roundel replaced the Union Jack, but with the colours in different positions from those used by the French. So the centre was red, then white, with blue on the circumference. (Barker, pp. 51–2.)

and landed behind the Allied front line, and the pilot and his observer escaped into a wood. Wilson considered landing to capture the aircraft but – not sure of his location and therefore which side of the lines he was on – observed what he thought was a German column of troops approaching. After he landed back at his squadron airfield, he learned that the cavalry were British. Meanwhile, another RFC aircraft piloted by Lieutenant Hubert Harvey-Kelly, more confident of his navigation, landed and claimed a plaque from the wreckage, though he later handed it over to Wilson. A few weeks later, Rabagliati received a Mention in Despatches for this achievement.[9]*

Over the next couple of months, warfare became less mobile as the armies established fixed positions and started to entrench themselves. The front line stretched some 450 miles from the English Channel, from the Belgian coast at Nieuwpoort through France to the Swiss border. This meant that cavalry could no longer be used to obtain information about enemy locations. Allied forces, therefore, became dependent on air reconnaissance for their information about German dispositions and troop movements, for both defensive and offensive purposes. The four RFC squadrons were reinforced on 27 August by an RNAS squadron from Eastchurch, which flew to Ostend. Shortly after their arrival, they carried out the first RNAS reconnaissance of the war along the Belgian coast, in support of a Royal Marine brigade. This was also the first air operation carried out by the Royal Navy.[10]

---

* Rabagliati had a colourful career. He later won an MC and an Air Force Cross and finished the war as a Wing Commander. He later joined Lloyd's, working on its Aviation Sub-Committee, and had a parallel career as an amateur racing driver, suffering and surviving a serious head injury while racing at Brooklands. During the Second World War, he served in the Secret Intelligence Service (SIS), working with the Danish and Dutch resistance. (See Mark Ryan, *The Hornet's Sting: The Amazing Untold Story of Britain's Second World War Spy Thomas Sneum* (London: Piatkus, 2009).) His nephew, Wing Commander Alexander Rabagliati, was also a pilot in the RAF in the Second World War, credited with twenty-one victories, before he was shot down and killed in July 1943.

As the front line was stabilised, the RFC found that German aircraft were attacking their reconnaissance flights with increasing frequency in order to prevent them from carrying out their tasks. These missions, either for observation to enable artillery to locate targets which they could not see directly for themselves or to provide the information which was required to create maps, made increasing use of photography. In the face of German attempts to frustrate or discourage their reconnaissance operations, there emerged a growing requirement to protect the aircraft involved – and, of course, to prevent the enemy from conducting the same activities themselves. This led to the development of fighter aircraft and the growth of aerial combat.

It was for this reason that 11 Squadron was designated as the first dedicated fighter squadron.

In those early days, aircraft were far too flimsy for their guns to be mounted on the wings: they needed to be positioned on the fuselage. Furthermore, no means had yet been developed which allowed weapons to be fired through the propeller of a tractor aeroplane, in which the engine was at the front. (Deflector devices and interrupter mechanisms came later.) So two-seater pusher aircraft were used for fighting reconnaissances. The records of 11 Squadron show that the decision that these early fighters 'must be two-seaters arose from the common belief that no pilot would be able to use a gun in the air as well as control his machine'.[11*] The squadron was equipped with the Vickers FB5, which was popularly known as a 'Gunbus', though that was a nickname which was generally disliked by those who had flown in them. The observer sat in front of the pilot, which

---

* Though it continued: 'It was soon evident that the fast and more manoeuvrable single-seater was the correct type of fighter. These fighting scouts first came into prominence when the German Fokker monoplane with the synchronised machine gun appeared in the summer of 1915, and which anticipated the British fighting scouts at about the same time.'

gave him a good field of fire, though the rear positioning of the engine made it vulnerable to attack from behind. Although it was slower than most of the German aircraft then in use, with a maximum speed of 65–70 mph, and took a painfully long time – around half an hour – to climb to its usual operating height of 9,000 feet, it was well armed and manoeuvrable and was treated with respect and caution by German pilots, who were often reluctant to engage with it. They had good reason: one of 11 Squadron's commanding officers, Lieutenant Colonel T. O'B. Hubbard, calculated that when he gave up his command at the end of October 1916, the squadron held the record for the greatest number of German aircraft brought down.

Moreover, the FB5 was easy to fly and had no significant vices to cause problems for unwary pilots. The French 100-horsepower Monosoupape Gnome engine was not initially popular with pilots because it had an alarming rate of failure. Indeed, Jack wrote that it never lived down its reputation for unpredictability and described how a senior staff officer at RFC's headquarters in France, Lieutenant Colonel H. R. M. Brooke-Popham, had written to the War Office to complain that 'a case has recently been brought to my notice where a pilot has had 22 forced landings in 30 flights in a Vickers machine'. However, a considerable improvement followed after some of the squadron engineers were sent to the Gnome works in Paris, where they watched the engines being made and received tuition in their maintenance (though certain parts still broke too often for comfort).[12] It is fair to say, though, that all Allied aircraft (during this early stage of the war, in particular) were prone to engine failure of some kind, and the Monosoupape was no worse than the others – though 11 Squadron claimed to enjoy the reputation of being the only Monosoupape squadron in France which could get the best out of its engines because of the quality of its mechanics at that time under Sergeant Major Littlejohn.[13] And there is plenty of anecdotal evidence to suggest that German aircraft engines were no different either in this respect. As for the weapons it carried when it arrived in France, the Vickers FB5 was equipped with a Lewis gun fixed on a moveable mounting, a specially lightened Lee–Enfield .303 rifle, an RL[*] tube for bombs and, in those early days, a few hand grenades too for good measure. So it was well capable of looking after itself.

Posed photograph of an observer, showing the mounting of his Lewis gun and the number of bracing wires required for the wings.
Source: 11 Squadron

As part of the plan to expand the RFC, it had been agreed in November 1914 that 11 Squadron should be created, and it was formed

---

[*] RL stood for the Royal Laboratory at Woolwich, where there was an ammunition workshop which had been producing armaments since 1695.

out of a nucleus from 7 Squadron, based at Netheravon and becoming a separate unit on 14 February 1915. After they finished their training at Brooklands, Gilbert and Jack were posted together to join it there a month later. The squadron was briefly commanded by Captain U. J. D. Burke, who was succeeded by Major G. W. P. Dawes, an experienced pilot who had served in France with 2 Squadron, which he had later commanded. Dawes was the first army officer to be awarded an aviator's certificate, No. 17, in July 1910.[14] He was also one of the first aviators to be sent to France, where he was posted with 2 Squadron in August 1914 and appointed a flight commander. During the retreat from Mons shortly afterwards, he and his observer Lieutenant W. R. Freeman were forced to land because of engine trouble some distance behind enemy lines. They took cover in a wood and avoided capture by the searching Germans. They also managed to escape German attention, as well as some British shelling which landed uncomfortably close to them, while they crossed the lines (which at this stage were still slightly fluid) and swam the River Aisne to safety, rejoining their squadron three days later.[15]

Jack painted a colourful picture of the impression which Dawes created: 'Slightly knock-kneed, a terror when roused, a master of unholy vernacular, a gay cavalier of outstanding military smartness, an addict of highly polished leather legging, and a devoted commander to those who served him truly.'[16]

The squadron was initially equipped with some Farmans as well as Vickers FB5s. The students started by gaining more experience on the Farmans – the product of Henri, not Maurice, but similar to Farman Shorthorns and generally regarded as reliable and easy to fly. Then they graduated to the Vickers, a handful of which had already been sent to France.

At this stage, the two brothers were moved into separate flights, because it was not thought wise for relations to serve too closely together. However, they shared a bedroom. Jack reckoned that during this period, Gilbert had not just caught him up but overtaken him on the way to achieving their wings, the final stage of their flying qualification. But in May 1915, before that point was reached, Jack had a bad accident. He was coming in to land and touched down slightly short, at a point where the ground fell away. The aircraft hit some ruts left in an unseen cart track which was hidden by grass, and his Farman bounced violently upwards, catapulting him out of his seat and then landing on top of him. Fortunately, he escaped serious injury, apart from a badly wrenched knee, and was given a few days off flying to give him time to recover. When he resumed flying, he found that although his skills were unimpaired, he had completely lost his confidence when it came to landing. He went up again numerous times to try to overcome this problem but without success. Since the squadron was shortly due to deploy to France, it was agreed that the best solution would be for him to abandon his flying training and to become an observer instead.

Observers in Vickers FB5s at this time had multiple roles. They had to provide ballast, to enable the aircraft to be properly balanced, and whenever the aircraft made a forced landing, they had to restart the engine once the aircrew between them had resolved whatever problem had brought them down in the first place and the pilot was back in the cockpit. (This was not always straightforward, and hapless observers were at risk of being left behind if their pilots misinterpreted their signals and started their take-offs before their observers were ready and in a position to get back on board.) Observers were navigators too, which was not an easy task, requiring the manipulation of maps in cold, cramped and very windy conditions and the ability to pinpoint their whereabouts when operating over strange and unfamiliar territory.

Observers also operated the weapons which the Vickers carried. But the Lewis gun at that time only contained forty-seven rounds in a drum, which did not last long – so observers would often be required to change the drum in freezing conditions during combat, when the aircraft would be providing anything but a stable platform, as the pilot manoeuvred to avoid fire from its opponent while seeking to get into an advantageous position to attack the enemy once the observer was ready to open fire again. What's more, of course, even though combat was often carried out at very close range, it was not easy to master the art of deflection shooting and to hit a target when both aircraft were moving in different planes and in different directions.

Jack in the observer's cockpit of his FB5, mounting his Lewis gun.

The observer was also responsible for keeping a look out for approaching hostile aircraft and for reconnaissance of enemy positions. As technology improved, this also included taking photographs and replacing plates frequently in a camera which was initially hand-held over the side of the cockpit and later fixed on the side of the fuselage. Replacement of the plates required considerable dexterity in the best of conditions, let alone those in which the aircraft was usually operating. So there were plenty of skills for Jack to master as an observer.

Jack preparing to test fire his Lewis gun into the ground in front of his aircraft. No health and safety in those days...

In the weeks before their departure, the crews practised cross-country navigation, where possible, across unfamiliar areas. And Jack had quite a few adventures. On one occasion, one of the main interplane struts, between the wings of his Farman, became detached. Jack's pilot therefore had to make an emergency landing, making sure that the field he chose contained no hidden ditches. They landed beside a farm, found that one of the holding pins of the strut had sheared, and in the absence of the farmer, persuaded the farmer's wife to let them rummage through his workshop and modify (with a hammer and a rasp) an old shackle which they used to reattach the dangling strut. On another flight, they decided to practise the procedure for dealing with the engine plugs oiling up, which required landing and some maintenance. Unfortunately, the site which they had selected for their landing turned out to be not the pleasant grass field they had anticipated but – as they found when their wheels sank into it right up to the axles – a water meadow. So, before the aircraft sank any further, Jack had to get out into a couple of feet of water and restart the engine in a great hurry, fortunately with success. They were further tested during other similar escapades.

The squadron left for France on 25 July, once it had acquired a full complement of twelve Vickers FB5s. They flew via St Omer to their first base at Vert Galand.* Eleven aircraft arrived safely, but the story of the accident-prone young man (whom Jack discreetly described as Second Lieutenant Fair A, to distinguish him from another pilot whose surname also started with A but who had a darker complexion) who was piloting the twelfth, deserves to be told in full.

Fair A stepped into the limelight, when the officers of 11 Squadron were ordered to parade in front of their mess at Netheravon, with their personal luggage, for inspection prior to departure. We had been warned that each officer would be limited to a weight of 120lb, and a gasp of amazement went up when Fair A made his appearance shepherding two perspiring batmen, carrying

---

* Probably best translated as 'an older man who actively chases women' or a 'go-getter'. It was a nickname apparently given to King Henry IV of France. Now known as Vert-Galant.

between them a mountainous valise, the like of which we had never seen before. When their load had been deposited, both batmen hurriedly beat a retreat, leaving its owner to face the inevitable music. I have already mentioned that our CO was a holy terror when aroused, so I can leave the reader to imagine the scene that unfolded when Major George Dawes came striding out from his office, snapping out instructions to left and right.

But for the unfortunate Fair A, this was only the start of his run of bad luck. Shortly after we had reached Vert Galand, when still only eleven of our pilots had reported their arrival, a telegram came through to say that Fair A had made a forced landing in a wheat field near Dover and would be late in crossing the Channel. The next day another signal was received to the effect that he had had another forced descent, and that his machine had landed rather heavily in a field of hops. Two days went by before a third message came in, to say that he had made better progress, but had once more been compelled to alight, by engine failure. His location was quoted as being a beet field not far from St Omer. The following morning, we received a final telegram, which read: 'Lieutenant A admitted hospital with fractured leg following further forced landing STOP This time in clover STOP.'[17]*

After the squadron had established itself at Vert Galand on 29 July, it started its operations straight away, carrying out patrols on the Hamel–Gommecourt line that same day. The squadron remained there for two months before moving briefly to Villers-Bretonneux and then Bertangles, where it stayed until the end of 1915. Vert

---

* In his book, Jack avoided naming the unfortunate who became the butt of Major Dawes's wrath, but his unpublished draft reveals that it was Lieutenant Gerald Allen, Second Battalion, Connaught Rangers. (RAF Museum, X007-5266/002.) Allen survived this encounter with Dawes, and the various accidents which followed it, and was later promoted to major in the RFC. (TNA, WO/371/1/57927.)

Galand was one of the sites which had been identified and recommended by Sykes during his reconnaissance in 1911. He had
obtained leave of absence and toured the countryside of northern
France and Flanders on a bicycle. Jack elaborated on that as follows:

I was astonished when, one day, I had been asked to sort some
confidential papers in our Squadron office, I came across a copy
of the War Office publication based upon Captain Sykes's detailed survey and discovered that not only the original aerodrome
we were then occupying but those being used by almost all those
other squadrons with which we were familiar on our part of the
front were described in detail in this booklet, which contained
carefully drawn sketches of the landing grounds, together with
accurate particulars of available buildings in the immediate
neighbourhood ... When we came to it in 1915, it was sown with
lush clover, and the whole Squadron had to fall in and march,
and counter-march, and march again, before it became really flat
enough for a Vickers Fighter, with two up and all its warlike
impedimenta to attempt to unstick from it and then clear the
line of trees at the far side, with any reasonable margin to spare.

The difficulty was, of course, to find suitable landing grounds
in the immediate proximity to equally suitable buildings. The establishment authorised for a Royal Flying Corps squadron was
138 other ranks (and nineteen officers) which is quite a lot of
square-footage when one comes to think about it in terms of
farms and their outhouses. And one did not just evict the farmers
and their stock just like that, and hope for the best. Selecting a
suitable landing ground was a complicated exercise.[18]

When they reached France, both the pilots and observers of 11

56

Squadron still had plenty to learn, not just about flying in often quite different climatic conditions and over an unfamiliar landscape but also about tactics and techniques for fighting German aircraft. Robert Hughes-Chamberlain, a former coffee planter who was nicknamed 'Old Nick', 'because he was tall, dark and saturnine',[19] provided a vivid example of the former:

> I was a bit late for going on patrol from Vert Galand, so I hurried to the airfield, put on my stuff, jumped into the machine with my observer and took off. It was already pretty foggy and within an instant I was out of sight of land. [The fog came down to eighty feet.] After climbing up to around a thousand feet, I found myself in blue sky, but the ground below was invisible under a carpet of cotton wool. Everywhere. I continued my ascent up to about 6,000 feet, but by this time I was frightened of getting lost, so I made for the lines and counted the minutes until I thought I had got there. It was about twelve minutes. Then I turned left to go up to the front, because I could see balloons sticking up out of the fog below. I didn't know whether they were our own or German, so I couldn't fire at them.
>
> After a while, I decided that it would be safe to turn left again and go back towards our side of the lines where I could try and find our aerodrome. But on diving down, I hit the fog again at about a thousand feet. I was worried that I might hit Amiens Cathedral, which would be a spiky place to end up, so I pushed her back up into the blue sky. When I reached 5,000 or 6,000 feet again, all my cylinders suddenly stopped firing. That settled it. I reckoned that I had to go down through the fog this time. After fiddling with the controls for a few minutes, the cylinders started up again. But by now, I'd decided that I was going down.

I came out of the fog next to a big wood, which towered up on our left, and nearby I saw a patch of green and thought 'that'll do' and I landed. I didn't have the foggiest idea where I was. It turned out to be a place called Pissy. We got out of the machine, and I told the observer to stay by the Vickers while I went to the nearest telephone. I found one in a cafe about half a mile away. I remembered that I hadn't had any breakfast, but when I put my hand in my pocket, I found that I'd left my wallet behind. After phoning the squadron, I said to the cafe owners, 'I'm very hungry. I have no money, but I'll see that you get paid.' They gave me coffee and everything else and were very courteous. Then I thought about my poor wretched observer, sitting along by the machine with nothing to eat. However, when I got back there, there was a tremendous crowd all around him and the aircraft. And the crowd was bringing all kinds of things for him to consume. So he was having a marvellous time.

Anyway, I'd landed on a strip of clover, which was growing from some very rough and uneven ground. On our right was a cornfield in full sway. So we climbed back into the Vickers and got started. However, our bumping over the uneven ground threw the maps which were in the cockpit up into my face. I couldn't see anything. I must have taken my right foot off the rudder, and we veered off into the cornfield. The corn wrapped itself round the Vickers' skids in such a way that the machine turned over, very slowly and very gently, onto its back. We fell out.

I went back to the telephone and reported what I had done. This annoyed George Dawes, the squadron commander, very much. He came along in the squadron car, and he could produce a blast of language, I can tell you. I said, 'There's a nice little cafe here, where they serve rather good drinks. Why don't you come along? And what's more, I've got no money, so you'll be stuck with the bill!'[20]

*An embarrassed Robert Hughes-Chamberlain standing
sheepishly in front of his overturned aircraft.*

Navigation sometimes proved to be just as much a problem for the Germans as it was for the RFC. In November 1915, Louis Strange and Freddy Small, both lieutenants of 5 Squadron, engaged an Aviatik* on the British side of the lines near St Omer. There was a brief exchange of fire, and the German aircraft stalled but appeared to recover, though it then landed without incident on the British side of the lines. Strange went to inspect his trophy. Though it had been hit a number of times, the Aviatik was essentially undamaged. It appeared that the pilot had come down at this point because he thought that he had reached the safety of German lines. His observer, who was a more senior officer (of the Prussian Guard), was enraged at finding himself taken prisoner. He broke away from

---

* A German reconnaissance aircraft.

his captors and attacked the unfortunate pilot, knocking him down and kicking him viciously before he was restrained and removed by British troops![21] The records suggest that this was an isolated incident...

The 11 Squadron combat reports during the first months after their arrival describe what must have been a frustrating series of experiences for their aircrew as they sought to engage with German aircraft – which initially proved particularly elusive* – and to work out suitable tactics for engaging with them. Almost all their encounters took place over the German side of the lines. Their first attempts to engage in combat took place at long range, over 300 yards, which was too far away for accurate shooting by inexperienced observers. (Most successful combats would take place at a distance of well under 100 yards.) The crews were not familiar with the different aircraft types the Germans were flying – on 11 August, Leonard Tilney and his observer saw what they both identified as an Avro and did not pursue it because they believed it to be friendly.[22] It was only on their return that they discovered that no Avros had been operating that day in the area of their patrol, so it must have been a German aircraft.

Towards the end of August, 11 Squadron was detailed to undertake more active photographic reconnaissance, occasionally well behind the German lines, and also some artillery observation. One aircraft fitted with wireless successfully cooperated with some French heavy artillery, enabling it to bombard some selected German targets. This pattern of a mixture of line patrols and reconnaissances was continued without significant incident during the Battle of Loos in September–October, which marked the largest

---

* For example, despite regular patrolling over a relatively small area, it was more than a month before Jack actually encountered a German aircraft.

British offensive of 1915, mounted together with a major French attack. During that period, 11 Squadron generally kept one aircraft airborne throughout the day, with the last one landing after dark.[23] This would have been no mean feat, for it would have required very precise navigation (with no assistance beyond a map and perhaps a compass) and a requirement for the runways to be adequately illuminated – and for long enough for pilots to be able to recognise them from a distance. That battle marked the first and only occasion during the war when British forces used poison gas. It was not successful, for a sudden change in the wind direction not long after the gas had been released meant that the gas was blown back from the German trenches towards the British front line. Jack, who was flying overhead at the time, watched as this happened. Although they were flying well above the poisonous cloud to begin with, they suddenly flew into a column of it as they were descending on their journey back to base and took in a few lungfuls before they realised what it was. Fortunately, they had not inhaled enough to have an adverse effect.

Crews often found that the German aircraft they were opposing could fly some 10 mph or even 20 mph faster than their Vickers, so could easily outdistance them if they did not wish to engage, which was frequently the case. Both Gilbert and Jack recorded separately several incidents when this happened to them. Gilbert gave a flavour of the frustration he felt and how he and his fellow pilots tried to deal with it:

It soon became clear that it would not be easy to get to close grips with the enemy. The first German machines sighted showed no inclination to contest their ground with the Vickers Fighters and, it being a simple matter for them to check us by pushing their noses down and making off at top speed on their own side of the lines, all sorts of weird and wonderful schemes to entice them across were evolved but without great success. The sight of our Lewis guns, then unstripped,* jutting out in front of our blunt noses, must have earned us a not altogether justified reputation for frightfulness – unjustified, for quite frequently, the Lewis refused to fire when invited or, having opened fire, ceased glumly after the first burst or two. Electrical heating had not yet been introduced, and the draught in the front of the Vickers was appalling, even on a summer's day – and the treatment that the Lewis gun received at the chilled hands of our observers cannot have made things easier for them. One of our number, in spite of this, took his gun down and placing it on his lap, completely reassembled it, while a Fokker monoplane from Bertincourt or thereabouts sat stolidly on our tail, not firing. Probably the Parabellum† was also suffering from one of the many complaints common to machine guns.[24]

Captain 'Pip' Playfair provided a graphic account of what could happen when a Lewis gun jammed when he was on patrol with Lieutenant A. L. Findley as his observer:

When over Buire an LVG‡ was sighted immediately overhead, about 300 feet above us. He opened fire and we replied, firing a drum and a half, when the gun jammed. It took between five and ten minutes to put the gun in working order. During this

---

* It later became the practice to strip Lewis guns of non-essential components in order to make them lighter. Although this was officially frowned upon, it became standard for most crews.
† A 9mm cartridge designed by the German Georg Luger and first used in the Luger pistol in 1902.
‡ Luftverkehrsgesellschaft (LVG) was a German aircraft manufacturer based near Berlin. It provided a large number of aircraft to the German Air Force in the First World War, many of which were two-seaters, used largely for reconnaissance and artillery-spotting purposes.

time, the LVG kept in front of us and fired back and to the side, sometimes coming as close as thirty yards. After about five or ten minutes, he turned back and went behind us. In the meantime, our gun was put right, and looking behind us we saw the LVG coming up behind us again. He was now on the same level as we. We let him come within about fifty yards of us, knowing that he could only fire backwards, and then turned sharply towards him and opened fire. After a drum and a half had been fired at him, a puff of smoke was seen to come from the machine, which immediately turned and dived down. Our machine had a flying wire broken, the propeller split and the planes being hit in several places with one internal bracing wire being cut. We are of the opinion that the machine must have been riddled with bullets as the range was so close and our machine was pointed straight at it so doing away with drift.* The enemy's machine went down at once.[25]

Those early reports contain several other similar descriptions of incidents when the Lewis gun jammed, though fortunately none of them had serious consequences.

Jack had an even more unpleasant experience, a few weeks later in the autumn of 1915, when he was on an operation on the other side of the German lines, and he and his pilot Lieutenant Hugh de Crespigny found that the wind was so strong that it was driving their Vickers back further behind the German lines, when they were at full throttle attempting to go in the other direction. They, together with Gilbert and his observer Thomas Donald, had been

---

* Otherwise described as the need for deflection shooting, or the technique of shooting ahead of a moving target, with the intention of intercepting and hitting the other aircraft at a predicted point.

detailed to act as escorts for another squadron which was going to bomb an airfield.

The wind was already blowing strongly when the two aircraft took off together to protect some BE2c bombers from 4 and 8 Squadrons, which were detailed to attack the airfield of Hervilly, near Cambrai. Jack soon lost sight of Gilbert. At this point, he remembered that Gilbert had told him how he had recently spent some considerable time varnishing the wings and tail of his Vickers and, as a result, calculated that he had added more than five miles an hour to its air speed. So it may not have been surprising that he easily outstripped Jack on the journey behind the German lines. Moreover, at this point, they were also overtaken by the bombers, which were also flying faster than they were. This meant that they were unable to climb above them and provide the protection that was required. They were unable to reach Hervilly by the time that the bombing started and so had to watch from a distance. As they manoeuvred around, Jack realised to his consternation at one stage that they were going backwards. The bombers – and Gilbert – overtook them on their return journey, waving gaily as they went, without realising the problems which he and de Crespigny were experiencing. Jack noticed a couple of Fokker fighters taking off from an undamaged part of the airfield but landing again soon afterwards, presumably because the flying conditions were too difficult for them to make an attack on the Vickers, which at this stage was going backwards at about twenty miles an hour.

From changes in the cloud formations below them, they worked out that the wind was veering and changing direction, and they adapted their course to try to take advantage of it. But there were few gaps in the clouds and for some time they were uncertain as to where they were. They also knew that they were about to run out of petrol, for they had a normal flying time of three hours and had already been airborne for fifteen minutes longer than that. (The tank was not normally filled to capacity, because of the problems which that sometimes caused with the pressure feed system supplying the engine. Fortunately, on this occasion, their tank had inadvertently been overfilled.) They dived into the cloud to gain extra speed, and when they emerged, found themselves crawling slowly over the lines in the right direction and were able to land safely at their own base. It took them some time before they could get out of the aircraft, and when they did so, their legs didn't work and they collapsed on the grass until some mechanics came to help them up.

Jack and de Crespigny received a reminder of how fortunate they had been, and of the fragile nature of the reliability of their aircraft, just four days later. After several flights with other crew, the two of them went out together again on patrol in the same aircraft, Vickers FB5 2876. On this occasion, they had just got as far as their own front lines when the engine failed completely, and they were forced to make an emergency landing in a safe spot just behind them. A good example of the fickleness of fate![26]

Gilbert provided an idea of the sort of tactics developed which gradually began to have some success in attacking German aircraft that were reluctant to become involved in combat. The squadron worked out that if their aircraft turned away from any German fighter which looked as though it might cross over the Allied lines, then once it had done so, they could very gradually and slowly edge round so as to attack it from the east, approaching from the German lines. The price to be paid for this would be that their aircraft would briefly become a target for German anti-aircraft fire, but then they would have a chance to climb unnoticed to a height above the intruding German aircraft. (A photograph, taken by Jack, of some hostile anti-aircraft fire near his Vickers is included in the plate section.) Though, Gilbert admitted ruefully, 'even then, those fish-tailed two-seaters had a knack of scuttling back to their own side of the lines, flying at a pace we found it next to impossible to keep up with'.[27]

There had already been some occasions when pilots had forced down, as opposed to shooting down, German aircraft. But it was Jack who gained the first victory for 11 Squadron, when he shot down an LVG on 5 September 1915. He described it in his first draft of his chapter on 'The War on the Westen Front', which he wrote after the war when working for the Air Ministry Air Historical Branch:

I was hugely, if secretly, elated when, after a succession of incon-clusive scraps all ending in the hostile machine concerned getting away apparently unscathed, I scored my first success on 5 Sep-tember over Le Sars on the Albert Bapaume road. After my pilot H. A. Cooper and I had gone into the CO's office to make out our report, a call came through from the Anti-Aircraft gunners on the line to say that our LVG had been seen to dive into the ground without attempting to flatten out. It was also the squad-ron's first enemy aircraft shot down, although paradoxically, since the hostile machine fell in its own lines, whither we had had to chase him, its destruction, although confirmed by eyewitnesses, was not allowed to count as a certainty.[28]*

RFC communiqué No. 9 provided rather more details[29] of what happened:

---

* This section of the history of 11 Squadron written by Jack was crossed out in the draft and not used in the final version. I assume that the reason was that he did not wish to be accused of sour grapes by complaining about the fact that the first victory of the squadron had been credited to someone else. This particular rule, preventing the claiming of hostile aircraft shot down behind German lines, was subsequently dropped.

Second Lieutenant Cooper (pilot) and Second Lieutenant Insall (observer), in a Vickers fighter, when patrolling near Gommecourt, sighted an LVG at 7,500 feet, they themselves being at 9,000 feet. The Vickers intercepted the LVG and got in front of it and above it. The hostile aeroplane then came straight at the Vickers and passed underneath, opening fire with a machine gun. The LVG then turned so as to get the Vickers on his broadside and dived past it. During this manoeuvre, he was fired on and then assumed a steeper angle (80°). When last seen, smoke and bright yellow flames were seen coming from his exhaust pipe above the engine. The Vickers could not follow, owing to engine failing to pick up. Reports of eyewitnesses to this encounter indicate that the German machine struck the ground while still in a deep dive.[30]

This was also confirmed in a report by Lieutenant Colonel W. S. Brancker, the officer commanding the RFC's III Wing, of which 11 Squadron was a part. He noted that 'the OC* 25th section AA guns appeared positive that the German machine attacked by the Vickers fighter on the previous evening reached the ground in a perpendicular nose dive'.[31]

Gilbert commented afterwards that the exchange of fire between the two aircraft had probably lasted no more than fifteen seconds. Most of the early combats of 11 Squadron were of that kind – short, sharp and swift. Dog fights, or more prolonged engagements, were then unknown, and the only time when aircraft were gathered together in numbers was when bombing raids were carried out, for the bombers would be escorted by a couple of Vickers, with the intention of providing some protection. Though, as Jack's experience

---

* Officer commanding.

illustrates, when his Vickers was severely impeded by strong winds, that did not always happen.

It was actually Lionel Rees, who in early 1915 was posted to command A Flight* of 11 Squadron, for whom Jack had considerable respect, who was subsequently credited with the squadron's first victory when his observer, Sergeant Hargreaves, shot down an Albatros several weeks later on 30 September. Continuing the account of his own success, given above, Jack provided this description:

And that was where Rees scored over Cooper and me for, on the last day of the month, while on patrol over Gommecourt (curiously, this was the point where we, Cooper and I, had sighted out LVG on the 5th), Rees, with Sergeant Hargreaves as gunner, encountered an Albatros two-seater very similar to the LVG and, after Hargreaves had emptied two drums into it in the course of the engagement that followed, the hostile machine went into a tight spiral. It then dived steeply and almost immediately a wing broke off, and the machine fell inside our lines from 5,000 feet, its pilot shot through the head.[32†]

Jack described Rees as 'one of the most accomplished pilots in the RFC, [who] like so many of the Corps' squadron commanders, took part almost daily in the unit's flying duties'. Jack did at least receive a Mention in Despatches for his victory, which was announced several months later and which must have been some consolation.[33‡]

---

* At this stage of the war, an RFC squadron would have three flights, usually of four aircraft each, so that a squadron would consist of twelve aeroplanes.

† Combat reports from 11 Squadron appear to show that both Rees and also Robert Hughes-Chamberlain had brought down German aircraft a little earlier than this in September, though they had also come down on the German side of the lines. (TNA, AIR 1//1219/204/5/2634/6.)

‡ However, the official history of 11 Squadron, written some time later, put this right and credited Jack with the squadron's first victory. (TNA, AIR 1/166/15/150/1.)

Jack at Bertangles on a cold winter's morning in November 1915,
probably taken by Gilbert.

Although by early November there had been some combats between the opposing aerial forces which had led to victories as well
as losses, the lack of what was seen as any consistent German willingness to engage was leading to frustration. Coincidentally, around
the same time, a Fokker monoplane had lost its way and after a
brief engagement was forced down and landed unscathed behind
the British lines near St Omer. It was exhaustively tested to see
how it compared for speed and manoeuvrability against the newly
developed Allied single-seater aircraft, such as the French Morane
Monocoque Scout, which were beginning to come into service. The

Fokker was found to be slower and less manoeuvrable, though it climbed more quickly and was better armed, with a generally reliable interrupter gear which enabled it to fire forwards through the propeller. These two factors and, perhaps, the consideration that because of the distinctive markings on the aircraft of certain German aces such as Manfred von Richthofen and Max Immelmann,* Allied pilots sometimes knew who they were up against, probably contributed to an extraordinary development. On one remarkable occasion, the RFC came close to proposing a duel with one of Germany's most successful fighter pilots.

The air combat reports for 11 Squadron for November 1915 contain a couple of unusual entries:

To: The Officer Commanding
      No. 11 Squadron

With reference to the attached message, the following instructions issued are for your information.

No. 13 Squadron has received orders to drop 6 copies of this message at various points in the German lines as soon as possible: No. 11 Squadron will arrange for an officer to be at the rendezvous daily, weather permitting.

(Sgd.)   B. C. Fellows, Captain
              For G. S. O. 3rd Wing, RFC.

And the attached message read:

---

* Immelmann and Oswald Boelcke, another German ace, both served in Feldflieger Abteilung 62 (the equivalent of 62 Squadron) at La Brayelle, near Douai. They competed with each other to see who could shoot down the most Allied aircraft. They both achieved their eighth victory on 12 January 1916, and were awarded Germany's highest decoration, *Pour le Mérite*. When these were presented to them on the same occasion by the Kaiser, Max received his first. For that reason, the medal came to be known as 'The Blue Max'.

Forwarded for information,
   (Sgd.)

In the Field   B. C. Fellows Captain
13 November 1915.   For O. C. 3rd Wing, RFC.

A British Officer-pilot is anxious to meet the redoubtable Captain Immelmann in fair fight.

The suggested rendezvous is a point above the first line trenches just East of Hébuterne.

The British Officer will be there from 10 a.m. to 11 a.m. daily from 15 November till 30 November, weather permitting.

It is understood that only one aircraft can be sent to meet this challenge, and that no anti-aircraft guns may fire at either combatant.

   Headquarters,
      Royal Flying Corps.[34]

This remarkable idea was the result of a suggestion by the 11 Squadron CO, Major G. W. P. Dawes, to Brancker, who took the idea seriously and put it up to RFC headquarters, who agreed. They referred it to general headquarters. No one expected it to be accepted, but Captain 'Pip' Playfair, with whom Jack often flew, told him a few days later that the CO had told him that he was to be detailed for the duel. Jack often flew with Playfair, as his observer, and hoped that he might be selected to join him. In the event, the message was never dropped – and the duel never took place. The reason for this never became known. But a few days later, an aircraft from another RFC squadron was brought down behind German lines. During their interrogation, the crew was asked which pilot had been selected to take part in the duel.[35] It is not known how the Germans had managed to find out about this plan, but it is another example of the effectiveness of their interrogation techniques. (See Chapter 4.)

That wasn't the only imaginative idea to be put up to RFC Headquarters or General Headquarters during that period which did not ultimately find favour. British airfields were now and then overflown by German aircraft, sometimes to drop messages about British aircrew who had been captured or killed (a courtesy which the RFC also sometimes performed reciprocally) but also to attack and machine-gun their own aeroplanes. A well-known Belgian pilot, Major Willy Coppens de Houthulst DSO MC, described a similar event in his autobiography *Days on the Wing*, when they were unexpectedly strafed.[36] He wrote that the aircraft passed no more than fifty feet away, and it was miraculous that no one was hit. Jack, a fluent French speaker, translated his book. He added a remarkable footnote to Coppens's description of this incident.

In 1915, the translator, then serving in a British 2-seater Fighter Squadron north of the Somme, submitted a scheme for an organised looting raid on a German aerodrome near St Quentin. The operation would infallibly have succeeded, had it been tried. A BE 2c Squadron was to land spare pilots who would have flown a number of the enemy's machines back. Engine-fitters were to be landed to start up the engines of the Aviatiks, and other aeroplanes known to be kept at the aerodrome selected, and those mechanics, and the spare pilots, were to receive training on previously captured specimens of these types. A Vickers Fighter squadron was to land machine-gunners armed with tripod guns, and the German Squadron was to be completely 'written off' – removed by air or burned. Prisoners were to be flown back, handcuffed. Photographs of the German aerodromes were available in the Royal Flying Corps, and a close study of the lay-out of the chosen ground had shown how easy the affair would have been. On a bad flying morning, the whole German squadron would have been present on the ground, and nothing could have prevented an overwhelming success. Retaliatory raids were to be provided against for several weeks thereafter, but it was essentially an operation to be conducted once, and once only. Alas, it was never tried![37]

This proposal contained the germ of a good idea, but there were probably too many unpredictable factors and risks to make it an attractive proposition for RFC headquarters to consider favourably. Had it been carried out, it would probably have been remembered as the first British special operation of the First World War, for the British did not develop any specialised force for this purpose until the Special Operations Executive (SOE) was created in July 1940. SOE found a use for Jack's fertile imagination, after he had initially been seconded from the Imperial War Museum (IWM) to work for Section D of SIS in September 1939, in a section creating black propaganda* for dissemination to neutral countries.[38] His work there will be described in more detail in the Epilogue.

---

* Black propaganda is a form of propaganda intended to create the impression that it was created by those it is supposed to discredit.

CHAPTER 4

WINNING A VC, CAPTURE – AND INTERROGATION

The events which led to Gilbert, then aged twenty-one, being awarded his VC took place on 7–8 November 1915. He and his observer Thomas Donald took off in his Vickers FB5 No. 5704 from Bertangles in the early afternoon on what his combat report[1] described as a Special Army Patrol (which was in support of an operation being carried out by another squadron near Bapaume). He climbed slowly to 7,000 feet. As they crossed the lines, he spotted a German kite balloon in the air some distance behind the German front and descended to attack it. His intention was to drop an incendiary bomb. (The bombs they carried were specially equipped with several triple pike hooks,[*] designed to enable them to catch on to the balloons. They could be launched through a tube.) However, Gilbert's position in the cockpit meant that the balloon was shielded from sight by part of the fuselage during the later part of his approach. By the time he saw it again, he realised that he

---

[*] A triple pike hook is a fishing hook with three hooks held together at 120 degrees from each other. In this case, they would have been considerably larger than fishing hooks, to try to ensure that the bomb lodged on the balloon skin in a way which would provide the maximum explosive impact.

was now out of position for an attack – not least because an anti-aircraft battery which was located near the balloon winch had already opened fire on him. He decided that it was not feasible to make another attempt.

Gilbert, therefore, climbed back up to 7,000 feet, his usual patrolling height. Before he reached that level, he sighted a German two-seater aircraft, which he identified as an Aviatik,* coming from a northerly direction and flying south and parallel to the trenches. It was about a thousand feet higher than he was. It was also flying faster – at that time, it was estimated to be capable of 80 mph. Gilbert, therefore, decided to turn back towards the lines and to get himself into a position where Donald could engage at fairly long range, by using his Lee–Enfield rifle so as to attract the crew's attention. He achieved that, because the Aviatik flew away towards the south-east. Gilbert steered south himself and engaged it again over Achiet, causing the German to increase speed and head in the opposite direction. Both aircraft then became involved in an intricate series of manoeuvres, as each tried to gain an advantageous position from which to attack the other. When this didn't turn out as he hoped, Gilbert steered away sufficiently to give the impression that he was not intending to continue to engage his opponent any further – an action which would have required him to fly further over the German side of the lines.[2]

The pilot of the Aviatik was lulled into a false sense of security by this move and turned to follow Gilbert on the assumption that he might not be seen to do so. When the German's approach brought

---

* It is not known what particular type of Aviatik this was, though it was likely to have been a variant of an Aviatik C or possibly a BII. Gilbert observed in his combat report that its 'wings were not swept back' and that it was armed with a machine gun. Incidentally, it was a type of Aviatik which was the first aircraft to be reported shot down with gunfire in aerial combat on 5 October 1914, by a French Voisin III.

him sufficiently close to the Vickers, Gilbert, who all the while had been climbing and was therefore at approximately the same height as his adversary, turned to engage him. The distance was short enough that Donald was able to use his Lewis machine gun (which had a similar calibre to the Lee–Enfield). The Aviatik immediately turned and dived away, heading in the direction of what Gilbert believed to be a rocket battery,* which was located near the kite balloon winch. However, Gilbert was able to frustrate him by cutting him off. At this point, both aircraft were diving almost vertically at a rate which was well above their normal diving speed. (In his combat report, Gilbert estimated it to be 90 mph.) Neither let up, and both aircraft were firing at each other. At this point, the Aviatik's engine stopped. Donald had to cease firing temporarily as they went through a layer of cloud, giving him the opportunity to change the drum on the Lewis gun. When they came out of the cloud, he resumed, and the Aviatik landed quite heavily in a ploughed field, west of Héninel.

The crew got out, carrying with them their machine gun. Gilbert assumed their intention was to fire back at him, as he had by then descended to a height of 500 feet. Donald fired a burst towards them, which discouraged this idea, and instead they made off towards some shelter. One of the crew was being assisted by the other, so had presumably been wounded by Donald's fire.

---

* This might have been a misidentification. RFC pilots quite frequently believed that they had been the target of fire from rocket batteries. Some doubt has been expressed about whether batteries of this nature existed at that stage. There certainly were attempts made to develop incendiary rockets for anti-aircraft purposes. These rockets were designed to carry incendiary materials aloft and ignite enemy aircraft. However, they were pretty basic and not particularly effective. But whatever they were, the batteries fired projectiles which were treated with considerable respect by Allied pilots – and even fireworks going off near a balloon would have caused problems to attacking pilots. Gilbert flew low over what he identified as another battery, when he was shot down the following month.

Artist's impression of the incident leading up to Gilbert winning his VC, a double-page magazine spread published in January 1916, shortly after Gilbert's VC was gazetted.
Source: Illustrated London News

Intent on destroying the Aviatik, Gilbert turned and dived lower. This gave Donald the opportunity to drop an incendiary bomb (one of those originally intended for use against the kite balloon), which left the aircraft wreathed in smoke. Their low-level activity had attracted plenty of attention on the ground, and concentrations of troops opened heavy fire on the Vickers. Even if they had had sufficient fuel to permit an ascent to a safer height before crossing the lines, Gilbert and Donald would have become an easy target not only to machine-gun and rifle fire but also to local anti-aircraft batteries, since they would have been climbing painfully slowly. Gilbert, therefore, decided to return at low altitude.

In an account written subsequently, Gilbert described what happened next:

As our speed was only 60–65 mph, we flew back about tree-top height, low strafing* all the way, and being fired at by every German weapon. Everything they had came up, and Donald sent all he had down. I tried to make the Vickers jink like a woodcock and just short of 'no man's land', I turned hard to port to be crosswind with maximum drift.† Halfway over, the engine cut out and I glided over a copse near Agny and pancaked‡ between two lines of trenches.

Frenchmen popped up and dragged us into a deep dug out. They entertained us as the shelling started and opened with a bottle of wine. We refreshed ourselves and listened to the running commentary of the regimental priest, who stood at the steps and reported the results of the shellfire. After some time, we were able to make a survey and examine the aircraft and found that the petrol tank was badly holed.³

The German shelling of the Vickers was assisted by a reconnaissance aircraft which had been sent over to act as a spotter and adjust range and direction for the gunners. However, even with this assistance and although around 150 shells were fired in the course of the afternoon and the evening, none caused any further damage. The French arranged for Gilbert to telephone back to the squadron

---

* A term used to describe the raking of ground troops or other targets (perhaps an airfield) with fire at close range, usually with machine-gun fire, from low-flying aircraft. The verb 'to strafe' came indirectly from the German 'Gott strafe England', meaning 'May God punish England', and was an anti-British slogan used by the German Army during the First World War. The term was humorously adopted by RFC pilots, who coined the term 'Zepp-strafing' to describe flights which they made for the purpose of attacking Zeppelin airships, and it gradually acquired wider usage.

† By this, he meant using the wind to push the aircraft sideways and help it to avoid ground fire. For a lightweight and low-speed aircraft like the Vickers FB5, it would have had quite a significant effect − particularly if the wind was fairly strong − which it presumably was in this case, otherwise Gilbert would not have undertaken the manoeuvre. It is now generally called a 'sideslip' and is most commonly used if landing in a cross wind, when, by steering across it, the pilot allows the wind to bring the aircraft back to align with the runway.

‡ Gilbert was already losing speed and would have adjusted the controls to bring the aircraft very close to stalling speed. As a result, the aircraft would have come down almost vertically, rather than going in a forward direction. It would, therefore, land flat, like a 'pancake' − though nowadays it also means landing with the undercarriage retracted.

office and report what had happened to Dawes, his commanding officer, who was some twenty-five miles away at Bertangles, 11 Squadron's base. He requested that Dawes organise the despatch of a replacement petrol tank, some suitably equipped mechanics and also a tarpaulin that could be used under Gilbert's supervision to erect a screen to facilitate repair work during the night without their being seen. As a further precaution against another round of shelling, the aircraft was moved some distance after dark to a new location. Gilbert also requested that French soldiers be deployed to fill in as best they could the shell holes close to his Vickers, which had been caused by the earlier intensive bombardment and were on his intended direction of take-off.

As dawn broke, he made another examination of the engine and discovered that two further rifle rounds had hit it. Fortunately, neither of them had caused any real damage, though one of them had bent an exhaust-valve tappet-rod, which, he later told his brother Jack sardonically, he did 'not consider to be in the best of taste'.[4] His own account continued: 'By dawn, all was ready, sandbags were in place on the gunner's seat and all the shell holes levelled up in front. I told them that I would take off immediately if the engine produced sufficient revolutions and they held up the tail to speed the take-off.' He had decided that the risks of taking off in these circumstances were such that he did not wish to be accompanied by Donald, his observer, as there was a high risk of crashing on take-off or being shot down by German small arms fire, as they could be an easy target at low level. So, in order to ensure that the weight was correctly distributed, he substituted sandbags instead.

However, in an anti-climactic moment, he found that the new tank did not maintain its air pressure. Further work was necessary to locate and seal off the leak. When he tried again, he found almost straight away, to his relief, 'that the engine ran like a bird'. So he decided to take off immediately, without warming up his engine first, as that might have alerted the Germans to what he was about to do. The French infantry who had assisted him, several hundred in number, emerged from their dugouts and trenches to see him off. When Gilbert was ascending from behind the protective cover of the copse, he deliberately showed himself to the Germans in their frontline trench. Predictably irritated and frustrated, they replied with a sustained volley of rifle and machine-gun fire. The watching French soldiers had to throw themselves to the ground in a hurry. Gilbert experienced no further problems as he returned to his base at Bertangles for what must have been a very welcome breakfast with his squadron.

Gilbert's VC citation, published in the *London Gazette* on 23 December 1915, read as follows:

War Office.

23 December 1915.

Second Lieutenant Gilbert Martin Stuart Insall

No. 11 Squadron, Royal Flying Corps.

For most conspicuous bravery, skill and determination, on 7 November 1915, in France.

He was patrolling in a Vickers Fighting Machine, with First Class Air Mechanic T. H. Donald as gunner, when a German machine was sighted, pursued and attacked near Achiet.

The German pilot led the Vickers machine over a rocket battery, but with great skill Lieutenant Insall dived and got to close range, when Donald fired a drum of cartridges into the German machine, stopping its engine. The German pilot then dived through a cloud, followed by Lieutenant Insall. Fire was again opened, and the German machine was brought down heavily in a ploughed field 4 miles south-east of Arras.

On seeing the Germans scramble out of their machine and prepare to fire, Lieutenant Insall dived to 500 feet, thus enabling Donald to open heavy fire on them. The Germans then fled, one helping the other, who was apparently wounded. Other Germans then commenced heavy fire, but in spite of this, Lieutenant Insall turned again, and an incendiary bomb was dropped on the German machine, which was last seen wreathed in heavy smoke.

Lieutenant Insall then headed west in order to get back over the German trenches, but as he was at only 2,000 feet altitude, he dived across them at greater speed, Donald firing into the trenches as he passed over. The German fire, however, damaged the petrol tank, and, with great coolness, Lieutenant Insall landed under cover of a wood 500 yards inside our lines.

The Germans fired some 150 shells at our machine on the ground, but without causing material damage. Much damage had, however, been caused by rifle fire, but during the night it was repaired behind screened lights and at dawn Lieutenant Insall flew his machine home with First Class Air Mechanic T. H. Donald as a passenger.[5][*]

Thomas Donald was awarded a Distinguished Conduct Medal for his part in this action.

---

[*] This latter point was incorrect, because Donald was not a passenger and Gilbert had decided to use sandbags instead to give him the balance he needed. It is not the only occasion when a citation has been found to contain factual errors. *The Victoria Cross and the George Cross: The Complete History: The First World War, 1914–1918, Volume 2* (London: Methuen, 2013) contains quite a few amendments to citations. However, these are generally of figures, and usually relate to dates, which can easily be cross-checked. It is much more difficult to pick up inaccuracies such as some of these, particularly where Donald was stated to have returned to base as a passenger, when he did not. I am drawing here both on Gilbert's notes, as well as on the account in my grandfather's book *Observer*.

Over half a century later, some comments were made about whether Gilbert's actions were really deserving of a VC. The source was Robert Hughes-Chamberlain, who had served with Gilbert in 11 Squadron.[6] He had been sitting in the squadron office when Gilbert rang Dawes, the squadron commander, to report what had happened and to request assistance in providing the necessary equipment to enable the aircraft to be repaired. In an interview with the Imperial War Museum in 1971, Hughes-Chamberlain said that Dawes had not liked Gilbert before this incident, though he did not know why. However, afterwards, 'he was racing about the place to get Insall the VC, to the French to get reports from them [and other] reports from all over the place. It made a very good story.'[7]

In an echo of the view which King George V had expressed to the recently returned escaper Lieutenant Peter Anderson in 1915, when the King told him he considered the bravery involved in escaping was, if anything, greater than that required on the battle-field,[*] Hughes-Chamberlain continued:

Well, they made a good thing out of it, but it wasn't a VC job in my opinion. It was very ordinary, shooting down a machine over the trenches. I should have reversed it. What he did in escaping from Germany was a VC job in my opinion. He told me the whole story one day at Dover when I was in command there and I always thought that was an extraordinary job. The other one was an MC job. He got them both, but the wrong way round.[8†]

---

[*] See Chapter 1, p. 8.

[†] A few months later, Hughes-Chamberlain had an extraordinary experience which well illustrates the vulnerability of so many early aircraft. By then in 24 Squadron and flying a de Havilland DH2, he was approaching the lines when his Monosoupape engine threw a cylinder, and the severed part went through his upper main spar and removed one blade of his airscrew. In the resulting vibration, the whole aircraft began to disintegrate, and by the time Hughes-Chamberlain reached the ground, there was little of it worth keeping. (Insall, *Observer*, p. 22.)

It is hard, more than a century after the events which they describe, to judge how much weight to give to these comments. Gilbert certainly displayed considerable courage in descending so low, when well behind the German lines, in order to ensure the destruction of the German aircraft which he had brought down. He would have known that he could not ascend to a safe height again without making his aircraft extremely vulnerable to anti-aircraft fire or attacks from other German aircraft, and that he would have to attempt to cross back over the lines at a very low level, where he would also be exposed to rifle fire. It was indeed a rifle bullet which punctured his petrol tank. Quite a few pilots in the RFC at that time would not have taken such a risk. For example, Major Frederick Powell, who had extensive experience in 5, 40 and 41 Squadrons, commented on Gilbert's action:

> Insall, who earned his VC in No. 11 Squadron in a Vickers fighter, he went out and shot down a German aeroplane which landed on the German side of the lines. Being so terribly aggressive, Insall followed him down, right down to the ground and then, as the pilot and observer ran out, he came after them and shot them up as they ran away. It depends how brave you were. If you were like myself, you sat up there and watched in the hope that he'd crash.[9]

We should also consider the risks involved in assessing the damage to his aircraft, and then supervising its repair, when it was out in the open and vulnerable to heavy German shelling. He – and the mechanics who actually carried out the repairs – were therefore exposed to considerable risk for some time. Gilbert also knew that the aircraft would be at even more risk when he took off the following morning. It was for that reason that he arranged for sandbags to be placed in the observer's seat, as there was no need for Donald to travel with him on the journey back to his base. But he couldn't resist the temptation to taunt the Germans for their failure to destroy his Vickers, by showing himself to them once he had taken off.

The achievements of Gilbert and Donald provided material which was subsequently used for propaganda purposes by MI7b, a little-known section of the Directorate of Military Intelligence which was set up in January 1916 to disseminate propaganda for both foreign and domestic purposes. Its staff included some members who subsequently became well-known authors, such as A. A. Milne, who wrote *Winnie-the-Pooh*. Most of its documents were destroyed at the end of the war, on the instructions of the War Office. However, one officer, Lieutenant James Price Lloyd, retained some 150 documents, which have survived. These include a series entitled 'Tales of the VC', which include a detailed handwritten account by Lloyd of the incident when Gilbert won his VC.*

Gilbert won one of just nineteen VCs which were awarded to officers in the RFC and (from 1 April 1918) the RAF, during the First World War, who were serving on the Western Front and in Palestine. Moreover, he won it at a stage when aircraft were underpowered, less robust and had limited capabilities for combat. So, engagements tended to be of short duration. Later in the war, when newer and more powerful aircraft were developed, the nature of aerial warfare – and the tactics used – changed significantly. Two other VCs were later awarded to pilots who had previously served with 11 Squadron and then been posted elsewhere. They were Lionel Rees, who was posted to be a Flight Commander in the then newly

---

* The collection provides an illuminating insight into the work of a rather obscure organisation, probably the least well known of the several working on propaganda during the First World War. The article about Gilbert may be viewed at: 'Gilbert Stuart Martin Insall and Thomas Ham Donald ['Tales of the VC']', Europeana, https://www.europeana.eu/item/2020601/https___1914_1918_europeana_eu_contributions_5375

formed 11 Squadron at Netheravon, before it moved to France. He was with 32 Squadron on 3 August 1916 when he took on a large group of German aircraft (which he had approached, mistakenly thinking they were British bombers). He engaged with them single-handedly and seriously damaged three before being badly injured in his leg. Yet he continued his attack and got to very close quarters, 'finishing by firing at the leading aircraft from no more than ten yards away'. German records confirmed his account of the combat.[10] His persistent aggression, witnessed from the ground by troops manning the 22nd Anti-Aircraft Battery, caused the whole German formation to abandon its mission and to return home.[11] Albert Ball, the RFC's leading ace with forty-four victories, served with 11 Squadron between May and October 1916, a period during which he earned two Distinguished Service Orders (DSOs) and an MC. He was shot down and killed in May 1917 and was awarded his VC posthumously, for a series of actions in the period before he died. His citation noted that in the period between 25 April and 6 May, he took part in twenty-six aerial combats, shot down eleven aircraft, drove down two more and forced several others to land. Moreover, 11 Squadron could reasonably claim that it had a number of other aces too.[12] The most successful were John Chick, who, remarkably, scored sixteen victories in only four and a half months in early 1918, and Eugene Coler, an American pilot who also scored sixteen victories (though over a slightly longer period) in 1918.*

---

* About 300 Americans flew in the RFC or RAF during the First World War (and others flew for the French too, most notably in the Lafayette Escadrille or squadron). Most joined before the United States entered the war in April 1917. There were a number from other neutral countries who also joined the RFC. One of the most notable was the Norwegian Tryggve Gran, a polar explorer and experienced aviator who was the first person to fly across the North Sea, from Scotland to Norway, in August 1914. He joined the RFC in the autumn of 1916, adopting the alias of Teddy Grant and posing as a Canadian to avoid compromising his neutral nationality. He served in several squadrons, including 44 Squadron (whose CO was 'Mother' Hubbard, who had previously commanded 11 Squadron), and was awarded the MC in March 1918 for his actions while carrying out a series of night bombing raids with 101 Squadron, in the course of which he suffered a severe leg injury.

However, a few days before the award of Gilbert's VC was announced, he was shot down and captured by the Germans.

On 14 December 1915, he and Donald were on patrol over Albert at about 8,000 feet in the same aircraft – Vickers FB No. 5704 – as he had been flying the previous month. They observed an enemy biplane approaching the German lines from the direction of Bapaume, and they turned immediately to attack it. Both pilots manoeuvred around each other in order to gain a more advantageous firing position and to avoid making themselves an easy target.

As will be discussed in Chapter 5, the British military has been described during the First World War as being deeply imbued with a 'nineteenth-century military ethos, which held that to be captured could have resulted only from the personal failing on the part of the soldier'.[13] That ethos permeated the Army Act of 1879, which warned of the death penalty for those who 'shamefully' abandoned their position or person to the enemy. The legislation dictated that all captured British servicemen would be subjected to an examination upon their repatriation, which would seek to establish the circumstances of their capture and whether the officer or soldier concerned might have deliberately surrendered. The records of some RFC officers – and all those who successfully escaped or were repatriated – show that they were required to provide an account of their capture to enable a judgement to be made about whether they had given up. After his escape to Holland, Gilbert was therefore required to make a statement about the circumstances in which he was taken prisoner. He provided the following account in November 1917:

No. 11 Squadron RFC was at that time maintaining a permanent patrol over the area Arras to the Somme River and I was detailed on 13 December 1915 for early morning patrol on Vickers Fighting Biplane No. 5074 with Corporal Thomas Donald RFC as gunner.

When we had been in the air for about 1 ½ hours, a hostile aircraft was sighted coming around ARRAS on the enemy's side of the lines and was observed to turn south towards Bapaume.

We crossed the lines in order to cut him off and, getting within range near Bapaume, opened fire with our machine gun. Our height at that moment was 8,000 feet, the height of the hostile aircraft (a tractor two-seater) around 7,000 feet. A dive at right angles to his line of sight brought us to close quarters and Corporal Donald opened fire as we turned right-handedly over the tail of the enemy machine. The latter then opened fire without altering his course, a bullet from his machine gun entering through the front of the Vicker's nacelle, passing fore and after through my observer's seat, cutting both the right aileron control cables, grazing my right leg and going through the petrol tank behind me. The engine, being pressure fed, immediately stopped.

The control lever was drawn over to the left by the remaining control cables (left), lateral control of the machine becoming practically impossible.

I reduced the dive to a slow glide of about fifty miles an hour and, instructing Corporal Donald to lean over to the left, contrived to turn west towards the lines, there being just sufficient control with the left ailerons to accomplish this.

On looking around I found that the hostile aircraft had disappeared. I think that our approximate position at that stage was 8 kilometres north of Bapaume.

We had glided about 500 feet when an AA [anti-artillery] shell, the first fired, burst close under the machine, hitting Corporal Donald in both legs and myself in the hip.

AA shells were then fairly plentiful as we approached a rail-head which I think must have been Achiet-le-Grand. I felt dizzy for a few minutes after I had been hit but regained full consciousness until we had landed.

We passed over Achiet and glided for some time in a westerly direction within sight of the trenches which looked nearer than they actually were. As we approached a small triangular wood, le Bois du Biez or possibly de Longeast, we were hailed by fire from a large rocket battery. The shooting was very bad at first. As we came over the battery, we could plainly see a set of about twenty stands in two rows which fired three to six rockets at a time. We were then at about 1,000 feet and their last burst bracketed us. I had to dive in order to avoid them. We continued gliding and came to earth on the other side of the wood, in a large field. The tyres burst and we lurched forward a bit; Corporal Donald and I got out of the machine and I got into his seat and loosened the incendiary bomb tube (which had been prepared for burning the machine with the igniting battery fixed to the tube). Corporal Donald pushed it up from below as it jammed. I got back to my seat and put a bomb in the tube; the bomb jammed in the tube and would not go off. I think it must have been shot through. While I was banging it, a German came up on a cycle and covered us with a pistol. I told him in German that I was coming down, and threw the contraption into the machine in the hope that it might ignite.

I was able to walk about six yards, clear of the machine should it catch on fire, and then lay down. The Germans who came up bandaged us with our field dressings and then took us off by horse ambulance to Achiet-le-Petit, where the nearest operating theatre was situated. The surgeon took a piece of shell weighing about 450 grammes from out of my hip and gave it to me as a souvenir. Corporal Donald had a smaller piece in his thigh. I saw him being operated on but was not allowed to speak to him until long afterwards, and we were kept apart, so I am not able to say how many wounds he had in all.* Subsequently we were sent to Bapaume and then to St Quentin.[14]

Sometimes the wheels of military bureaucracy can grind exceedingly slow. Gilbert submitted the account of his capture on 22 November 1917. It was not until 8 August 1919 that he received a letter from the Secretary of the War Office stating that the Army Council had informed him that 'his statement regarding the circumstances of his capture having been investigated, the Army Council considers that no blame attaches to him in the matter'.[15]

But other parts of the military bureaucracy reacted more quickly. Rather unusually, the file containing Gilbert's report (as well as similar reports from other officers who had also either escaped or been repatriated) also contains extracts from an MI1a report about his capture and treatment in the weeks afterwards, before he was sent to Germany. (MI1a was the organisation which in the late autumn of 1939 was transformed into MI9, responsible for helping British PoWs to escape, but at this stage the role which it played was more analytical than operational, and it was largely concerned with gathering information about the treatment of prisoners after capture, their medical treatment where relevant, as it was in Gilbert's case, and conditions in prison camps.) While the information which was provided to them by Gilbert was not very detailed, it was recorded on 26 September 1917, barely a fortnight after his arrival in Britain:

---

* Donald's wounds were actually fairly light, for he was discharged from hospital within ten days and sent to a prison camp in Germany. Gilbert was to be in hospital for several months.

I was shot down by AA fire in the neighbourhood of Bapaume and was taken to hospital at Achiet-le-Petit, where I had a slight operation under ether. I was taken in a motor ambulance to Bapaume. In Bapaume, I was put in hospital, where I remained for about a fortnight, being with the German wounded and being treated about the same as they.

From Bapaume, I was taken in a hospital train to St Quentin, where I was kept until just after Christmas. I was still a bed case and was transferred to Cologne in an ordinary train, a bed having been made up on the seat.

At Cologne, I was put in Hospital No. 6. Here the officers had a room to themselves and were treated fairly well, though we were not allowed out even when we were convalescent.[16]*

Gilbert (second from left) *with other convalescing prisoners in Cologne.*

---

* From early 1917 onwards, which is around the time that MI1a became active, a number of reports from other officers about their capture are also accompanied by extracts from MI1a correspondence adding useful details which the more substantial (and later) reports about the circumstances of their capture do not contain. It was also at this time that the Foreign Office began to copy MI1a on correspondence about British prisoners of war in captivity in Germany and elsewhere, to be found on files in the FO 383 series.

The statement which Gilbert provided about his capture did not include any reference to an extraordinary coincidence which had occurred just after he had got out of his Vickers and collapsed on the ground. One of the German stretcher-bearers who was called up to take the injured pair to hospital for treatment recognised Gilbert. They were both hockey players and had taken part in a match against each other not long before the outbreak of war, when the Paris University Hockey Club, to which both Gilbert and Jack belonged, had visited Hanover in March 1914, little more than eighteen months previously. (A German photograph of this remarkable encounter, taken just after Gilbert's capture, is included in the plate section.) This man accompanied Gilbert as he was taken on a horse-drawn ambulance to a field hospital at Achiet-le-Petit, where Gilbert was operated on successfully to remove the shrapnel from his buttock. Afterwards, the stretcher-bearer stayed with Gilbert overnight and looked after him.[17] The following morning, Gilbert was taken by ambulance to Bapaume, where he remained for about a fortnight in a hospital where the other patients were all German. At this point, he and Donald were separated, and they did not meet again until after the war. However, Donald had a chance encounter with another RFC pilot, Captain Herbert Ward, in the railway station at Aachen. In late November, Ward had been wounded when shot down with Lieutenant Sidney Buckley (of whom more is discussed later in Chapter 9) and was being transferred to a prison hospital in Cologne.[18]* At the time of this meeting, Donald had recovered sufficiently from his wounds and was discharged on 24 December to be sent to Germany.[19] He was moved to Stendal, some seventy-five

---

* Like Jack, Ward either fooled the recruiting officer or more probably connived with him, so that he could join up at the age of seventeen. He was trained as a pilot and commissioned into the RFC in June 1915 shortly afterwards and was posted to 16 Squadron in France. He was captured less than six months later.

miles west of Berlin. Gilbert, meanwhile, was moved on a hospital train to St Quentin, where he spent a fortnight before being sent to Cologne Hospital No. 6, where he was confined with other Allied prisoners and spent the next two months convalescing.

At Cologne Hospital No. 6, Gilbert shared a room with a dozen other British officers, one of whom was another RFC lieutenant called Grey. The food there – an extremely important consideration for prisoners – was, Gilbert considered, fairly good.[20]

Quite a few RFC officers described how, after they had been brought down and captured by the Germans, they were taken to an officers' mess and well entertained by their pleasant and well-informed hosts. This happened sufficiently often to suggest that it was considered to be a technique capable of providing worthwhile information. A British interrogation of a captured German pilot shows that the Germans had carefully worked out the best way to do it:

When a British flying officer is captured, he is at once taken to the nearest Flight Casino (or Mess). He lunches and dines, perhaps for several days, with the Mess. No actual interrogation takes place, but the Flying Corps Intelligence Officer from Corps headquarters temporarily attaches himself to the Mess in question. No captured flying officer is ever put through a formal examination or asked a direct question during this process.

The British interrogator added: 'In view of his own loquacity, prisoner, Hans Baldamus,* was not asked whether much information

---

* Lieutenant Hans Baldamus came from Saxony. He was serving with 201st Artillery Flight when he was shot down. Not long before his capture, he had been awarded a high Saxon decoration for two successful flights when spotting for the artillery in July and August 1916.

was derived from captured British officers'! His interrogation certainly produced plenty of valuable information, perhaps especially on German wireless procedure from aeroplanes, though he also described their interception of signals from British aircraft:

> The enemy* derives intelligence from wireless signals emitted by our aeroplanes. There are wireless stations down the front, specially detailed to intercept our signals. The principal intelligence so far gained has been in regard to the concentration of our aeroplanes at a given point, and in warning batteries and localities that they are about to be shelled. Many lives have been saved in the prisoner's own corps in the latter way. Prisoner was not certain that intelligence as to the location of our batteries was obtained by the interception of our wireless calls, but he thought it highly probable. 'You will never be able to do the same with us,' he added, 'because we have no system, whereas you have a uniform one all down the front.'[21] [A photograph of this document is included in the plate section.]

Further proof of Baldamus's loquacity – and immodesty – was provided when he was asked who were considered to be the best German aviators and worthy successors to Oswald Boelcke and Max Immelmann, the two most outstanding German fighter pilots up to that time, who had both been killed in the previous few months. He named five, including Immelmann's brother Franz – and himself! He was able to provide the precise details of the numbers of Allied aircraft which each of the five had shot down, revealing that he was second on the list. (He did not mention Manfred von Richthofen,

---

* I.e. the Germans.

who at that point was only just beginning to establish his reputation as an ace.)

Since he was destined to spend three months in hospital, Gilbert did not have a chance to experience the sort of hospitality which Baldamus had described. However, surviving German military archives, mainly in Karlsruhe, provide a fascinating account of the interrogations which he and Donald underwent.* Their records also provide some revealing details of the way in which the Germans treated their prisoners. The files include information about the aircraft responsible for the damage caused to Gilbert's Vickers and describe the competing claims of the anti-aircraft battery which was also seeking the credit for having shot him down.

On the whole, German interrogations were more extensive and thorough than those of their British counterparts, which tended to concentrate on a smaller number of prisoners, often singling out those who appeared to be disaffected or vulnerable in some other way, as Baldamus clearly was. The Germans also prepared a remarkably long and detailed questionnaire, which ran to sixteen pages – though there were separate sections for different nationalities and occupations. The section for airmen included a range of questions about anti-aircraft fire, its effectiveness, whether it had caused more concern to captured pilots than German aircraft and whether its effectiveness had led to changes in British tactics. It also included several questions about the issue of weather reports.[22]

---

* The central German military archive, and the bulk of German records, were held in Potsdam. They were destroyed by RAF bombing in April 1945. However, certain states (Bavaria, Saxony, Württemberg and Baden) held their records in geographically and administratively separate archives in their own capitals, and many of them survived. Fortunately for my research, Gilbert was shot down in the sector of XIV Reserve Corps. This was originally from Baden, and its papers are therefore in Karlsruhe. If he had landed elsewhere on the front, he would have been in a different sector and a few exceptions would have been in an area whose records would have been most unlikely to survive. I am most grateful to Dr Tony Cowan for his assistance in tracking down and providing me with these records, and for his explanation of how relevant German military records were organised.

The Germans found that airmen were often particularly rewarding subjects for interrogation: 'We have found from experience that the enemy aviators, and the British in particular, are most inclined to chat and give answers to their German counterparts. That is why the interrogation of enemy flyers should be conducted only by the airmen who are attached to the intelligence office.'[23] Colonel Walter Nicolai, who was the head of the German military secret intelligence service between 1913 and 1919, also observed:

> The airmen on both sides were bound together by technical interests and a certain sporting spirit. In addition, many were quite young and the English and the French airmen were often recruited from inferior material ... and their news was all the more valuable because airmen often had exact information regarding strategic conditions.[24]

Notably, Nicolai also observed that the effects of wounds and shattered nerves varied a great deal. The better-trained English prisoners would 'show greater powers of resistance than the French or the Belgians ... and the Englishman [could] be silent and completely obdurate'.[25]

Though not always. The shock of capture, often in quite brutal circumstances, could be very unsettling, especially if accompanied by generous hospitality from apparently unthreatening fellow aircrew, who spoke the same sort of language. And questioning techniques could be subtle. It was the same for both sides, and it is not so very surprising that prisoners – especially those well treated in these circumstances – sometimes did give quite a lot away. (Moreover, at this stage in the war, RFC aircrew were given little or no advice on how to behave after they had been captured.) German archives contain a report on Second Lieutenant H. T. Kemp of 11 Squadron, who was shot down in flames by Max Immelmann in January 1916, just weeks after Gilbert's capture. Kemp suffered a head wound and Second Lieutenant S. C. Hathaway, his observer, was killed. Kemp somehow managed to jump clear just as the aircraft crashed. Immelmann landed nearby, to see the results of their combat. In an act of chivalry, he sat down with Kemp and they smoked a cigarette together while watching the aircraft burn. Kemp was later treated for his injury and afterwards well entertained by Immelmann and other officers. During these meetings and subsequent interrogations, he provided information about the effectiveness of anti-aircraft batteries as well about the Fokker fighter. Moreover, from the collection of papers he had unwisely carried with him when flying on this sortie, the Germans were able to establish details identifying four RFC squadrons on the front opposite them as well as a balloon detachment and an aviation park, plans for a corps reconnaissance in the area and some of the movements of Lord Kitchener, who had recently inspected the 2/9th Middlesex battalion in Maidstone.[26]

Later in the war, intelligence organisations began to provide briefings to RFC aircrew on the need to avoid carrying personal papers with them when taking part in operational sorties. But even then, mistakes were still made. In May 1917, Lieutenant James Bennett of the Royal Naval Air Service was flying in a seaplane as an observer, when it was forced to land in the Channel, as a result of engine failure during a patrol to locate German submarines. One of the submarines which he had been searching for surfaced and took him and his pilot prisoners. Fortunately, however, he had time to go through his pockets and destroy the papers he had with him.[27*]

Second Lieutenant Kemp somehow managed to keep a diary of

---

* It is possible that RNAS squadrons such as his, which were not based on the Western Front and therefore were not in general at such a great risk of capture, were not considered to be such a high priority for briefing.

this period, and it describes the extent of persistent German questioning, first in Bapaume:

> I was taken off and questioned by a group of young officers and noted that one of them was better informed about what was happening in Britain than I was, and that he spoke English very well.
>
> At 3 o'clock my journey began again. I was taken in a car from Bapaume to St Quentin. Accompanying me was a nephew of that Baron von Bissing,* about whom there had been much agitation in England some months before. At St Quentin, the events of Bapaume were in part repeated. I had tea with some staff officers and was immediately pumped by them on all topics. It is remarkable that a number of them can speak good English and how active an interest some of them took in British affairs. It was the hobby – or duty – of one young officer to follow our home politics and on this topic he was far better posted than I.
>
> Having served my purpose, I was delivered to another room for removal to St Quentin prison. The accompanying officer knew English and spoke it fluently. He had lived in London for several years and had a thorough knowledge of British affairs. We drove to the hotel where dinner was served, then to the hospital and then to the prison.
>
> [The following] morning there returned my officer of artillery† – who had conducted me to the prison – and we talked, passing the time. At half past twelve, lunch was brought, again from the hotel.[28]‡

---

* A Prussian general who was appointed Governor General of Belgium in November 1914 and whose behaviour was divisive and controversial. He also signed the warrant for the execution of Edith Cavell.
† Who would no doubt have been interested in continuing his questioning about the effectiveness of German anti-aircraft batteries.
‡ There are plenty of references in literature about the Second World War describing the extent to which the Germans continued to use this technique, for example the extent of hospitality shown by the German fighter ace Adolf Galland to the legless pilot Douglas Bader, after he had been captured.

Gilbert was interrogated several times. He refused to give any details about the airfield where he was based or where he had come from. He thought that the aircraft which had shot him down was an LVG. Both Thomas Donald and Gilbert provided information about some of their colleagues. Neither of them had a good opinion of one of them, an officer called McLean in III Wing (which controlled the activities of both 11 Squadron and 4 Squadron) who was on the staff of the commanding officer, Brigadier General Sefton Brancker. They thought that he understood nothing about aviation. Donald went further and described him as generally unpopular. Gilbert was also willing to discuss the relative merits of German aircraft which he had come across. He said, for example, that the Fokker monoplane was a very capable machine because of its high speed. He did not think much of the German biplanes, which were then being deployed. Kemp, incidentally, also later told his interrogators that he had a very positive view of the Fokker machine, assessing it as 'absolutely superior to the British machines. Above all, they are much faster. Their main advantage is the good location of the machine gun.'[29]

In general, Donald was rather more forthcoming in his answers to his German interrogators, identifying the senior officers in his and other squadrons and their locations, as well as details of some of the military deployments in his sector. He also provided quite full details about weather forecasts, stating that his squadron received weather reports in the morning, at noon and in the evening by wireless telegraphy from the Eiffel Tower, Dunkirk and London. There was a receiving station near Marieux from which reports were distributed by motorcyclist. Like Kemp, Donald also provided information about German anti-aircraft batteries, a subject of particular concern for German intelligence at this time, because of uncertainties about how effective they were. In December 1915, the army circulated a document addressing criticism that their anti-aircraft fire was ineffective given the manpower and resources devoted to it. The paper explained the difficulties of developing its use, at a time when the science of anti-aircraft gunnery was starting from scratch. The document also included prisoner statements on the effectiveness of anti-aircraft fire and why its results would not always be visible to ground troops. Donald told his interrogators that the German artillery shot 'excellently on British planes'. His aircraft had been hit on various occasions. He added that British aircraft tried to avoid coming under German artillery fire. The Achiet anti-aircraft battery was particularly feared, although Donald had little knowledge about the effectiveness of other batteries. He added that as far as he knew, no special flightpaths had been established: on the outward route, they flew as high as possible.[30] On the same subject, Kemp said that German anti-aircraft fire was very accurate and pilots were very wary of their batteries. He always tried to fly between them. A few days before his capture, he had flown over the anti-aircraft batteries at Achiet and Grévillers. He was amazed how quickly the anti-aircraft guns found his range.[*]

The German records of Gilbert's interrogation also show that (presumably because of competing claims by those involved) those who questioned him went to some trouble to establish whether it was the aerial combat or anti-aircraft fire which had brought his Vickers down: their investigation lasted several weeks and included a statement from the commander of the anti-aircraft battery at Grévillers which had fired at Gilbert. He observed that the British

---

[*] It is a reflection of the value placed by the Germans on Donald's report that it was included in a summary of seventeen statements about German anti-aircraft fire obtained from captured airmen, which was circulated on 27 December 1915.

aircraft had suddenly lost height and changed direction, so he had opened fire with his battery and the 10 cm gun which was attached to it. After 'a well-aimed salvo', Gilbert's aircraft descended even more steeply. He was confident that it was the engagement with German aircraft which had been the first cause of the aircraft starting to come down and that he had reported this by telephone to corps headquarters. He left to experts to judge the extent to which the injury to the pilot had also contributed to them having to make a forced landing. In a subsequent interrogation, Gilbert said that the petrol tank was holed during combat, which caused the engine to stop. He confirmed that he was only hit by anti-aircraft fire during his descent. Gilbert had been given the shell fragment, after it had been extracted by the doctor operating on him, and showed it to First Lieutenant Tillemanns, who conducted his first interrogation. This fragment was later recovered from him for expert examination, as the Germans wished to confirm what sort of gun had fired it. It was indeed identified as a 10 cm calibre.[31]

The pilot who shot Gilbert down was Captain Zander of the 9th Field Reconnaissance Flight, whose observer was Lieutenant Lerche. He was flying an Albatros.* Gilbert's Vickers was carefully examined. An inventory revealed details of the instruments it carried (airspeed indicator, rev counter, clock, compass, fuel indicator and pressure gauge), a Morse key, two incendiary bombs with igniters, a Lewis gun with nine drums of ammunition, a German Mauser pistol and a British carbine with magazine. (These weapons had all

---

* Although Gilbert and Donald were by then a reasonably experienced crew, neither was well trained at aircraft recognition. Gilbert thought that he had been shot down by an LVG, while Donald told his interrogators that it was a Fokker. It is quite likely that the Germans were also affected by the same difficulties, for the files in Karlsruhe contain accounts of a second aircraft, believed to be a French Farman, which was shot down on the same day, at very nearly the same time and in very nearly the same place, whose (unidentified) crew suffered similar injuries. (Generallandesarchiv Karlsruhe (hereafter GLAK), 456 F7/107 folio 176 and folio 197.) Perhaps this was also a similar misidentification.

been recovered by the 9th Field Reconnaissance Flight, presumably as trophies.) There was also a map case with maps which was delivered to XIV Reserve Corps headquarters. A physical examination of the aircraft showed that apart from the holed petrol tank, splinter perforations and a trivial defect in the undercarriage, it was perfectly serviceable. It was disassembled on the spot by the 32nd Field Reconnaissance Flight and was to be used for test purposes.[32]

It is remarkable how infrequent the references are to German interrogations in the accounts provided by escaped and repatriated British prisoners on their return to Britain. Their reports are often very detailed – in Gilbert's case, it runs to eleven pages – but other than a few references to hospitality provided to RFC officers in German messes and the questioning which accompanied it,[33] they provide scanty information on this aspect. And there is often no mention at all of the interrogations prisoners faced, even of those who were captured before the end of 1916, when MI1a might have started to take an interest in the subject and whose records have generally either remained classified or been destroyed. So it seems reasonable to conclude that at least during the first part of the war, members of fighting services were not warned about the dangers of interrogation because the War Office did not wish to raise the possibility of their surrendering, and also – despite the valuable reports which were being obtained through interrogation of German prisoners – the War Office was not paying sufficient attention to German interrogation techniques.

Jack had also been out on a patrol at the time when Gilbert was shot down, so heard almost immediately of his failure to return from his mission. The family endured a worrying month before they received a postcard through the Red Cross with some minimal details, which were all that Gilbert was permitted to provide, informing them that he was a prisoner, though wounded. A couple of months later, Jack received a letter from him, written in carefully chosen terms, which Jack (who of course knew him very well) was able to interpret as meaning that he was intending to escape as soon as he had recovered sufficiently to do so. For example:

> He mentioned the fact that he would soon be able to extend the length of the few short walks which he had already been able to indulge in the ward he was in, qualifying the extent he foresaw with the words 'very considerably', and then making some quite harmless comment on the scenery visible from the windows of the lazarette.* It did not take me very long to get the message. The gist was that he was shortly being sent to a prisoner of war camp and could do with any maps we could get hold of showing the approaches to neutral frontiers.[34]

Gilbert was a little over optimistic in his assessment of when he might be ready to start to prepare an escape. He took nearly nine months to recover from his wound and to regain sufficient fitness to be able to become involved in planning an escape, and so he was only able to make a start when he was transferred to Heidelberg in August 1916. But the family's response to this letter marked the beginning of their involvement in supporting Gilbert in his attempts to escape, in seeking to obtain the equipment which he needed for his projects and in finding safe ways by which they could send maps, compasses and other items to him carefully concealed in parcels in ways they hoped would minimise the chances of their detection in searches by his German captors. Gilbert had not been

---

*   Term for a hospital.

in a position where he could specify which areas of which frontiers would be of particular interest to him. So Jack's initial enquiries and research were necessarily rather general. These will be described further in Chapter 6.

At the end of February, Gilbert was discharged from hospital in Cologne and sent to a camp in Mainz, which was a clearing station for prison camps. The food there was not good and much worse than he had received in hospital in Cologne. The lavatory accommodation was very bad and primitive, and such insanitary conditions were another frequent cause of complaint for prisoners. Later in March, he was transferred to his first proper prison camp at Fort Prinz Karl at Ingolstadt, Bavaria, where he was to spend the next six months.

CHAPTER 5

DEATH – AND LIFE – IN PRISON CAMPS

M uch has been written about the conditions experienced by Allied prisoners in prison camps in Germany during the Second World War, the achievements of prisoners who managed to escape successfully, sometimes in remarkable circumstances, and the tragic outcome for some of those who were unfortunate enough to be recaptured, particularly the fifty RAF officers who were murdered by the Germans after the Great Escape from Stalag Luft 3 in March 1944. Russian prisoners were treated much worse than Allied captives, with extreme brutality, to such an extent that some 3 million of them died. (Russia had not signed the Geneva Convention in 1929, so Russian prisoners had no protection at all.) Moreover, as Professor Matthew Stibbe has commented, 'the horrors of the Nazi concentration camps have overshadowed everything that came before'.[1]

Much less is known about what happened in the First World War. Although the Geneva Convention had not by then been signed, there were already some existing international agreements (the Hague Conventions of 1899 and 1907) which governed the treatment of prisoners of war. Among the articles in Chapter II, there were the following provisions:

Article 4. Prisoners of war are in the hands of the hostile Government, but not of the individuals or corps which capture them. They must be humanely treated.

Article 6. The State may utilise the labour of prisoners of war according to their rank and aptitude, officers excepted. The tasks shall not be excessive, and shall have no connection with the operations of war.

Article 7. The Government into whose hands prisoners of war have fallen is charged with their maintenance. In the absence of a special agreement between the belligerents, prisoners of war shall be treated as regards board, lodging and clothing on the same footing as the troops which captured them.

Although there were some camps where prisoners were treated humanely, the Germans certainly did not observe the strictures of those articles. Prisoners were often starved, ill-clothed, kept in unhealthily and dangerously unsanitary conditions, denied proper medical treatment (and often any medical treatment at all), beaten, overworked (twelve-hour shifts in coal mines and salt mines were not uncommon), ordered (with threats to enforce compliance) to work on the production of items which had a military purpose, sentenced to long periods of solitary confinement for no reason other than the whim of their captors – and sometimes subjected to extreme violence such as bayonetting or even, in the case both of escapers and those who failed to respond quickly enough to the commands of their captors, shot out of hand.

We do not know with any real precision quite how many British and Allied prisoners were either captured or died in German captivity, or how many Germans were captured or died in Allied hands. In the later stages of the war in 1918, the German Army, disintegrating under pressure, stopped registering newly captured prisoners. And an unknown, but significant, number of prisoners were shot after capture, as they were being escorted away from the lines. Moreover, many of the records for the rest of the war were destroyed by Allied bombing during the Second World War. So estimates vary. But Professor Heather Jones, in her authoritative evaluation of this subject, concludes that the most realistic number of British (including empire) and French prisoners of war held in camps in Germany was 520,579 French and 175,624 British captives. Though, she points out, even the latter figure is based on incomplete records of the number of British prisoners who were repatriated. There are fewer differences for the figures of German prisoners held in France and Britain, though discrepancies remain. She takes a relatively reliable estimate as being some 392,425 Germans held by the French and 328,900 captured by the British.

On that basis, she concludes that the estimated maximum death statistics for French prisoners would be 7.48 per cent, based on 38,963 deaths out of 520,579 Franch captives, and a British death rate of 7.07 per cent, based on 12,425 deaths out of 175,624 British captives. For Germans held in France, the maximum estimated death rate comes out at 6.42 per cent, that is 25,229 deaths out of an estimated total of 392,425 prisoners. However, in Britain, the figure is substantially lower: if the highest estimated number of captured prisoners is 328,900, and the number of deaths some 10,000, then the maximum death rate would have been 3.04 per cent.[2]

It is also worth bearing in mind that captivity was less dangerous than service for soldiers on the front line, where the death rate for British infantry on active service during the war was 12.9 per cent, compared with 16.8 per cent for French soldiers and 15.4 per cent for German troops. This might help to explain the resentment which was felt about prisoners, who were seen to be less at risk in captivity than those who were serving in the tranches, even if their daily lives were generally really quite unpleasant. For though prisoners were not quite at such risk of being killed in combat, they were much more vulnerable to humiliating, degrading and debilitating treatment, particularly in Germany.[3] And it had post-war consequences, too. In France, for example, returning prisoners were excluded or at best marginalised in official commemorations of the war, where emphasis was given to the heroism and sacrifice of those who had fallen in battle and on the grief felt by their families.[4]

While this chapter will concentrate on describing the conditions which Gilbert and other British and Allied prisoners experienced in German prison camps, it is also appropriate to acknowledge that harsh treatment was also sometimes meted out to German prisoners as well, and that the injustices, sufferings and privations were not all one-sided.

The lower death rate of German prisoners in British custody does not mean that the British were entirely blameless in their treatment of German prisoners. Both sides were quite overwhelmed in the first months of the war by the large numbers of both civilian internees (more than 50,000 in Britain, compared with some 10,000 in Germany), and an additional complication for the Germans was the huge number of prisoners whom they captured during their early advances. Neither side was prepared for these influxes, overcrowding was rife and facilities were inadequate. For example, conditions at the German camp at Sennelager in September 1914 were described thus: 'It was an open field enclosed with wire ... There were no tents or covering of any kind. There were about 2,000 prisoners in it – all British. We lay on the ground with only one blanket for every three men.' At Hameln during the same period, 'prisoners were lodged for the first six weeks in trenches covered with canvas awnings. The bedding consisted of shavings and each man had one blanket ... The dirt and vermin etc. were frightful. Washing facilities consisted of one tap for 7,000 men.'[5] In Britain, German civilians were sent to an internment camp in Douglas, on the Isle of Man. Originally built as a holiday camp, it had a capacity of 2,400. But within a month of its opening, the number of inmates had risen to 3,000. Conditions worsened and there was discontent not only about overcrowding but also about the quality of the food and the harsh discipline which was being enforced. This culminated in a riot on 19 November, when the guards opened fire, killing five prisoners and wounding nineteen others. The British government commissioned a senior American diplomat, Chandler Hale, to investigate what had happened, and published his report as it largely exonerated the authorities. Subsequent research has shown that Hale's report was superficial and played down the problems which caused the complaints.[6]

The British government was also responsible for taking the lead in introducing the first serious use of reprisals. They did so in early 1915, after the Germans had begun their campaign of unrestricted submarine warfare. This provoked a strong reaction in Britain, and Winston Churchill, the First Lord of the Admiralty, announced that Britain would retaliate. He instructed that in future all captured

German submarine crews would be placed in detention barracks as 'criminals', rather than in camps as 'honourable prisoners of war'.* Thirty-nine German submariners were so detained. Churchill argued that the sinking of naval or merchant shipping without warning was an act of atrocity which should mean that captured prisoners would forfeit their rights under the Hague Convention. Notwithstanding the extent of public support which this measure attracted, the Foreign Office began to question its wisdom, fearing (with justification) that it might have adverse consequences for British prisoners in Germany, as retaliation was being threatened. But their reservations were removed when the German campaign grew in intensity – on 31 March, twenty-nine ships were sunk in a single day. Shortly afterwards, the Germans did indeed retaliate, putting thirty-nine British officers (many of them from prominent families) in prison. *The Times* did its best to stoke public opinion further, quoting 'rejoicing' in the German press at this action[7] and – in a leading article – equating the German imprisonment of these officers with their use of poison gas at Ypres.[8] But concern about the treatment of British prisoners led to growing reservations, particularly after the American Ambassador to Germany, James Gerard, was permitted to visit them and reported that they were being held in small cells, some no larger than eleven foot by four foot. Although Churchill robustly maintained his attitude,[9] the tide began to change, despite the sinking of the *Lusitania* in May, which caused widespread revulsion. After Churchill resigned in June,

---

* Churchill had had experience of being a prisoner of war, because he was captured by the Boers when working as a war correspondent during the Boer War. Conditions in his camp in Pretoria were not unduly arduous, and he was permitted to buy newspapers, cigarettes and beer. He escaped after four weeks captivity, in December 1899, avoided intensive Boer searches and travelled 300 miles to safety in Portuguese East Africa. When Major C. V. Fox successfully escaped from Germany in June 1917 and founded a dining club whose members were those to have made a successful escape, Churchill was invited to join and often attended their gatherings.

following the reverses in the Dardanelles, and was replaced as First Lord by Arthur Balfour, the Cabinet agreed that the segregation of submariners in this way should be discontinued and that they would in future be treated as ordinary PoWs.[10]

The use of reprisals continued to cause problems throughout the war, though not to the extent which this incident achieved. Sometimes they were much more trivial, but they still nonetheless had the capacity to make a significant difference to the conditions in which prisoners lived. Because of the limited options available to belligerents beyond the battlefield, the punishment of prisoners became an attractive method to right a perceived wrong perpetrated by the enemy or to force the enemy to refrain from the use of some 'uncivilised' weapon or policy. For example, insufficient or inaccurate information about conditions in German prison camps led the British to prohibit the use of tobacco among German prisoners and reduce German officers' pay in British prisons, because the Foreign Office believed the Germans had instituted similar policies in their camps. The Germans retaliated against the British for the use of 'hard labour camps', when the British sent German PoWs from England to work on the docks at Le Havre, by sending four times as many British PoWs to work in Libau, in German-occupied Russia.[11] Gerard also reported that sometimes, too, the commandants of German prisoner of war camps took things into their own hands and ordered reprisals against British prisoners on the basis of rumoured ill-treatment of German prisoners or civilian internees in the UK. There is no evidence to show that individual British commandants behaved in a similar way.[12]

Interestingly, though rather belatedly, in July 1918, the War Cabinet set up a subcommittee, chaired by Lord Newton, to review the effectiveness of reprisals. It noted the equivalent (or occasionally tougher) German reactions to measures such as the stricter treatment meted out to submariners, and their response to the transfer of German prisoners to France to work there (which they considered to be harsher and inappropriate). It also recorded that in February 1918, in view of 'the many petty annoyances and improper treatment to which many British officers had been subjected' in certain camps in the Tenth Army Corps district,* commanded by General Karl von Hänisch, the British government had retaliated 'by subjecting all German officers in the Northern Command to equal annoyances and by withdrawing privileges'. However, the Germans simply retaliated further. The subcommittee noted just two instances where retaliation, or the threat of retaliation, had produced satisfactory outcomes. The first was when the merchant ship SS *Caledonia*, under the command of Captain James Blaikie, was torpedoed and sunk by the German submarine *U-65* in December 1916. The crew captured Blaikie, who had attempted to ram the submarine in self-defence after it was torpedoed and while it was sinking. The British government threatened reprisals 'if the German Government should see fit to execute Blaikie, as they had earlier executed [Captain] Fryatt'. (Captain Charles Fryatt, who was in command of SS *Brussels* in March 1915 when it was attacked by *U-33*, had attempted to ram the submarine, which dived to avoid him. He was later captured by the Germans, court-martialled as a *franc-tireur*[†]and executed.[‡]) The Germans took no action against Blaikie. The other concerned an issue early in the war when following German ill-treatment of Russian prisoners, the Russian government placed German officers

---

* These included Ströhen, the last camp which Gilbert was sent to in May 1917.
† A term generally used to refer to guerilla fighters who operate outside the laws of war.
‡ This caused a large protest in London and led the War Cabinet to consider the confiscation of all German property in the UK as a reprisal for his murder. They explored whether the French and Russian governments would be willing to support this or possibly other measures, though without result. (TNA, CAB 42/17/1.)

in camps for other ranks. It was noted that this had apparently been successful. The subcommittee concluded that whereas the threat of reprisals in the cases of individuals had achieved success, 'whenever we have embarked upon a system of collective reprisals, the results from our point of view have been thoroughly unsatisfactory'.[13] It is hard to resist the conclusion that it was a pity that this lesson was not learned earlier.

A different sort of example, though, is provided by the increasingly effective Allied economic blockade. The Allies hoped that such a blockade could help starve the German civilian population into submission and, therefore, that it would be an appropriate measure. The German response was that this provided a justification for ensuring that the diet and nutrition in their prison camps should reflect conditions on the German home front more generally.[14] The Foreign Office took the view that the diet, which consequently was provided, would just about keep men doing little work alive but prolonged exposure to it would result in 'serious prejudice' to the health of captives.[15] And, of course, most of them were engaged in demanding labour.

The consequence of such an inadequate diet for many prisoners meant that they lived on the verge of starvation, especially if they were working. It has been estimated that by the end of 1916, at least 1.1 million prisoners of war were employed in some form of labour, with about 340,000 working in industry and trade and over 630,000 in agriculture.[16] And they were sometimes doing so in very dangerous circumstances. In retaliation for the British supposedly having sent German prisoners to work within five miles of the Western Front, the Germans sent British prisoners to work within just a couple of hundred yards of the Russian front line. As author John Lewis-Stempel highlights:

The work was clearing snow out of German trenches and cutting timber for nine frostbitten hours a day. When they weren't dodging Russian machine-gun bullets that is. The rations were two-fifths of a three-pound loaf a day (the only solid food), one cup of coffee and a bowl of soup. Accommodation was in a dugout. 'We were like skeletons: shoulder bones, hip bones, knees and elbows were horribly prominent.'[17]

Some prisoners died before this reprisal was lifted.

It was little better for those prisoners who were sent to work on forced labour gangs. As Lewis-Stempel quotes:

We began our day by being walked on and walloped with sticks while it was still dark. Then we were shoved into lines of four men and issued with a drink of coffee made with burned barley. A piece of bread was the day's ration, but as most of the fellows were nearly mad for food the first one got the most – if he was strong enough to keep it! Our work would carry on until about five in the afternoon … On arriving at the lager* we were issued with another meal. This meal consisted of stewed something. At first this was sometimes macaroni with a little meat mixed with it. By about June it became dried vegetable. This mess of pottage consisted of turnip skins dried almost to resemble chips of wood, chopped up like sawdust and mixed with boiling water.[18]

In fact, it was often much worse than that, because of disease and overworking, as well as a poor diet. When the Committee on the Treatment by the Enemy of British PoWs recommended that

---

* The camp.

protests should be made about the lack of food being given to prisoners at Wittenberg camp, where there had already been significant problems with typhus, as we will see, the Foreign Office declined to intervene out of concern that to do so might in its turn raise awkward questions about the British naval blockade. James Hope, a Lord of the Treasury, was more candid when asked in 1917 if British prisoners in Germany were being slowly starved to death. He stated that 'the rations allowed by the German Government to British prisoners of war are undoubtedly insufficient ... It is, however, doubtful whether the rations are worse than the diet available for great masses of the German civil population.'[19] Notably, and reflecting a realisation that retaliation could be counter-productive for British prisoners, he added:

Reprisals in connection with a matter of this kind can only be justified if they are likely to prove effective; and, without prejudice to any future action that may be necessary, I am authorised to express the opinion that to enter now on a course of competitive ill-treatment of prisoners in the matter of feeding would be a policy for which the enemy are better adapted by temperament and tradition than ourselves.

It would seem that the Germans did try to feed their prisoners according to a dietary model designed to maintain their basic health. Increasingly, however, they did not have enough food to be able to do so.[20]

Food parcels were a saving grace for many British prisoners. In the first years of the war, it was up to families to provide them, once they had been notified (usually by the Red Cross) that their relatives had been captured. But gradually, the process became more formalised, leading to the formation of a Red Cross-run Central Prisoners of War Committee, which by the end of the war was employing 750 staff. It aimed to provide each prisoner with three 10lb parcels of food and 13lb of bread once a fortnight. By the end of the war, it had been largely responsible for sending over 9 million food parcels and 800,000 clothing parcels to prisoners abroad. Moreover, despite the food shortages which were prevalent in Germany, most parcels – about four out of five – reached their intended destinations. But nonetheless, many thousands of prisoners never received parcels – and withholding them was a frequent German punishment. In such cases, for those doing heavy labour, the consequences could be dire. Prisoners on penal hard labour, who were required to do twelve-hour shifts, were sometimes given a daily diet which amounted to less than 750 calories, barely a quarter of the normal recommended daily calorie intake for men leading a normal life. This led to much suffering. For example, one prisoner, Sapper George Waymark, weighed twelve stone six pounds when he was captured: by the time of the Armistice, he weighed a bare eight stone. But he survived.[21]

Disease, particularly communicable disease, took the lives of many Allied prisoners in German captivity. The most notorious – and most deadly – was typhus. The worst outbreak was in the camp at Wittenberg, which held more than 17,000 prisoners in conditions where there was severe overcrowding. There were 700 or 800 British captives, and rather more French, but the majority were Russian. The different nationalities were forced to live together – and worse, the commandant insisted that each British prisoner should share his bedding with both a French and a Russian prisoner as well. Sanitary conditions were wholly inadequate, with just one water tap per compound of more than 2,000 men. There was minimal clothing – and many prisoners lacked boots or socks too. The winter of 1914–15, when the typhus epidemic struck, was exceptionally severe, which compounded the difficulties. And the Russians arrived infected with lice, which spread quickly, as did the infectious disease they carried. (The Russians had gradually built up some immunity, so it was the British and French who were most affected.)

When, in late December 1914, the disease started to cause significant fatalities, the German commandant evacuated the camp of German personnel, putting it in quarantine and isolating it completely, so sentries were posted no closer than fifty yards from the perimeter.[22] Food supplies were simply pushed through or thrown over the wire. No medical treatment whatsoever was provided: the camp doctor entered the camp only once in the course of the whole epidemic.[23] After a month, six British doctors from the Royal Army Medical Corps were sent into the camp.* They were so horrified by what they found that one of them broke down:

Dead and living were lying next to each other in crammed, dimly lit huts; since there were no stretchers, the sick were moved around on table tops on which the men ate. These could not be cleaned because there was no soap. Some who had survived typhus succumbed to gangrene because there were no blankets, socks or shoes to keep them warm. Almost everyone was grey, pallid and running with lice.[24]

---

* The Geneva Convention of 1906 had stipulated that medical personnel were not to be treated as PoWs, though if required to do so by the enemy, they could be required to continue to carry out their duties under the direction of the enemy but should then be sent back to their own side at the earliest opportunity. This generally did not happen, though it had the advantage for prisoners in circumstances such as these, that there were trained medical staff available to care for them in camps where the Germans were not willing to provide their own.

It took more than six months before the epidemic ended in Wittenberg, and by then three of the RAMC doctors – Major Fry, Captain
Field and Captain Sutcliffe – as well as ten of the volunteers who
assisted them, had died. American diplomats were initially prevented from inspecting the camp, but after Ambassador Gerard had
eventually managed to do so, he described Wittenberg as the worst
camp he had ever visited.[25] We do not know for certain how many
deaths it caused altogether, but of the 1,975 cases of typhus thought
to have occurred in Wittenberg, there were at least 185 fatalities. The
conditions in Wittenberg may have been the worst, because of the
very significant overcrowding and the callous lack of any attempt
to provide treatment, but the typhus epidemic also ran amok in at
least another thirty camps during much of the rest of 1915 and was
also especially serious in Gardelegen. The camp there contained
over 11,000 prisoners, there were some 2,000 cases of typhus and
some 300 of them died.[26] And Heather Jones quotes an interesting
statistic from a German source showing that between mid-August
and mid-September 1915, the overall number of British prisoners
in Germany dropped by 417, which could be taken to suggest that
British prisoner deaths from typhus may have cancelled out any net
German gains achieved by capturing more prisoners of war.[27]

There were plenty of deaths from other communicable diseases
such as pneumonia, which resulted in 1,389 recorded deaths, and
tuberculosis, which killed 485 prisoners among an overall total of
at least 2,735 recorded deaths. Medical negligence, indifference or
sometimes brute sadism would certainly have contributed to those
losses. A doctor at Güstrow regularly refused to help English prisoners, saying, 'If they had not come into the war, they would not
be there.' And operations, including amputations, were frequently

performed without anaesthetic.* This happened to an Australian officer in the prison hospital at Würzburg: 'I shouted out and struggled violently, breaking the operating table.' He had both his legs sawn off.[28] Though, in other cases, prisoners were cared for much better. Lieutenant Bertram Ratcliffe was captured in September 1914, when he was shot through the lung. The treatment he received over the next few months varied from indifferent to excellent. He ended up in Ingolstadt. Although his wound had healed, he had no movement in his right arm or hand, and a German nerve specialist told him that an operation would be necessary if he was to recover the use of his arm. This was performed under anaesthetic in the local military hospital, where he subsequently spent two months, making a full recovery.[29]

Threats and violence, usually beatings, were fairly commonplace in most prison camps, though there were some where a benevolent commandant discouraged it. But there were also more serious incidents when prisoners were bayoneted. This happened several times at Ströhen, the camp from which Gilbert successfully escaped. The circumstances in which Gerald Featherstone Knight, a fellow member of 11 Squadron with whom Gilbert had served, was bayonetted by a German guard, will be described in Chapter 10.

But there was worse than this, for there were quite a few examples of cases where prisoners were cold-bloodedly murdered by the Germans. Major C. V. Fox (who himself later made a successful escape from Schwarmstedt, as will be described later†) provided a vivid example of an incident in Brandenberg. Able Seaman

---

* As Gilbert was to discover when he was in Heidelberg, when his undiagnosed appendicitis caused peritonitis, and his subsequent operation was performed without an anaesthetic. See Chapter 7.

† Fox was so badly beaten by guards when he was recaptured after an earlier escape attempt from Crefeld, that he lost an eye.

J. P. Genower had been confined there in a detention block, together with some Frenchmen and Russians, when a fire broke out. Other prisoners called to the guards to release them, which they refused to do. Those inside were driven by the flames to one end of the building, which contained a window. Genower tried to escape through it, but a guard who was watching ran up and bayoneted him in the chest, causing him to fall back. Seeing this, the prisoners rushed the building and by force of their numbers managed to evacuate some of those inside, but most of them, including Genower, died.[30]

Escapers sometimes suffered the same fate. Second Lieutenant Harold Medlicott was captured in November 1915, when a blinding snowstorm led to engine trouble which caused him to land behind German lines while carrying out a reconnaissance. He was indefatigable in his determination to win back his freedom, making a record fourteen attempts to escape* during the next two and a half years. Eventually, the Germans got fed up with him. After he and Captain Joseph Walter had been recaptured following an escape from Bad Colberg in May 1918, the camp adjutant, one Beetz, detailed eight guards to go and collect them. They were brought back on stretchers, dead. The German version of events maintained that they had tried to escape again and were shot. However, a tame guard told the British prisoners that Beetz had become infuriated with their escaping activities and had issued instructions that they should be killed. It is not therefore surprising that a British request to examine their bodies was refused.

Another example involved Captain William Morritt, East Surrey Regiment, with whom Gilbert made an unsuccessful attempt to escape from Crefeld in May 1917, which will be described

---

* This was unmatched, though Claude Templer, who later escaped successfully with Gilbert from Ströhen in August 1917, came closest to that figure, with thirteen attempts.

in Chapter 8. Following their recapture, he was transferred to Schwarmstedt. Within weeks of his arrival, he dug a very shallow tunnel. The undersoil, being of peat, was easy to work with. The Germans, who must have been very annoyed by two successful escapes at that camp within the previous ten days, somehow got to hear about Morritt's intention and made their preparations. On 27 June 1917, when making his exit from the tunnel, Morritt was shot dead by a sentry at point-blank range and another escaper with him, Captain Frederick Moysey, was also shot and badly wounded in the arm.[31] Moysey reported that the Germans who arrested him were all fully dressed: since this incident occurred in the early hours of the morning, he considered that it provided further evidence that they were anticipating an escape. The prisoners were able to identify the sentry who shot Morritt as Wolf, who was promoted to under-officer a few days later.[32] No retribution was ever taken against him either during or after the war. Morritt was, at least, allowed a military funeral.*

Inveterate escapers or those who irritated the Germans by their uncooperative attitudes were sent to *straflager* (punishment camps). There were several of them – Clausthal, Ströhen, Holzminden and Schwarmstedt – in the Tenth Army Corps military district commanded by General von Hänisch, who encouraged a harsh regime. Conditions in these camps were the cause of more complaints during the latter part of the war than almost any others, because of their oppressive and punitive regimes, overcrowding and excessive punishments for those who escaped and were recaptured or even

---

* There are some rather poignant details about Morritt's capture in late August 1914, given what happened to him later. An order to retreat was given but never reached him, so his company was attacked by the Germans from the rear as they got round behind him. Taken unawares, he was shot three times, several other bullets passed through his field glasses and clothes, and the Germans then shot at him again to finish him off but hit his sword, which broke and turned the bullet, saving his life. He was not to be so lucky the next time he came under fire.

for those who were discovered attempting to escape. Gilbert was one of many who experienced those difficulties.

Remarkably, despite significant initial misgivings, both Britain and Germany agreed to meet at The Hague for conferences facilitated by the Dutch in 1917, and again in 1918, to discuss the conditions under which their prisoners of war were held and treated. One particular concern for the Allies was the excessive German punishments for prisoners who had attempted to escape and been recaptured. The problem was that it was accepted that the law to be applied in dealing with the offences committed by prisoners should be the military law of the capturing state. And German military traditions and rules were much stricter than those of the British, so Allied prisoners were liable to fare much worse than their counterparts in British custody. It was agreed that some of their practices should be changed and that existing sentences should be remitted – which had a fairly immediate benefit for Gilbert, who (as will be described in Chapter 8) was serving a five-month sentence at the time for an earlier escape attempt. Other changes were also agreed, which ultimately led to the closure of Ströhen and Schwarmstedt and the removal of General von Hänisch from his command. Further changes were agreed at a second conference in The Hague, in July 1918, but the ratification process in Britain was protracted and came too late to make any difference before the end of the war in November.

CHAPTER 6

GETTING OUT – AND GETTING HOME

The rapid and successful German advance in overwhelmingly large numbers during the autumn of 1914 resulted in almost 20,000 British troops being captured within the first three months of the war.[*] To be captured in those circumstances must have come as a considerable shock to army regulars, for whom surrender would have been a betrayal of their long traditions and of their comrades – notwithstanding the fact that during this period, it came as a result of military operations that did not unfold as planned, rather than through any lack of spirit or determination. It was also something for which they were unprepared, for no information was given to troops leaving for France on how to give themselves up. To do so would have risked making surrender, instead of fighting to the last round, a not dishonourable option.[2] That this was the opposite attitude to the one which the War Office wished to inculcate was demonstrated in the language regarding surrender used in the 1907

---

[*] Although this was a significant number, it was significantly outstripped by the number of troops who surrendered during the rapid German advance during the spring and early summer of 1918, when well around 120,000 more were taken prisoner, of whom 100,000 were captured in March alone.

Manual of Military Law and repeated in subsequent editions. This made clear that it was a court-martial offence under the Army Act to 'display the white flag in the presence of the enemy' without specific orders from HQ or indeed to be 'taken prisoner, by want of due precaution'.[3]*

The military authorities in Allied countries did all that they could to discourage surrender by making clear that after the war or on return following a successful escape, the circumstances of an officer's capture would be examined. The French Ministry of War promulgated to all senior officers a decision taken by the commander-in-chief in November 1914 that

> any <u>unwounded</u> soldier who has been taken prisoner will, upon his return from captivity, be the subject of an investigation, with a view to determining whether there is reason to bring him before a court of inquiry (on the grounds that he surrendered, deserted to the enemy, or abandoned his post in the presence of the enemy), and then to take disciplinary sanctions against him.[4]

There were additional provisions about the behaviour of officers. The Canadians went further – all their troops, regardless of rank, were required to report on the circumstances of their capture following their return home. The British War Office decided only to investigate what happened to officers. Though, the fact that, by 1917, the process of its inquiries generally took some two years to complete (as it did in Gilbert's case) suggests that by then, it may not have been given a high priority.

---

* Aircrew were not issued with parachutes either, also for the reason that it would make them less willing to fight – although it would not have been easy to make parachutes small enough to fit into the cramped cockpits of that period, though the Germans managed it. Balloon observers were issued with parachutes, because they were more vulnerable, and their baskets were big enough permit them to be worn.

Nonetheless, the War Office retained concerns about unjustified acts of surrender throughout the war. Lord Alfred Milner, Minister without Portfolio in David Lloyd George's War Cabinet, signed off a memorandum by the Army Council in May 1918 which expressed alarm about the way in which sections of the press were reporting public attitudes towards some of those who had been taken prisoner. It stated that officers and men who had been wounded or incapacitated could rightly claim sympathy.* But unless someone who was unwounded and captured could justify his act of surrender, it would be 'if not a military crime, then at least a lapse from the high standards of the past which had enabled the British Army to assist in building up the British Empire'. Milner continued:

> During the present war, a large number of surrenders have taken place which, if evidence could be produced, would be found to have been without any justification, and records exist indicating that when those concerned are released, drastic steps should be taken to deal with them for their behaviour ... Those officers and men who surrender while unwounded should be looked upon as having failed to carry out their duties as soldiers to the full.[5]

However, the problem caused by the lack of guidance from the War Office about the circumstances in which surrender might be acceptable was that there could be no guidance provided either on the subject of escape. The *Manual of Military Law* made clear that it remained a court-martial offence if anyone 'fails to rejoin His

---

* John Lewis-Stempel observes that the casualty level in some units during the Battle of Le Cateau in August 1914 was as high as 70 per cent and that, overall, some 25 per cent of British prisoners captured in the First World War had been wounded. 'There is, however, no absolute and direct correlation between wound rates and surrender rates; Scottish regiments famously bled buckets and yet were among the least likely to *"Hände hoch"*.' (*The War Behind the Wire*, p. 4 and pp. 306–7.)

Majesty's service when able to rejoin the same'.[6] What 'when able' meant was not explained, which left it up to the officers concerned to decide whether or not to try to escape.

The consequence of this lack of clarity was uncertainty and disagreement. For example, Lieutenant Duncan Grinnell-Milne, RFC, commented that when he arrived in the camp at Mainz, he found that among the older prisoners, there were very few who had any intention of trying to escape. This was partly due to their ill-treatment, which had lowered their morale and their physical fitness, but also due to the advice given to them by senior officers in the camp. Several of them believed that it was almost impossible to get out of the camp and quite impossible to cross a neutral frontier to freedom. Moreover, the German authorities had informed them that in the event of anyone escaping, very severe reprisals would be taken against those remaining. Eventually, quite a lot later, the senior British officer (SBO) called a meeting to canvass about the question, and the majority opinion was in favour of not hindering such activity.[7] In other camps, it was even worse. When Captain Philip Godsal arrived in Torgau in October 1914, he discovered that following some problems with their German captors,

> the senior British officer practically undertook to maintain order among the other British officers and to see that none escaped. When I arrived, the senior British officer was Colonel Gordon VC, Gordon Highlanders,* and the German commandant's name was Braun ... The arrangement was, I believe, made between these two. Anyway, Colonel Gordon practically ordered us not to escape. Our roll call was called by a British officer, and I

---

* Colonel William Eagleson Gordon VC CBE. Godsal added that he believed that Colonel Gordon had been severely wounded in South Africa and had been in ill health ever since.

understand that when Major Yates [*sic*] escaped, he was reported missing by some British officer to the commandant.[8]

A slightly different interpretation of Gordon's actions was provided by Second Lieutenant Henry Le Grand of the Intelligence Corps, who was also incarcerated in Torgau. He observed some years later that a number of the older officers in Torgau suffered with mental illness as a result of their captivity. It was this which led Colonel Gordon to order officers not to escape. (Though not everyone obeyed. Lewis-Stempel points out that 'almost symbolically, while Gordon was decrying escaping, Lieutenant Claude Templer,* in collaboration with Lieutenant A. B. W. Allistone, 6/Middlesex Regiment, was digging a hole under his very feet'.[9]) Gordon was apparently concerned that it would be harder for those left behind if some did escape. Le Grand also reported that when Major Yate escaped, he was in all probability lynched by German civilians – though the Germans officially announced that he had committed suicide.[10]† One of Gordon's successors as SBO at Mainz, Colonel S. C. F. Jackson DSO, of the Hampshire Regiment, reported that he was regularly asked by the German authorities to exert his influence for the maintenance of discipline among British officers. He would reply that he was quite ready to do this, on the understanding that he would never consider it his duty to dissuade an officer from escaping, nor would he take any steps to prevent an officer from doing so.

In another case, Lieutenant Beverley Robinson, of what was by then the Royal Air Force, was being taken to Aachen for what he

---

* With whom Gilbert later escaped successfully from Ströhen.
† There remains some uncertainty about the circumstances in which Charles Yate, or Yates, died. It has not been possible to identify him.

expected would be an exchange. He knew that two fellow prisoners had sought permission from the SBO to escape and were absolutely forbidden to do so. Consequently, he did not ask for permission and simply got out of the camp and crossed the border successfully. In his War Office interview after his return to London, he stated that he considered that his attempt was not only justified but it was also a duty. He complained that the War Office had never provided a ruling on this point. Had there been, he was certain that other attempts would have been made long before. The absence of any ruling was the sole reason which had prevented them.[11]*

There were more extreme examples in some Turkish prison camps, where conditions were often very harsh.† Some camps were situated in remote locations, meaning that escapers would need to travel long distances over barren, largely deserted and hostile terrain in attempting to regain their freedom. When four officers escaped from Kastamuni (about 200 miles north-east of Ankara, near the Black Sea) in late 1917, the other prisoners were moved to a more remote location at Changri (in the same area) and the Turkish commandant warned that any further escape attempts would result in a further move to an even harsher environment. The British SBO, Colonel H. R. Annesley, tried to persuade the other

---

* Robinson was interviewed in 1918 by Victor Cavendish-Bentinck, whose job at this stage required him to debrief those who had escaped successfully. During the Second World War, in December 1939, Cavendish-Bentinck was appointed chairman of the Joint Intelligence Committee (JIC). A little earlier that year, in October, the JIC had received a proposal written by Major J. C. F. Holland of Military Intelligence Research (MIR), recommending the creation of a separate organisation under the War Office to facilitate the escape of captured prisoners from German and Italian prison camps. Cavendish-Bentinck had been involved in the work of the JIC since June 1939, so it is highly likely that he would have been involved in the consideration of this proposal and that he would have taken into account his experience of interviewing escaped PoWs over twenty years earlier when assessing it – and the outcome was the creation of MI9.

† Although Turkey had signed the 1899 Hague Convention, it was not a signatory to the 1907 Hague Convention, which slightly modified some of the specifications concerning the treatment of captured prisoners. British government attempts to negotiate with Turkey over the treatment of British prisoners were slow to bear fruit. A Cabinet meeting in October 1917 noted that the Turks had only accounted for 4,000 to 5,000 out of a total of 10,000 British prisoners, judging that the remainder had probably died as a result of the treatment which they had received while in captivity. (TNA, CAB 23/4/20.)

prisoners to give their word that they would not attempt to escape. Those who agreed, and who later provided a written undertaking not to escape, were moved to a different camp, but a third of the officers refused, ignoring a written order not to try to escape, and they remained where they were.[*] In another Turkish example, the SBO in Yozgad (about 100 miles east of Ankara) became aware in early 1917 that Cedric Hill, an Australian officer in the Royal Flying Corps, was about to attempt an escape from there. He put strong pressure on Hill to give his word that he would abandon his attempt, warning him that if he did so, it would endanger not only his own life but the lives of other prisoners as well. Hill felt obliged to give his word not to proceed.[12†]

In the absence of an unambiguous policy directive on the subject, there was a broad spectrum of opinion among captured British officers in German camps about the extent of their responsibility to escape if they were fit enough and able to do so. Most of the incidents described above demonstrate the difficulties which could be caused by a difficult and negative SBO. In many other camps, this was not the case. Officers were then left to decide for themselves whether they were in a position to try to get away. And the results were consequently quite varied. It remained a subject of debate even after the end of the war. As Michael Harrison, who

---

[*] A court of inquiry after the war concluded that Colonel Annesley had behaved somewhat precipitously towards those who refused to give their word but that he and other senior officers were not to blame for their actions to safeguard the welfare of the prisoners in the camp.

[†] Hill later found an alternative and quite remarkable means of escaping successfully. Together with a fellow officer, Lieutenant Elias Jones (a Welsh lieutenant in the Indian Army), they convinced their Turkish captors that they were mediums adept at operating a Ouija board for supernatural communication. Taking advantage of the greed of the Turkish camp commandant, with promises of buried treasure via the Ouija board, the two men managed to engineer the circumstances of their imprisonment to favour their escape. Eventually, they persuaded their Turkish captors they were insane and, after being moved to a hospital for the mentally ill in the summer of 1918, the two men played their roles as lunatics so successfully they also fooled the doctors and were returned home, where they arrived shortly before the Armistice. Jones described their experiences in *The Road to En-Dor* (London: Hesperus, 2014), one of the best escape books of the First World War.

escaped successfully with Gilbert from Ströhen, observed more than a decade after the end of the war that 'different opinions "still existed" as to whether it is right or not for a prisoner of war to try to escape'.[13] Harrison was one of a small number of officers who had successfully escaped during the First World War, who provided advice and assistance to MI9 after it had been established at the beginning of the Second. A. J. Evans, another successful escaper in the First World War who also assisted MI9, commented on the dispiriting consequences which could affect those who declined to become involved in escaping. He observed that many prisoners deteriorated mentally and physically as a result of their imprisonment, while very few suffered similar symptoms in the Second World War as a result of 'barbed wire disease'.[14]

By then, the attitude of the War Office had changed, and the concept that it was an officer's duty to escape had become well established.

This, and the support provided to prisoners by MI9, helped to instil a much more widespread determination among prisoners to find ways of regaining their freedom during the Second World War. A far higher percentage of prisoners in this war sought to escape – but according to Evans, the number which succeeded was smaller than it had been between 1914 and 1918 (though see below).[15] He gave several reasons for this. The number of available destinations had declined and far more of Europe – in particular, Holland – was hostile territory. The Germany Security Police, better known as the Gestapo, was an efficient and ruthless organisation, meaning that security was tighter and escaping prisoners faced more challenges. Camps were more secure and harder to get out of. And the range of books written after the First World War by prisoners describing how they had got away meant that the Germans had a pretty good idea of the range of techniques which had been used successfully and which might be used again.[*]

So how did those Allied prisoners who were intrepid enough to contemplate escape set about doing it? What were the problems which they needed to overcome?

They faced three quite different problems:

- Getting out of their prison camp, usually by going over or through the barbed wire fences or walls, exiting through the gate by bluff or concealment, or by tunnelling.
- Negotiating their passage through hostile German territory without being detected, and equipping themselves beforehand with enough escape equipment and food, as well as appropriate clothing, to make that possible – and concealing it during frequent searches.
- Getting across the border into a neutral country, usually Holland, sometimes Switzerland or far more rarely Scandinavia, either overland to Denmark or by sea to Norway or Sweden.

Getting out of well-guarded prisons, usually either camps, sturdy old fortresses or other buildings which had previously had some military use, was almost never straightforward. It was much easier for someone to escape when they were outside the camp, where supervision might not be quite so close. So officers sought opportunities to swap identities and places with soldiers in other camps who went out on agricultural working parties (as C. V. Fox did) or posed as orderlies. Lieutenant R. J. Fitzgerald, Gloucester Regiment, and

---

[*] Apart from *The Road to En-Dor*, the other two classics which particularly stand out are M. C. C. Harrison and H. A. Cartwright, *Within Four Walls: A Classic of Escape* (Barnsley: Pen & Sword, 2016), and A. J. Evans, *The Escaping Club* (Stroud: Fonthill Media, 2012).

Lieutenant G. P. Harding, RFC, did this successfully to get out of Ströhen in September 1917. Having already dressed as orderlies, they cut through the barbed wire fence to get into the orderlies' camp next door. That evening, they walked outside the camp to a pump to wash themselves, as orderlies were permitted to do after finishing work. And then they simply ran off: the old sentry who was supervising use of the pump was taken by surprise, so did not fire at them, and was unable to chase them. Their journey to the border was uneventful, though Harding lost his boots and some of his clothing when swimming the River Ems, which made the last part of his journey rather uncomfortable.[16] Quite a few prisoners jumped off trains which were transporting them from one camp to another, as H. S. Ward and H. F. Champion succeeded in doing (and separately A. J. Evans and S. E. Buckley as well) when they were, fortuitously, relatively close to the Swiss border. The fact that the number of ordinary soldiers who made successful escapes was much higher than that of officers is largely explained by the fact that they could slip away from a working party relatively easily.

Acquiring the knowledge to navigate their way through Germany towards a neutral border took escaping prisoners time and was often obtained during previous unsuccessful attempts and then shared. It was no coincidence that nearly half of those who did manage to escape successfully had already made two unsuccessful attempts, as Gilbert had done, so were familiar with many of the difficulties which they would have to negotiate. Wing Commander C. E. H. Rathbone, RAF, one of those who successfully escaped through the tunnel at Holzminden in July 1918, put it quite succinctly: 'I may say that escaping entails many hardships, coupled with long periods of cells. A first attempt very seldom succeeds, and it is only by paying great attention to every small detail that one can hope to achieve one's object.'[17]

'Prisoners' universities' such as Fort IX at Ingolstadt, where Evans spent time, would have been enormously useful for learning about potential techniques for getting out of camps, as well as other relevant skills. On his first escape after his capture in July 1916, Evans got almost as far as the Dutch border. As a result, he was transferred to Ingolstadt, where the Germans collected many of the prisoners who had unsuccessfully tried to escape already, so that they could keep a closer eye on them. These totalled some 130 out of 150 inmates. Evans calculated that when he arrived, at least 75 per cent of these were scheming to find means of getting out again. They all reckoned that they had been caught through ill fortune and were determined to do better the next time. The most frequent subjects of conversation, which were rarely out of the thoughts of the great majority of them, were escaping and how it should be done, what to beware of and what to risk, what food to take and what clothes to wear, how to get maps and compasses, how to look after your feet (because of the distances to cover and the need for adequate footwear) and how to light a fire without smoke, where to cross the frontier and what route to take and a hundred other things connected with escaping. Each man was ready to give the benefit of his experiences, his advice and his immediate help to anyone who asked for them. In fact, wrote Evans, 'we pooled our knowledge, and the camp was nothing less than an escaping club'. He continued:

There were in the camp, mainly among the French, some of the most ingenious people I have ever come across. Men who could make keys that would unlock any door; men who could temper and jag the edge of an old table knife so that it could cut iron bars; expert photographers (very useful for copying maps); engineering experts who would be called in to give advice on any tunnels; men who spoke German perfectly; men who shammed insanity perfectly and many like myself who were ready to risk a bit to get out but who had no parlour tricks. One man had escaped from his prison camp as a German officer; another had escaped in a dirty clothes basket and another had been wheeled out of the camp in a muck tub.

He added: 'It can well be understood that the Germans, having collected into one camp 150 officers with the blackest characters, took considerable precautions to keep them there.'[18] In fact, very few managed to get out of Fort IX and not one succeeded in getting across the frontier. However, when later the Germans distributed the most aggressive prisoners among other camps, nearly 50 per cent of them escaped and many got home – which was a powerful demonstration of the unusual sort of university education which Ingolstadt had provided!*

The French, incidentally, had some significant success as escapers and achieved far more home runs than the British were able to manage.† Sometimes British and French prisoners escaped together. Henry Cartwright‡ and Anselme Marchal very nearly made it but

---

* Future French President Charles de Gaulle (who altogether made five unsuccessful attempts to escape) was among the other inveterate escapers who were held there, whose number also included Roland Garros and the future Soviet Marshal Mikhail Tukhachevsky.

† It has not been possible to establish precisely how many French prisoners succeeded in escaping in the First War. However, a Cabinet paper of 4 October 1917 records that by that time, 480 French prisoners had made home runs. (TNA, CAB 23/4/19.) A separate Cabinet paper of the same date records that 141 British prisoners (twenty-two officers and 119 other ranks) had achieved the same result. (TNA, CAB 24/28/12.) It seems reasonable to assume that these sorts of rates would have been maintained during the last year of the war, when conditions for escaping gradually became easier.

‡ Also an escaping partner of Michael Harrison, who got out of Ströhen with Gilbert.

mistakenly thought that they had reached Holland and were several miles inside Dutch territory – but were arrested right on the border. Cartwright discovered afterwards that his compass had become wet,[19] and the needle was partially frozen, so it did not provide accurate readings. He thought that they must have roamed around the frontier for several hours and crossed and recrossed the border several times during that period. In February 1918, Marchal subsequently got away successfully with Eugène Roland Garros, who had earlier designed an effective interrupter gear, protective deflecting metal wedges which were fitted over propeller blades and enabled guns to be fired forwards.[20] (Incidentally, just as Blériot was the first to cross the Channel, so Roland Garros was the first to fly non-stop across the Mediterranean and he also shot down at least four German aircraft.*) Unfortunately, the Germans learned about his interrupter gear when his engine failed, and he was captured in April 1915. The Dutch aircraft designer and manufacturer Anthony Fokker[†] studied it and was then able to develop an even more effective interrupter system which gave the Germans a temporary advantage.

But prisoners still had to find ways of acquiring their essential escape equipment, especially maps, compasses, torches and perhaps files and wire cutters as well – and also disguising their clothing so that it did not look military. In the absence (in the early years) of any official organisation to help them, they would have needed to rely on assistance from their families in obtaining what was needed and devising means of sending it to them which would defeat the scrutiny of their guards. To achieve this, they needed to be able to communicate safely, without attracting German attention. How to

---

* He was shot down and killed in October 1918, and the tennis centre in Paris which was built in the 1920s was named after him.
† Fokker, an aviator as well as an aircraft designer, had moved to Germany before the war and remained there, building a significant number of aircraft which were used by the German Air Force.

do that? Later in the war, some far-sighted officers prepared codes which they shared with their families, which they might use with them if captured. Later still, MI1c provided briefing on devising suitable codes, as will be explained in due course. But during that early period, prisoners had to rely on their own ingenuity and luck. Some tried but without success.[21] Gilbert tried a different technique. He used milk as an invisible ink and, knowing that the Germans tested letters for different such inks by passing them through some special iodine-fume cabinets, he wrote his messages on the inside of the envelopes. But his family did not realise what he was doing and did not detect them. Then his father, Gilbert senior, received a visit from one of his former patients, a widow whose son was a French Army officer incarcerated in a German prison camp.* He had sent his mother a coded message, using a cypher system they had devised together before he left on active service. This requested her to get in touch with Gilbert's parents and to pass on the details of this cypher. Gilbert senior then re-examined all the letters the family had received from Gilbert and found that he had indeed sent them a coded instruction, telling them 'to apply heat to all the *envelopes* which he had sent'. They did so by using a domestic iron and found messages on the inside of just about every envelope which they had received.[22] Jack kept a file containing all the messages which Gilbert had sent in the course of his captivity, either by secret writing, occasionally by use of a code or sometimes by some other even more imaginative means, as will be described in Chapter 7. Jack calculated that they totalled over 5,000 words. These messages did not just include Gilbert's requirements for escape equipment; they sometimes contained intelligence, too. For example, probably

---

* A reference in Gilbert senior's papers suggests that this was very probably a Madame Ducellier de Brabandes, whose son was imprisoned with Gilbert in Ingolstadt.

by bribery or theft, Gilbert managed to get hold of a copy of the latest German infantry training manual and passed on descriptions of the most important sections. Jack typed them up and sent them on to the appropriate department dealing with that subject.[23]

The use of veiled, or cryptic, language was also sometimes effective, provided it was interpreted correctly by the recipient. Gilbert used it in a letter to Jack when he was still in a prison hospital in Cologne, suggesting that he would soon be leaving for a prisoner of war camp and would welcome maps showing the approaches to neutral frontiers. Jack visited the Cartographic Department of the British Fourth Army and was given about thirty huge maps, providing a supply which he was able to draw on when sending Gilbert what he specifically needed over the next year and a half. When required, they were reduced and printed on tissue paper.[24] Gilbert was able to secrete these during searches and still had some of them with him when he arrived in Heidelberg in August 1916. The knack when using veiled language in this way was to devise a means of concealing the key phrase or request in a sentence which would not arouse the curiosity of the German censor enough to make him suspicious but which would puzzle friends or family at home to such an extent that they would realise the significance of the reference. A simple example, also quoted by Lawrence Wingfield, who was to escape from Ströhen not long after Gilbert, was the following, written by Henry Cartwright: 'I know young Ambrose [which was not his name] better than you do, and I know you've hit on the very thing he wants … If you want to please him, send him some of the pictures of the edge of the dear old Cheese country.' This worked, and he was soon sent some maps of the Dutch border.[25] Cartwright did even better when he wanted a compass which needed to be luminous, to replace one already supplied, which the Germans had found: 'I have lost the dear little copy of "Lead, Kindly Light" which you sent me. I should so like to have another, but the one which you sent me was much too good considering how easily such small volumes get lost, but I did love the illuminated capitals.'

He thought that the censor might have thought the endearment a bit sloppy, but it worked, and a luminous compass arrived by return of post.[26]

Other prisoners developed their own simple codes. For example, Lieutenant Geoffrey Lamb, of the King's Liverpool Regiment, adopted a very simple one, using the first letter of each sentence in the letters he wrote home to spell out a message. He wrote a letter from Fort IX, Ingolstadt (for he was another inveterate escaper), requesting that a large-scale map of the Swiss frontier be sent to him. He also asked for a pair of wire cutters. His family approached a company manufacturing powdered milk and asked for help with concealing this contraband. The company obliged, though it proved necessary to return the tin and ask for it to be done again because the wire cutters rattled when the first tin was shaken![27]*

Other prisoners did much the same. For example, there is a letter in the Imperial War Museum archives written in July 1916 by Harold Medlicott to Herbert Ward, whose escape is described below. In it, Medlicott asks for a compass, a map, money and wire cutters. Unfortunately, the explanation describing how his code worked has not survived – though his statement that 'I have received the £5 which you have sent me, but not the nail scissors which I rather want' was probably his reference to money and wire cutters.

A. J. Evans was one of the first who was savvy enough to

---

* Lamb was repatriated and interned in Holland in June 1918.

anticipate the possible need for coded communications. When he was on his last leave in UK before he was shot down in July 1916, he had arranged a very simple code with his parents. He used this to request that his mother send him maps of the area between Ingolstadt and the Swiss frontier. She had some difficulty in buying the right maps, so his father contacted an old friend, Colonel Clive Wigram, who was private secretary to King George V. The King was much intrigued and instructed that the maps should be obtained and sent to Evans. They arrived safely at Fort IX, with some being baked in the middle of a large cake and others concealed in a packet of Oswego flour. Unfortunately, the maps only covered the country south of Ingolstadt and when Evans later escaped with Captain Sidney Buckley, also RFC, it wasn't until the fifth night of their journey that they reached Gunzenhausen, which featured on the very edge of the maps. Previously they had often got lost, and Buckley had had to climb up on Evans's shoulders to read signposts in the hope they could recognise one as being on the map.[28]

The acquisition of maps was critical. Prisoners became adept at copying them, so the number in circulation increased. Wingfield used plenty of them during his escape from Ströhen. He noted that they were tracings of ones which belonged to a brother officer in the camp, though he did not know how they might have been obtained. He added: 'Many curious parcels arrived from England, and despite the strict censorship to which our parcels were subjected and the frequent barracks searches by our captors, they never succeeded in confiscating all the wire cutters, files, compasses and maps which undoubtedly existed in the camp.' Lieutenant James Bennett, an RNAS officer, obtained his maps in an unusual way:

I wrote to my brother and told him I intended decorating the wall over my bed with some pictures from home, and would he go to the photographers called Stanfords in Long Acre and get a copy of the photograph of my Rolls-Royce car they took in 1915.

My brother thought I was crazy but went to see Stanfords, who turned out to be map makers. Upon showing my letter to the head of the firm, he advised that he knew what was wanted, and would pass my request on to the proper quarter.

About six weeks later I received a very affectionate letter from a man whom I had never heard of, who said that he had met my brother and then wrote two or three pages of what seemed to me to be a lot of nonsense. I read the letter again and tried to find a possible hidden message. Eventually I was successful, and the coded message told me to look inside the handle of the badminton racquet, and to take care to destroy the letter after noting the address.

A parcel arrived [containing a badminton racquet] and sure enough, after taking off the leather binding at the end, and removing the leather pad, I saw a wooden plug which I pulled out, and then out came some maps and a compass, with a message to burn the racquet to avoid the scheme being discovered.*

Bennett was later to use the equipment when he escaped successfully through a tunnel out of Holzminden in July 1918. In the meantime, he used a clever means of hiding the precious delivery, borrowing an idea which he knew that Gerald Featherstone Knight had first thought of in Ströhen. He built a false ceiling beam from

---

* Bennett either never found out, or at least certainly never revealed, which intelligence organisation had been involved in helping him. It seems quite likely that he asked his brother for this assistance on the recommendation of a fellow prisoner who had already received similar help, and thus he asked his brother to visit Stanfords because he could be confident that the management would pass on the request to whichever of MI1c or GHQ1b was in touch with the firm and capable of making these arrangements.

cardboard and painted it with cornflour until it matched those on either side of it. His room was searched on at least four occasions by detectives from Berlin, but the hiding place was never discovered.

On another occasion, Bennett took the opportunity to send a letter home via an officer who was being repatriated and interned in Holland, who was able to forward it to his family. He included a detailed shopping list of the escape equipment which he still needed. He also provided advice about how best to conceal items which were being sent to him in parcels: 'If sending something in a cake, see that it is an oblong one and put stuff in the end, not the middle, they always cut through the centre. It's the same with bread.' He added, of Holzminden, that not only was it a hard camp to get out of; it was also located a long way to the border. A prisoner had got to within fifteen miles of the border recently but was starving and had to give himself up.[29] (A photograph of part of this letter is included in the plate section.) That touched on another difficulty for escaping prisoners in the First World War. Most of them travelled on foot and had to carry everything with them which they might need. The further away they were from the border when they started, the greater the amount of food which they would have to carry with them, for there was only a limited period of the year when they would be able to supplement their provisions by foraging for vegetables or fruit from the land – as Gilbert was able to do during his escape from Ströhen in August 1917.

Incidentally, prisoners quite often asked fellow captives who were being repatriated either to Switzerland or Holland to carry private mail for them, sewn into the lining of a coat or well enough hidden elsewhere in their luggage to defeat German searches. Gilbert used this method successfully too, writing to a Mrs Verard in Cours de Rive in Geneva, who found a way of passing on his mail to Gilbert senior.[30]

The final challenge for escapers was to get across the border. The border areas were intensively patrolled by sentries, and the approaches would not only be closely guarded but also protected by hidden obstacles such as trip wires. Moreover, by the time the escapers reached that point, they would have been out and on the run for days if not weeks, very probably exhausted, because they would have been sleeping out in the open with very little cover, and extremely short of food, if they had not run out completely. So there would have been a temptation to get on as quickly as possible – and in their likely state, if they did that, then they would have been prone to errors of judgement and to making poor choices, which all too often would lead to their recapture, as happened to Marchal and Cartwright. Sometimes they thought that they had crossed the border when they had not and approached local farmers who turned out to be German, and sometimes they did not realise that they had crossed the border (which was not often well marked) and went back into Germany where they were arrested.

Gilbert, Michael Harrison and Claude Templer were well aware of these risks. So they made sure that they were as fit as possible before they escaped and were also able to supplement the food they carried with them by stealing farm produce (including some milk, a rare treat) during their journey. So when they got close to Holland, they did not attempt to cross the River Ems and the border straight away. They spent time reconnoitring to find the most suitable cross-ing point.

Fortune is said to favour the brave, but there were certainly plenty more very courageous officers, who had also shown resilience and determination, whose attempts were frustrated by sheer bad luck. But there were a good few too who benefited from the other side of the coin – such as Lawrence Wingfield experienced when he met an Alsatian sentry on the River Ems who, instead of arresting him, showed him the best place to cross. (See Chapter 1.) But luck sometimes combined with the most extraordinary coincidence, as Captain J. A. L. Caunter, of the Gloucesters, discovered after he had escaped on his own from Schwarmstedt in June 1917 and was making his way to the Dutch border:

And now happened the most remarkable thing that could well have fallen to the experience of anyone outside a novel.

I was walking along a hedge very slowly, watching a German in the distance, when suddenly I thought I heard my name being spoken very clearly and distinctly. Again I heard it and this time I was certain, and immediately thought that I was imagining it and that I was really going mad. I was told afterwards that I clutched my head with both hands. It was an awful shock to hear this, after not having seen anyone or been with anyone who knew me for two and a half days, and having crossed two rivers and got miles from the camp in which my only acquaintances and friends in Germany were locked up. I turned round and then I heard it again coming out of the hedge, and not only my name this time but an exceedingly English sentence which told me that I was a something fool, and that I was to come back. I promptly did so and found Major C. V. Fox DSO and Lieut. Blank* lying at the bottom of the hedge. I at once joined them, and I naturally thought that all the officers from the camp had escaped and were spread far and wide over Germany, and that I had found a couple of them without being unduly lucky. However, that was

---

* This was Lieutenant J. O. Groves, RN. See John Lewis-Stempel, *The War Behind the Wire*, p. 234. However, Groves is not mentioned in the account given by Fox in his debriefing following his return to the UK. (WO 161/96/20.) Caunter's debriefing (WO 161/96/19) does not, unusually, give any details at all of his escape.

not the case. Fox and Blank had escaped sixteen hours after I did, but while I had been hung up between the ambush and the first bridge for four hours, they had pushed ahead and crossed both rivers and got to their present hiding-place at daybreak.[31]

The three of them decided to team up and travel on together, though Groves dropped out near the border and subsequently gave himself up, as he was having difficulty walking and given his condition, he was also not sure that he could swim across the Ems. When Caunter and Fox got across this obstacle, Fox (like Harding had also done) lost his boots in the river, but Caunter was able to lend him a pair of thick socks. They decided to cross the border separately to improve the chances of at least one of them making it over. In the event, they both did. Caunter was later awarded an MC, while Fox received a Mention in Despatches.

The first successful British escaper of the First World War was the improbably named Major Crofton Bury Vandeleur, Scottish Rifles, who escaped from Crefeld more than a year before Gilbert was captured, in December 1914. Having pinched the uniform of a German officer and walked out through the gates, he caught a train most of the way to the Dutch border, during which, in an act of remarkable effrontery, he smoked cigars and (for he was a fluent German speaker) chatted with the German officers whom he was accompanying. He crossed the border without trouble and returned to London. Legend has it that he turned up at his club in St James still wearing German uniform.[32]* For this remarkable achievement, he was awarded a DSO after the war.[33] Vandeleur's panache and

---

* After Vandeleur's escape, the commandant ordered as a reprisal that all prisoners should hand over all cigarettes and tobacco which they happened to have in their possession, and smoking was banned for the next three months. Permission to buy wine and tobacco was also withheld for the same period. (TNA, WO 161/96/33.)

effrontery was never quite matched during the Second World War, though the attempt which probably came closest to it was made by a Royal Navy lieutenant, David James. He described it thus:

> Owing to the large number of uniforms to be seen in Germany, I resolved to attempt to escape in full British naval uniform, carrying a card purporting to be a Bulgarian naval identity card in the name of I. Bagerov, a trade name which will be remembered long after my own is forgotten.

(He was probably right, even though he did make a name for himself as a Conservative MP, serving for twenty years after the war.) James got as far as the port of Stettin on the Baltic before he was caught. However, after the standard punishment of a spell in solitary confinement, he managed to escape again soon afterwards, disguised this time rather more prosaically as a Swedish sailor, and made it successfully to Sweden.[34]

The next Allied officer to make it back to Britain was Major Peter Anderson, 3rd Battalion (Toronto Regiment), Canadian Expeditionary Force. He was actually born a Dane but had lived for most of his life in Canada. He was captured at Ypres in April 1915 and escaped from Bischofswerda in Saxony, which he described as the best prison camp in Germany, five months later in September, though he generously overlooked the fact that the camp interpreter, whom he described as a very lazy man, who instead of censoring letters as he was supposed to do, just destroyed them – Anderson calculated that around thirty of his letters failed to arrive. He spent much of his time in prison gathering the equipment he needed for his escape, much of which was donated by fellow prisoners. He got out by crawling over the stables and then – using a grappling hook – he climbed over three high wire fences and past two lines of sentries. It took him seven hours to do that. There were few successful escapes at this stage of the war, and Anderson had several things in his favour. He was well over the normal military age, so did not attract attention or suspicion. He had been a woodsman and hunter in Canada, so was used to living in the open and keeping out of sight. He had learned plenty of German while in captivity, and could speak reasonable Danish, further factors which enabled him to avoid attention. He walked for more than 100 miles, so got well away from the area where searches might have been looking for him, before he started travelling by train.[35] On his journey back, he went through Frankfurt, Hamburg, Berlin, Denmark, Sweden and Norway and thence from Bergen back to Newcastle. He experienced no problem in getting over the German frontier into Denmark, though he added (tongue in cheek) that 'the sentries were four deep'.[36] Once in London, he had the audience with King George V which was earlier described in Chapter 1.

No other British officer succeeded in emulating Vandeleur and getting back home until Herbert Ward, RFC, achieved it with Hilary Champion, another RFC officer, in April 1916, when they were being transferred from Vöhrenbach to Heidelberg prisoner of war camp. There had been so few British escapes up to that point that German security was still quite lax. Ward explained that, remarkably, it was possible to buy from the prison canteen a map which covered the area up to the Swiss frontier. The Germans discovered this and recalled the map, but it had already been copied by a French fellow prisoner, from whom they acquired a version. On the following day, they were put on a train to Heidelberg. Some Russians, with whom they were travelling, helpfully provided a distraction, enabling them to sneak off the train while

From right to left, Gilbert with his brothers Jack and Cecil in 1900, dressed in the fashion of the time. After Gilbert was captured in 1915, Jack in particular would play a key role in smuggling equipment and information to him in German prison camps, which facilitated his escape attempts.

Jack and Gilbert (*right*) in 1914, when they played hockey for the University of Paris against other student teams in northern Europe. After the outbreak of war, one of those matches was to have unforeseen consequences for Gilbert, when he came face to face with one of the Germans whom he had previously played against.

It often took both horsepower and manpower to launch an aeroplane in the early years of aviation. Gilbert's photograph of an early Maurice Farman aircraft shows it being towed out using both, probably in 1912.

Gilbert's first and rather indistinct attempt at aerial photography, taken during a flight with Farman in 1913, showing horses and the shadow of his aircraft in a field below. These early aircraft were fragile and often mechanically unreliable.

The twelve Vickers FB5s of 11 Squadron lined up at Folkestone, prior to departure for France on 25 July 1915. All of them save one arrived at their base at Vert Galand without incident. The journey of the twelfth was full of mishaps, and the progress reports supplied by the pilot provided humour to the rest of the squadron – and irritation to his commanding officer.

An aerial photograph taken by Jack behind German lines, showing the black puffs of German anti-aircraft shells which were exploding around them.

An FB5 left upside down in a clover field – the aftermath of pilot Robert Hughes-Chamberlain's accident. He had tried to take off through a cornfield, but the corn wrapped itself around his skids and he performed an acrobatic loop, which fortunately did not injure him or his observer and left the aircraft largely undamaged.

An 11 Squadron Vickers FB5 on patrol behind German lines near Bapaume in 1915. This photograph was taken from another 11 Squadron Vickers at a height of 9,000 feet.

This German photograph of Gilbert was taken shortly after his capture and is surely one of the most remarkable images of the First World War. He is lying on a stretcher and the medical orderly at his feet was known to him; they had played hockey against each other in Hanover the previous year, in the spring of 1914.

Source: The Great War Aviation Society

Gilbert's Vickers being examined after his forced landing by German officers, who are standing on the far side of the fuselage behind the wing.
Source: The Great War Aviation Society

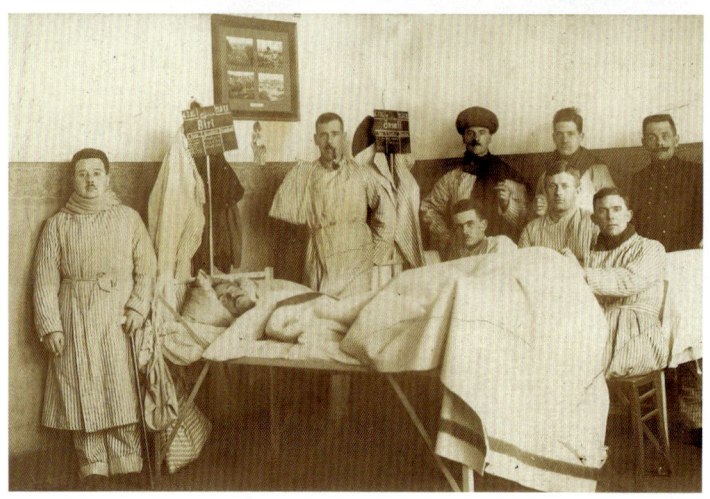

Gilbert, seated third from right, with fellow injured prisoners in a hospital in Cologne. The patient standing on Gilbert's right, at the head of the bed, is Lieutenant J. W. Reynolds, who travelled with Gilbert to Ingolstadt prison camp, where they were both imprisoned until Reynolds was repatriated on medical grounds in June 1916.

24. **Opinion of British Aviators.**—Prisoner said, "You seem to be magnetically attracted to any German aeroplane you see, and never weigh the situation. I saw one of your machines take on one Fokker, then two Fokkers, then three Fokkers, before being shot down at Lille. We do not look for fights unless it is our duty. With us a machine should return without a fight, unless it is specially sent up to fight. To return without a fight and with our work done, is the test with us."

GERMAN WIRELESS PROCEDURE FROM AEROPLANES.

(a) The enemy derives Intelligence from Wireless Signals emitted by our aeroplanes. There are Wireless Stations down the front, specially detailed to intercept our signals. The principal intelligence so far gained has been in regard to the concentration of our aeroplanes at a given point, and in warning batteries and localities that they are about to be shelled. Many lives have been saved in prisoner's own Corps sector in the latter way. The warning is done by telephone. Prisoner was not certain that Intelligence as to the location of our batteries was obtained by the interception of our Wireless calls, but he thought it highly probable. "You will never be able to do the same with us," he added, "because we have no system, whereas you have a uniform one all down the front."

(b) The enemy is *not using* Compass Stations for the purpose of locating hostile artillery aircraft. Prisoner knew the functions of this apparatus and remarked, with evident sincerity, "The Zeppelin uses the Compass Station in order to find out where it is. Why should we use one? When we are over Bapaume, we know perfectly well we are over Bapaume."

(c) A few isolated aeroplanes are now fitted with receiving apparatus. Prisoner has himself experimented with one, but found it unsatisfactory owing to the amount of signals heard.

An extract of an extremely valuable British interrogation report of Hans Baldamus, a captured German pilot. This section reveals differences in attitudes to combat, how effective the Germans were at obtaining intelligence from Allied pilots' radio transmissions and how such information was used.
Source: Vincennes Military Archives Centre

J. Just a line by the way on the Q.T. When you receive it let me know by referring to it as letter from J. This is a pretty hard camp to get out of, & when out it's a jolly long way to the border. A fellow got to within 15 mls the other day but was nearly starving and had to give up. These camps are surrounded by barbed wire with armed guards at about every 30 yards. So to get out one must have a pair of wire cutters small but very sharp so that you can cut very quickly. also small luminous compass & large scale map showing x the cross roads. German paper money is also very useful, should like say 50 or 100 mks in 10 mk notes if you should be able to get these from "Cooks" before I get home. If anyone calls on you or mother mentioning my name. You will be able to get a few tips from them & I know

Part of a letter from Lieutenant James Bennett to his mother, smuggled out by an officer being repatriated to Holland, requesting wire cutters, a luminous compass, a large-scale map and 100 German marks – items which would be essential for a successful escape.

Courtesy of James Bennett's family

A portrait of Gilbert painted by a French prisoner in Fort Prinz Karl in Ingolstadt, which Gilbert posted to his family in Paris from his next prison camp, Heidelberg. He used the package as a means of sending a long, concealed message home.

The message (*top*) which Gilbert sent from Heidelberg, showing how it was wrapped round knots which he had extracted from the wood of the painting's box. This photo also includes his tunic, turned inside out to appear civilian, which he used in his escape from the camp at Ströhen.

Image via Imperial War Museums

ABOVE The two knots which Gilbert drove out of the wooden frame, together with the wood from which they were taken and a surviving fragment of the message.

LEFT A metal container holding maps, prepared by the Insall family to be sent to Gilbert, though this one was never sent. The text reads: 'PofW Germany 1915–1917. Maps prepared for despatch (to be soldered in bottom of food tin, after sealing).' It was signed by Gilbert after the war.

LEFT The underside of the secret container, showing the maps inside and the flanges, which would have been used to attach the container to the bottom of a food tin.

The exterior of the cell at Crefeld prison camp in which Gilbert served his sentence of fourteen days' solitary confinement, extended, without reason given, to twenty days. The interior of the cell was even darker and gloomier. Taken by Gilbert on a return visit after the war.

After months of careful planning, Gilbert (*right*), Claude Templer (*left*) and Michael Harrison (*second left*) successfully escaped from Ströhen and made it safely to neutral Holland. They are pictured here in September 1917 with Gerald Featherstone Knight (*second right*), who escaped separately, during their quarantine in Enschede, Holland. The bearded man in the middle is thought to be a representative of the Consul General in Rotterdam, who had come to oversee their release.

Gilbert being awarded his Victoria Cross by King George V on 26 September 1917.

Image via Imperial War Museums

Gilbert in 1968, at a reception to mark the fiftieth anniversary of the founding of the Royal Air Force.

The author in front of a replica Vickers FB5 (*left*), the first aircraft flown by 11 Squadron, at the RAF Museum in Hendon, and a Typhoon (*right*) of XI(F) Squadron at RAF Coningsby. The FB5 weighed about a ton, had a speed of 70 mph and took half an hour to climb to 9,000 feet. The Typhoon weighs about twenty tons, has a speed of over 1,500 mph and climbs to 9,000 feet in seconds. Both, though, are representative of cutting-edge technology in their time.

it was stationary. The war had now been in progress for nearly two years, and apart from Vandeleur and Anderson, no one else had so far succeeded in regaining their liberty – yet here were these two young officers, neither of whom spoke German, claiming that they had jumped from a train in broad daylight while it was standing at a station and had then walked into Switzerland within two days, without being challenged. It was hard to credit. As a consequence, they were treated with extreme suspicion by the intelligence officers who questioned them on their arrival there, and again when they reached Paris. Quite unusually, too, despite the enterprise which they had shown, they received no medal or other recognition at the end of the war.[37]

Later that year, Lieutenant Claude Ridley successfully managed to get back to Holland from occupied France, though strictly speaking this was not an escape but an evasion, because the Germans never actually arrested him, though one did lay a hand on him. On 3 August 1916, Ridley undertook a mission to drop a French agent, Victor Marie, behind the lines. He suffered an engine failure near Cambrai and had to make a forced landing. Marie knew the area well and during the next few weeks was able to arrange for the two of them to be hidden in safe houses in a series of villages. Though many of Marie's friends and relatives were arrested, the pair managed to avoid detection – sometimes by a whisker – by the Germans who were looking for them. They had a number of hair-raising escapes, having to jump out of a back window as searching troops came through the front door, staying in houses where Germans were also billeted and nearly being arrested by sentries on several occasions when they were moving from one safe house to another.[38] Such journeys were fraught because of the large numbers of Germans around – in Hermies, a village of 2,000 inhabitants where they stayed, there were also quartered a German general, fifty officers, 100 gendarmes and 300 soldiers. Ridley and Marie eventually managed to cross the intensively patrolled border into Belgium and caught a tram towards Brussels. During this journey, Ridley was accosted by a suspicious gendarme who tried to detain him, but he hit him in the face and jumped off the tram when it was travelling at full speed, managing to avoid serious injury. At that point, he was separated from Marie, but he linked up with a Belgian who assisted him with the final stages of his journey. This involved climbing very carefully over a highly dangerous electrified fence and regaining his freedom in Holland. He was later awarded a DSO for this feat.[39]*

The experiences of Lieutenant Cecil Blain, RFC, during his captivity and his eventual escape illustrate quite vividly many of the challenges which have been described here and the imagination, versatility and determination which a prisoner might need to solve them. Blain was captured in August 1916, as a result of engine failure, not enemy action. He and his observer managed to destroy their aircraft before they were taken prisoner. They were initially confined in the old fort in Cambrai, where conditions were foul and dysentery was rife. After a couple of days on minimal rations, they were taken to headquarters for interrogation and thence to Bapaume airfield, where they were allowed to inspect and climb into German fighters, while their hosts unavailingly tried to inveigle them into comparing notes on the various gadgets they found on them, compared with what they had on their own. They were

---

* War Office bureaucracy caught up with him in November 1917, when he was instructed to provide the Army Council with an account of his capture the previous year. He had earlier been debriefed by an intelligence officer who instructed him not to discuss the details of this episode with anyone else. So the report he provided was less than comprehensive, comprising five curt sentences and stating that he had never been a prisoner of war. It took an intervention by the general commanding 6th Brigade RFC, where he was then serving, to persuade the War Office that Ridley's report reflected earlier instructions, and his rather cavalier attitude was overlooked.

sent to Gütersloh and thence to Osnabrück. Here they were kept for several weeks in what was described as quarantine, in rooms with whitewashed windows where no one was allowed to see out. They eventually discovered that they had been sent there to be shot as a reprisal of some sort. This was presumably linked to the treatment of German submariners in British custody, though the reason was never spelled out to them and nothing further happened.

Blain's thoughts quite quickly turned to escape. He and his close friends thought that the first priority should be to acquire a compass, maps and wire cutters. They concluded that rather than trying to bribe a guard, it would be better to find a way of asking their families to send them what they needed in parcels. Like Gilbert had done, they decided to use invisible writing with milk on the envelopes, rather than on the letters inside. But they needed to find a way of warning their families what they were doing. So Blain's next letter home read:

> My dearest Mother,
>
> I am so sorry to account for the los of my letters home to you but hop this one will rive soon telling you that I am very fit and well. I ccannot tell you how I long to be ome again etc. etc.[40]

The missing and duplicate letters spelled 'search all envelopes'. His mother did so and found a message written in milk on the inner flap of the envelope, requesting a compass. She did as he requested and sent Blain a compass concealed in a tin of Pascall's Crème de Menthe and, separately, a map which arrived safely hidden in the bottom of a box of chocolates. On the same day that the chocolates arrived, Blain discovered that there was a large manicure set for sale in the canteen, which included an enormous pair of nail clippers.

He bought it and found that the nail clippers cut wire like butter. Soon afterwards, he also acquired a compass from a newly arrived officer who had managed to smuggle it in. But just as they were on the point of attempting to break out, they were betrayed by a fellow prisoner, a Maltese officer, Captain Allouche. The Germans ransacked their room in their search and they lost almost all of their escape gear. Blain was held largely responsible and sentenced to solitary. After his release, he and the other frustrated escapers got their revenge by dousing Allouche with a mixture of coal dust, water, ashes and anything else they could find, including a large tin of treacle. For this, they were sent to Clausthal in the Harz mountains, in Northern Germany, south-east of Hanover, and told they would be court-martialled. Their trial resulted in a fine of 500 marks or fifty days in prison. Not much of a choice.

Blain escaped again from Clausthal and as usual was given a spell in solitary confinement. However, this was not much of a punishment as he and the other prisoners were able to get out and socialise as the cells were not properly guarded. It wasn't only the cells which weren't well guarded. Blain found a room which was thought to be used by the Germans for storage, opened it with a skeleton key and found that it contained some extremely old (1811) brandy, food and other supplies. It was there that they hid much of their contraband, for example the typewriter and stamps which they used for forging passes. (Stamps were made by using the lid of a round tin, a two-mark silver piece and a child's printing outfit which had been bought in the canteen.) After Blain had been let out of solitary, he bribed a venal guard to supply him with a civilian suit, an electric torch, a railway map and a timetable. He also managed to get hold of a steel saw and a pair of wire cutters. He escaped again from Clausthal and this time got to within a couple of hundred yards of the Dutch border. He described the German sergeant who captured him as one of the finest men in Germany, who told him quite how close he had come to freedom, before providing him with several decent meals before he was taken back to prison. One of the infamous Niemeyer twins (Heinrich) was running Clausthal by then, and Blain was quite harshly treated, though he successfully managed to palm (and retain) a compass and some money when he was stripped and searched, before he was sent off to do another stretch in solitary. Thereafter, he was transferred briefly to Ströhen and to Neunkirchen before ending up in Holzminden, where the commandant was the other Niemeyer twin, Karl, disdainfully known as Milwaukee Bill, because he had spent time in the United States and spoke poor English with a nasal American accent.* Blain was involved in building the tunnel there, which was the largest successful British mass escape during the war. For digging implements, they used table knives to remove the soil and a cold chisel and bits of rake to get through the stone. Ventilation was provided by bellows, which were made with the leather of an old RFC flying jacket, with the air shaft constructed from biscuit tins, from which the bottoms were removed so that they could be joined together. They stole bed-boards from the beds of fellow prisoners to support the roof of the tunnel. Despite the ventilation, digging conditions were not pleasant, because there were rats – plenty of rats. Blain described their effect on him: 'There were many rats living in the tunnel, and meeting one of them and seeing the glitter of beady eyes in the semi-darkness was a feeling of revulsion which was only

---

* Karl and Heinrich Niemeyer had lived in Wisconsin for seventeen years, only returning to Germany when the United States entered the war. They were both harsh and unrelenting characters who were given jobs as commandants of punishment camps which were the most strictly run and where prisoners were generally very poorly treated.

surpassed when one of the vile and foul creatures scurried over you.'[41]

It took nine months to complete the tunnel, and on 23 July 1918, twenty-nine prisoners escaped. Ten of them succeeded in getting over to Holland. They included Blain, who travelled with two other RAF officers, Captain David Gray and Lieutenant Caspar Kennard, and who crossed the border together on 16 August 1918.

But despite the support which was provided to them by their families and friends, and some impressive improvisation, imagination and determination on the part of the captives themselves to take every opportunity to get away, the number of escapes by British officers from German camps during the first two years of the war was disappointingly low, though many of those who both got out of camps and escaped successfully were RAF officers. The more occasions when prisoners escaped and acquired experience which they were able to share if they were recaptured, the more other escapers could benefit. Furthermore, when the two intelligence agencies, GHQ1b and MI1c, began to become involved, and to play a significant role in coordinating the work which was being done, providing additional advice and assistance, things gradually improved further. Very little has been written about their role, apart from coy references in some of the post-war stories written by a few of the most prominent and successful escapers themselves. This subject will be discussed in more detail in subsequent chapters, but it is worth highlighting here a previously unpublished description of the difference made by these agencies which was provided by Henry McWilliam, who escaped with Gilbert from Heidelberg. After their recapture, Gilbert and McWilliam were moved to Crefeld in March 1917, where British prisoners were being concentrated:

It was at the time of our arrival that many moves to and from this camp were taking place. Apparently, Berlin wished to have all, or nearly all, the British officers in Germany in Crefeld. Why, we did not really know, but there had been rumours of peace (or an exchange of prisoners at least) and as Crefeld was only 18 kilometres from the Dutch frontier we thought that it was possibly so that transport to Holland would be simplified ... Gütersloh was the largest camp before these moves, with about 180 officers, Crefeld had some 120. These all arrived, with others from Freiburg, Rosenberg, Gnadenfrei, Ingolstadt etc. One interesting fact about this move, was that before it took place, very few attempts to escape had been made by British officers. They were mostly in camps like Heidelberg and Ingolstadt, which were very far from any frontier and, like us, had very little information about methods, maps, routes etc. The French were the most well off in this way, as they were very well supplied with many useful things and much data by their Government and friends. These things were almost unobtainable in England, and also the French Government seemed to encourage efforts of this sort, while ours discouraged them, both in the censorship regulations, the supply of information and in the granting of permission to send things.

At the time of this move [to Crefeld] things seemed to change. We were getting far more attention from home.* I believe that measures of considerable importance and interest were decided upon in this connection. The fact remains, that whereas only twenty or thirty attempts had previously been made by English officers to escape during the whole war up to then, very nearly

---

* Although he did not succeed in making a successful escape from Germany, McWilliam was one of those who received some significant assistance from MIıc, as will be described in later chapters.

that number were made while on the way to Crefeld alone. One party, who were twenty-four strong when they left Ingolstadt, arrived only sixteen strong at Crefeld railway station, where the absence of the other eight was noticed for the first time. Of these eight, five reached England, and two were caught actually on the frontier, having crossed it and returned by accident. The other man had to give up because he was out of condition.[42]

The eight referred to by McWilliam jumped off the train when it arrived in Crefeld station on 5 April 1917, at about 8 p.m., when it was dark. There was, remarkably, no guard in their compartment, and their carriage had stopped short of the platform, so their departure was not noticed in the confusion as the other prisoners alighted. They left in two groups, one led by Captain E. F. Briggs and the other by Lieutenant D. Stewart, both RFC. Both groups subsequently split up. Briggs crossed the border two days later, early on 7 April, and Stewart and Lieutenant Gilliland were almost as quick. Both were spotted and chased by sentries, who fired at them but fortunately missed.[43] Lieutenant B. Ratcliffe, 1st West Yorkshire Regiment, who had been travelling with Briggs, was captured by a sentry shortly afterwards when he was just at the border. Ratcliffe tried to convince the sentry that he was Dutch. The sentry replied that in that case, he would be fined thirty German marks for being in that area without authority. Ratcliffe then negotiated with the sentry and succeeded in bribing him with the same amount to let him go. Whether or not the sentry swallowed his story, he willingly pocketed the money and also showed Ratcliffe the best way to cross the border, warning him about a second sentry who was positioned about 200 yards away.[44] None of these reports – indeed none of the reports in the WO 161 series based on debriefs of escaped or repatriated prisoners – make any reference to the support from home to which McWilliam refers.

McWilliam continued:

> Three others, out of many who jumped off their respective trains in this way, got over at that time, while only about six English-men had got over before since the beginning of the war. During the time that I was at Heidelberg, nineteen attempts were made, including our own, five English altogether participating, and of these nineteen none got over, and only one succeeded in reaching the frontier.[45]

It was certainly the case that as the war progressed and more knowl-edge of escaping techniques was acquired and shared, and more support became available, the number of escape attempts increased. Though that didn't necessarily mean that the proportion of success-es rose. It's simply not possible to calculate with any precision how many escapes were attempted. Lewis-Stempel notes that memoirs and evidence taken by the Government Committee on Treatment by the Enemy of Prisoners of War provide details of some 3,000 escapes and attempted escapes from Germany and elsewhere in occupied Europe. He considers that a reasonable estimate might be that somewhere between 5 and 10 per cent of all British prisoners held captive in Germany or on the Western Front made at least one escape attempt. That would mean that there were probably more than 10,000 escape attempts made altogether.[46] How did that com-pare with results during the Second World War, when the number of successes was enhanced by the significant contribution played by MI9? This needs to be done with caution, for just as Lewis-Stempel's figure is tentative, so the estimates for MI9 are similarly quite rough.

As a consequence, the calculations can be no more than indicative. In January 1944, Brigadier Norman Crockatt, the chief of MI9, told an audience (of newspaper correspondents to whom he was giving a privileged and private briefing, so that they understood the need to avoid any public reference to his organisation) that he reckoned that one in four officers and men of all the prisoners in Germany 'had been at large' already.[47] There were some 170,000 British and Allied prisoners in German and Italian hands during the war, of whom the 50,000 in Italian captivity were later taken over by the German Army after the Italian surrender. If the rate of escape attempts continued broadly as Crockatt had estimated, then there would have been about 45,000 escape attempts between 1939 and 1945, five or ten times as many as there were in the First World War. And there were approximately 3,000 successful escapes made in western Europe, compared with about 570 in the First World War. We are not looking to judge who did best in this comparison – but it seems reasonable to conclude that the results look really quite impressive in both wars.

Although we are primarily concerned here with conditions in camps in Germany, we should consider briefly what happened to Allied prisoners in Turkey, too. There were very few successful escapes, for the terrain, the distances which needed to be covered and the difficulties to be surmounted in a country where foreigners really did stand out all presented significant obstacles. So those who did manage to get away had some impressive stories to tell. The remarkable achievements of Hill and Jones, recorded in *The Road to En-Dor*, has already been mentioned. One prisoner, A. J. Evans, was a prisoner in both countries. As described above, he had escaped successfully with S. E. Buckley from Germany in June 1917 and was subsequently posted to Turkey, where he was once again shot down and captured in March 1918. He took an opportunity to escape again but was ill-prepared, lacking food or water, and his physical condition deteriorated so much that he eventually had to give himself up. He remained a prisoner until the Armistice.

Captain R. J. Tipton, RFC, and three army officers, Captain E. H. Keeling, Captain H. C. W. Bishop and Captain R. T. Sweet, escaped from Kastamuni* (some 260 miles east of present-day Istanbul) and set out in August 1917 to walk 110 miles to Bafra, on the Black Sea coast, with the intention of stealing a boat and sailing to Crimea. (They carried with them a makeshift sail, made out of a sheet, a towel and the linings of two suitcases, as well as an axe head for making a mast.) When questioned by villagers, they posed as German soldiers. The party frequently lost their bearings as they walked through difficult and undulating terrain, and they marched more than 200 miles before they got to the coast, where they were recaptured. As they were being marched back to Kastamuni, they and the soldiers escorting them were ambushed by a group of young Turks, most of whom had fled to the hills to avoid conscription. They were led by a political opponent of Enver Pasha, the Turkish Minister of War. Three of the escapers were rescued, but the fourth, Sweet, became separated in the confusion and was subsequently recaptured. The escapers' saviours also wanted to get out of Turkey, so both parties went back together to the coast, managing to avoid the large number of Turkish troops searching for them after the ambush. Eventually, after marching another 150 miles, they found a boat (though it was barely seaworthy) and managed to sail to

---

* Now known as Kastamonu.

Crimea and freedom. Their journey had taken forty-nine days. Tipton rejoined the RFC, but he was badly wounded in combat in March 1918 and died shortly afterwards.[48]

A further group of British officers escaped from Yozgad, high up in the inhospitable Anatolian mountains 150 miles east of Ankara. One of them, Captain Archibald Cochrane, RN, a submariner, had arranged, when he was at a previous camp, that a naval vessel would be at an agreed rendezvous off the coast on specific dates at the end of August 1918. Twenty-six officers decided to break out in four separate groups and try to get to this point. Leaving on 7 August, Cochrane helped to lead a group of eight of them on an arduous journey over more than 400 miles to the coast, once being attacked by brigands. They had many vicissitudes and close shaves, but they eventually reached the coast. However, they arrived later than the date agreed for them to be picked up. Shortly afterwards, thirty-five days after their escape, they found a tug in which they were able to sail to Cyprus, a voyage which took four days. Most of them finally reached England on 16 October, after a journey of two and a half months.[49]

It was generally much more difficult for German prisoners to escape from Britain during the war. There were no neutral borders, such as those to Holland or Switzerland, available to them and so they would have to smuggle themselves onto a ship sailing to a neutral country, of which the closest was Holland. German prisoners made fewer escapes than British prisoners, but there were some imaginative ones. We do not know whether GHQ1b or MI1c studied German methods to see whether they had developed techniques which might be copied by British prisoners in Germany. But the security of German prisoners, as well as the prevention of their escapes, was certainly a subject of continuing concern to the British government and was raised regularly in the War Cabinet.

Of particular interest is a detailed paper of 5 October 1917, reporting on the findings of a court of inquiry considering a successful escape by tunnellers from Kegworth camp the previous month. It was put up by Lord Derby, the Minister for the Army.

There were certainly reasons for concern. The report started: 'The Court of Inquiry which was held shows that this is the third tunnel which has been attempted during the last six months. The other two were discovered.'[50] Although another tunnel was suspected, its entrance could not be discovered despite frequent inspections and searches. The use of a geophone (a listening device) provided no evidence either. After the escape, the Deputy Chief Constable of Leicester was taken into the hut from which the escape was mounted, placed within three feet of the mouth of the tunnel and asked whether he could see any signs of disturbance. Despite spending much time searching, he could not. There was clear evidence that the entrance was well disguised. A key problem for tunnellers is the concealment of the earth which has been dug out. Here, the Germans had also found an effective way of achieving this: the camp authorities could not work out where such a substantial amount could have been concealed. They only succeeded when they called in the foreman of works who had built the camp, who suggested that it might have been hidden above the ceiling of the lecture theatre, as indeed it was – in a large area which the authorities had not known about. The prisoners had no proper implements and used a jam pot and a piece of zinc shaped like a trowel to dig a tunnel more than forty yards long and two foot six inches high.

The German escape took place during an air raid, when the lights were extinguished. Although prisoners were not permitted money other than small copper coins, one man had managed to conceal seven pounds, having given his word of honour that he had no money. (Which suggests some naivety on the part of those who did not search him properly.) All of the escapers had managed to acquire plausible civilian clothes, though it was not clear how they had done so. They had also made compasses out of metal cut from a lightning conductor and had maps which were detailed, though it was not known how they had obtained the original map from which they had made copies. The food which they carried had all arrived in parcels from Germany.*

Most British prisoners who were contemplating escape and acquiring the equipment they needed to do so would probably have been reasonably impressed by what their German counterparts had managed to do, in equally unfavourable circumstances. Indeed, it may be of interest to see how their preparations compared with what Gilbert and his fellow prisoners did when excavating the tunnel for their escape from Heidelberg earlier in 1917. (This will be described in Chapter 7.)

While not complacent, the court of inquiry's paper provided some interesting comparisons as to how the number of German escapers contrasted favourably with the position in other countries. It noted that at that moment, in October 1917, there were some 242 German prisoners at liberty in France, who had escaped from French prison camps and not yet been recaptured. However, out of a total of 2,020 officers and 42,815 soldiers in camps in Britain, the report stated that only one officer and two soldiers were known to have succeeded in making it back to Germany.

So far as we know, this latter figure is incorrect. Only one German prisoner had escaped by October 1917, who turned out to be the only

---

* The investigation was thorough and detailed, and lessons would no doubt have been learned. No evidence has been found to suggest that the Germans undertook similar investigations after Allied PoWs escaped from their camps.

person to achieve success during the whole war. This was Gunther Plüschow, a colourful and larger-than-life German Air Force pilot who began the war fighting the British in China and who attempted to return to Germany by sea, via the United States. He was captured when his ship made an unscheduled stop in Gibraltar, and he was sent to Donington Hall in Derbyshire in May 1915. Plüschow had no map or compass and did not even know exactly where the camp was. This did not stop him teaming up with naval officer Oskar Trefftz and breaking out of the camp on 4 July 1915, with the intention of travelling to London and stowing away on a ship sailing to neutral Holland. They concealed themselves in the large park surrounding the camp, which was not patrolled at night, and their fellow prisoners fooled the guards at the evening roll call so they were not missed. They walked to Derby, split up and caught trains to London, where Trefftz was caught. Plüschow read headline newspaper reports of his escape, which provided an accurate physical description and details of his clothing, adding that he was particularly smart and dapper in appearance. He therefore sought to avoid detection by sleeping in the gardens of large private houses and discarding some of his respectable clothes, lest they draw attention to him, and by altering his appearance:

I threw my beautiful hat into the river, and later my collar and tie ... After that a mixture of Vaseline, bootblack and coal dust turned my blond hair black and greasy; my hands soon looked as if they had never made acquaintance with water; and at last I wallowed in a coal heap until I had turned into a perfect proto-type of the dock labourer ... In this guise it was quite impossible to suspect me of being an officer, and 'smart and dapper' were the last words anyone could possibly have applied to me.[51]

Plüschow did not know how to find a ship to take him to Holland, but – by one of those huge slices of luck which can make the difference between freedom and recapture for an escaper – he overheard a conversation between two passengers on a bus and learned that a fast Dutch steamer departed for the Port of Flushing from Tilbury Docks every afternoon. He tried to steal a dinghy to row down to Tilbury, but it was not seaworthy and started to sink, forcing him to try to jump to safety. However, he ended up instead falling into a thick layer of viscous, clammy and malodorous mud and consequently appearing – and smelling – even more disreputable. The following day, he tried again, found another dinghy and reached Tilbury. But he was too late to catch the Dutch steamer and had to watch it disappear into the distance. So he hid nearby overnight and then waited for a suitable moment before rowing over to the boat scheduled to depart the following afternoon, the *Juliana*. He boarded it by scrambling up a massive steel anchor cable onto the deck – which was no mean feat and would have required courage, strength and balance. Caution was still needed, for there were sentries on board, but he was eventually able to hide himself under the tarpaulin of a lifeboat, where he spent the voyage, successfully avoiding detection. He arrived in Holland on 13 July, after a journey lasting nine days.[*][52]

---

[*] No German prisoner succeeded in escaping from Britain during the Second World War, though Franz von Werra, an enthusiastic and indefatigable escaper, has surely earned an honourable mention. Von Werra, a Luftwaffe fighter pilot, was captured in September 1940. He escaped three times, on the third occasion through a tunnel and out of a camp in Swanwick, in Derbyshire. He took with him his flying suit, pretended to be a Dutch pilot and managed to talk his way not only onto the base at RAF Hucknall, near Nottingham, but actually into the cockpit of an aircraft, claiming that he had been cleared to take it up for a test flight. He was detained before he could take off and was later sent to Canada. He escaped again, by jumping out of a train while being transported to another camp, and crossed the St Lawrence River, reaching safety in the then neutral United States in early 1941. While the American and Canadian authorities were negotiating his extradition, German diplomats smuggled him out of the United States into Mexico, and he eventually returned to Germany in April 1941. Von Werra resumed flying, serving on the Russian front and was later transferred to the Netherlands, where he was killed in a flying accident in October 1941.

There were other German attempts that came very near to success. In August 1917, six prisoners got out of a camp in Alnwick, on the coast of Northumberland, and stole a boat in which they tried to get across the North Sea. They made good progress but were sighted by a trawler, which reported them, and they were subsequently picked up by a destroyer 150 miles east of the Tyne.[53] And one other attempt, though it ended up as a near miss, is worth mentioning because if it had succeeded, it would have been one of the most imaginative escapes of the war – and for reasons of geography, would have been extremely difficult for a British escapee from Germany to replicate. Hermann Tholens, a senior officer on the German cruiser *Mainz*, was captured in late August 1914 and was held in Dyffryn Aled camp in Denbighshire, north Wales, where most of the other inmates were submariners. The camp was not far from the coast. Tholens conceived the idea of arranging for a German submarine to meet him at an agreed point on the coast and bring him back to Germany. He took advantage of an exchange of prisoners to send a message to the commander-in-chief of the German submarine flotillas, outlining his idea and suggesting the most westerly point of Great Orme's Head, north-west of Llandudno, as a rendezvous. This was accepted and the timings (two successive nights in August 1915) and other details were worked out in a series of letters using veiled language. Tholens and two other prisoners (one was Heinrich von Hennig, a submarine commander whose boat had been sunk after reconnoitring Scapa Flow) escaped from the camp the evening before and made their way to the coast. But on the first night, they found that they could not get down to the shore, and although the submarine approached to within 100 yards, it did not see the agreed signal they made with a lamp from the cliff top. After a careful reconnaissance the following day, they made their way down to the shore on the second night and gave their signal again. This time, the submarine came in closer than was expected but was hidden from their view by a protecting ledge of rock, so it could not see the signal which they were making. The three men were all captured shortly afterwards.[54]

CHAPTER 7

TUNNELLING OUT
OF HEIDELBERG

Gilbert spent ten weeks in hospital, mainly in Cologne, before he was judged to be fit enough to be discharged and sent to a normal prison camp. But his earlier optimism that he would soon be able to start preparing an escape, carefully hinted at in his letters to Jack, proved to be ill-founded. He was still having difficulty in walking – to such an extent that several months later, he was examined by a medical board to determine whether he might be a candidate for medical repatriation. It would take more than six months before he would be fit enough to make any realistic plan to try to get away.

At the end of February 1916, he was sent to Mainz, which was a clearing house for prisoners before they were sent to other camps. He had little to say about it that was good, making adverse comments about the food – 'much worse than in hospital' – and the lavatory facilities, which were primitive. (A frequent complaint.) After a few weeks, he was sent to Fort Prinz Karl in Ingolstadt, in Bavaria, much further south, where he arrived in April. Ingolstadt had originally been a fortress city, and several of the forts had been turned into prisons. Fort Prinz Karl was built in almost the same way as Fort IX, where the inveterate escapers were held, though it had two floors and was on higher ground. So it should have been less damp. Gilbert was one of three British officers (the others were Lieutenant J. W. Reynolds, 8th Lincolns, and Captain C. A. Anderton of the Manchester Regiment), all of whom had been serious hospital cases, who were transferred at the same time. None were yet fit, and all had difficulty walking, but they were made to march the ten kilometres from the railway station up the hill to Fort Prinz Karl.* They were the only British officers sent initially to the camp, together with some 200–300 French and Russians, though others arrived later. Their living conditions were most unpleasant. The curved roof of the fort, and the lack of adequate drainage, meant that any rain which fell just soaked through the ceilings. It came down the walls and across the floors, which were always damp. Moreover, their room was next to the kitchen and all the rubbish and greasy waste was carried through an open drain across their floor.[1] As a result, commented Gilbert, 'rats were common, too, and the place stank'.[2]

The German food was inedible, but fortunately parcels started to arrive and they were able to buy a small stove to do their own cooking. Two men had escaped just prior to Gilbert's arrival, and security was increased as a result, but none of the three were in a position to make an attempt to get out anyway.[3] However, as mentioned in Chapter 6, during this period Gilbert was able to establish reliable and secure means of communication with his family, who started to send him maps and other necessities for escaping. What's more, he was able to find ways of concealing them when he was transferred

---

* Reynolds had been badly injured by a shell splinter in his foot and gunshot wounds to his arm (which necessitated amputation), prior to his capture in September 1915. He had shared the same ward with Gilbert in the prison hospital in Cologne and was eventually repatriated at the end of June 1916. (TNA, WO 161/95/53.)

to his next prison camp, Heidelberg, in August. Two photographs included in this book's plate section show one example of the way in which this was done. The maps selected for despatch were folded very tightly and packed into a purpose-built tin container, which was sealed. Using the flanges which were attached to it, the tin would then be soldered, in a false bottom, to the underside of a food container. A coded letter would then be sent to Gilbert, warning him what to look out for. (The particular container shown in the plate section was one which the family had prepared, which was never sent to him.) Although the Germans gradually became aware of many of the techniques which were used to smuggle contraband into prison camps in parcels, and tried to frustrate them by opening the parcels and carefully examining their contents, the prisoners used all sorts of ways to avoid scrutiny. These included simple distraction of the German parcel examiners or the use of skeleton keys to break into the room where the parcels were held, pinching the containers they wanted and substituting harmless alternatives. (In Gilbert's case, in Heidelberg, they used a skeleton key made from an aluminium spoon.) Another method was for the officer to make up a dummy parcel, addressed to himself and looking as though it had been sent through the post, and arrange for a cooperative British orderly to introduce it into the parcel distribution hut, where he would then substitute it for the genuine parcel. Or the contraband might be so well concealed that the prisoner would have no concern that it might be found.

In June 1916, while Gilbert was still at Fort Prinz Karl, he was told that he and another British officer were going to Fort IX the following morning to see a doctor. It was raining hard, but they were required to walk the whole distance, some twenty kilometres. On arrival, together with other British prisoners already at Fort IX, they were carefully examined by a medical commission consisting of two German and two Swiss doctors. Gilbert was not told the reason for this – but at least he and his fellow prisoner were allowed to travel back by train, though at their own expense. It later transpired that the purpose of the commission was to consider the cases of prisoners with injuries thought sufficiently serious to justify repatriation on medical grounds. Gilbert, and another British officer, Captain C. Hutchinson of the 8th Royal West Kent Regiment who was already at Fort IX, were told that they had passed and would be sent to Constance,* for a second and final examination. This happened a few weeks later, when a larger group of them were transferred there. They were not told the results but were all moved on to Heidelberg, where the successful ones awaited the arrival of the Germans with whom they were going to be exchanged. On the eve of their departure for Switzerland, eleven out of twenty-seven (including Hutchinson) were told that they had been successful. The others, including Gilbert, stayed in the camp there.[4]

Heidelberg prison camp, where Gilbert was imprisoned from August 1916 to March 1917.

---

*   Now known as Konstanz.

A photograph of Gilbert taken in Heidelberg prison camp.

Heidelberg was a newly built camp which in the course of the war accommodated between 250 and 350 officers, the higher figure being rather more than its capacity. They comprised different nationalities, around fifty of whom were British at the time that Gilbert arrived. The quality of the food and the accommodation was tolerable, with electricity and heating stoves and adequate coal supplies during the cold winters. Prisoners were not segregated according to nationality, and there were generally between eight and ten in each room. Medical facilities were poor, though, as Gilbert was later to find out to his cost. The commandant was a reasonable man and the discipline was fairly lax. On one occasion, some of the badly injured officers who were awaiting repatriation were allowed by the commandant to go out for a drive, though after complaints from local inhabitants, this was not repeated. At the time of Gilbert's arrival, there were just three roll calls, or *appells*, a day. Prisoners were counted in their beds each day at around 6 a.m. and again in their beds at 10 p.m., and there was one further *appell* during the day, though another one was added during the late afternoon, providing some inconvenient additional scrutiny for those wishing to escape and to conceal evidence of their departure for as long as possible.[5]

The story of how Gilbert, together with Henry McWilliam and Brendan Jolliffe, escaped from Heidelberg has never been told before.* It is worth relating in full because it illustrates the extraordinary range of challenges which escape-minded prisoners had to overcome not just in establishing secure lines of communication with their families or friends,† to obtain the equipment they needed, but also a quick eye and fleetness of foot, a clear head and the ability to think very quickly when confronted with sudden problems which needed fast reactions, as well as grit, determination and toughness when pushed to the absolute limits of exhaustion. And, of course, luck. On this occasion, they didn't have quite enough of the latter.

When Gilbert arrived in Heidelberg, he was able to smuggle in a good collection of contraband, not just maps but also other escape equipment. This alone would have made him welcome, for the small number of escape-minded British fellow prisoners whom he met there had hitherto been hampered in preparing plans for getting out. Despite numerous attempts, none of them had yet been able to establish successfully any coded exchanges with their families

---

* This account of the building of the tunnel, and the subsequent escape of Gilbert, McWilliam and Jolliffe, draws on personal knowledge, private family papers, some references in *Observer* and papers of the McWilliam family, which are in the Liddle archives in Leeds University. I am grateful to the McWilliam family for permission to quote from them and in particular to use the sketches made by Henry McWilliam which vividly illustrate some of the methods they used when constructing their tunnel.

† This was during the first half of the war, before organisations were created to support escape activities, which will be described in Chapter 9.

or friends, so they had been unable to arrange supplies of escape equipment. And while there had by then been a small number of escapes, no one had succeeded or even managed to get very far away from the camp. Gilbert quickly established a close relationship with Henry McWilliam, a Royal Navy officer who was captured after his ship had been sunk by a mine in May 1915, with whom he was later to escape. McWilliam commented on how their attitude to escaping had been invigorated:

> Up to the arrival of Insall, I had been unable to make any definite plans of escape, owing to lack of material and, above all, of any means of getting the material. I had several times tried to establish a code with Home but had not succeeded, and the censorship of parcels was rapidly becoming more strict. However, the arrival of a man armed with real maps and compasses, and with much valuable information about other people's attempts and experiences, put an entirely different complexion on the matter. We at once set to work ... Every evening, we used to discuss our plans, how to get clear, how to travel, how much food to take, where to make for on the frontier, and a hundred other ideas and details.[6]

Based on an assessment of the methods which other escapers had used, they quite quickly established two principles they would follow once they had got out of the camp. They would only travel on foot and they would always plan to hide and lie up during the day, walking only at night, and – if possible – never travel on main roads or through villages. (These were sensible precautions, though they would later find out that in practice they couldn't keep to them.) Travel by foot would be much slower, but the risks of travelling by public transport were much greater. Identity checks were common, and they did not have the means to forge identity documents and other passes. Although Gilbert was a fluent German speaker, the group could not have passed more than the most cursory scrutiny. They also decided that they would aim for Switzerland, and in particular for the Schaffhausen salient, for which Gilbert already had a map. They also knew – a tribute to the effective means by which such valuable information was circulated between camps – that several other prisoners had already got out of Germany successfully through this area. To assist with their preparations, Gilbert wrote to Jack (who had by then recovered sufficiently from his injury to return to work for the RFC in Paris) to ask for some further maps, wire cutters, compasses, torches and a water bottle.

To do so, he devised an extremely imaginative – and very probably unique – way of sending a much longer message back home. While he had been at Ingolstadt, a French artist, who had been experimenting with portrait painting, persuaded Gilbert to sit for him. The outcome was a painting which, although it wasn't a work of art, was at least a reasonable likeness (the portrait is included in the plate section). Shortly after Gilbert was moved on to Heidelberg, in September 1916, he persuaded the camp commandant to allow him to send the portrait home. The commandant apparently felt that there might be some public relations value in agreeing to this, and the camp carpenters constructed a suitable box, made to Gilbert's specifications, which included the choice of wood selected for it. This wood included several knots. Gilbert selected two of these knots and drove them out. Jack continued:

He whittled away the centre of them until only a thin spindle remained. He then prepared a narrow strip of paper about one yard in length, which he completely covered in minute handwriting.

The completed strip he then wound tightly around the reduced centre of the knot, and secured the latter in its hole with some form of glue ...

When the portrait reached its destination, my father had to extract all the knots in the box before he discovered those referred to in a coded letter he had already received from Gilbert.[7] [Photographs of the message, the knots and the wood which they were extracted from are also included in the plate section.]

The message which Gilbert sent was as follows:

My Dear All, Have received all things OK but only parts of map, as they went to last Camp[*] and were forwarded after selection by people there. Most of course were no good here. Could you send the same kind of this region to Switzerland and scale 1:200,000 or better still 1:100,000 if possible, especially for the frontier. Rest assured I am not taking any silly risks. Wire cutters, German money most useful, and more batteries for lamps,[†] also bulbs. Water bottles could come in biscuit box quite safely as you have already sent things. A-------[‡] still worse off at FPX[§] – very bad there. He sent me a note in forwarded parcel,[¶] and things are much worse (food). Here we never get a bit of meat, but vegetables are fairly good. There is supposed to be a meat ration, but it is put in the soup or mixed with the vegetables (potatoes and

---

[*] Ingolstadt.

[†] Torches, necessary for map-reading at night.

[‡] 'A-------' was Captain Charles Anderton, of the Manchester Regiment, in which the poet Wilfred Owen also served.

[§] 'FPX' has been incorrectly transcribed. It should be 'FPK', an abbreviation of Fort Prinz Karl, Gilbert's previous camp at Ingolstadt. Gilbert senior, incidentally, was in contact with the parents, relatives and friends of a number of fellow prisoners of Gilbert, including Anderton, Templer and Thomas Donald, though no substantive correspondence between them has survived.

[¶] An intriguing indication of how relatively quickly prisoners had worked out how to communicate among themselves when in different camps, without German knowledge. See Chapter 8.

cabbage) and we never see it. I think it is given to the *Landsturm*.[*]
If any civilian complicity could be arranged with say Dutchmen
or Swiss, it might make things easier.[†] Love to all. Cheerio.[8]

Some of these requests took time for Jack to meet. In particular,
the request for wire cutters. In a separate message, Gilbert had further specified that he needed a pair capable of cutting half-inch
diameter wire, substantially thicker than ordinary barbed wire. No
British wire cutters were produced which could meet that specification. But Gilbert was insistent that they were essential, so Jack
continued to make enquiries. Eventually, through one of his French
contacts, he was put in touch with a director of the Peugeot car
company, who invited him to a meeting where he was presented
with a large paper-wrapped bundle, containing huge, double-acting[‡]
cutting shears, about the size of gardeners' hedge clippers and fitted
with massive double-lever jaws. They were about eighteen inches
long, including their wooden handles, and Jack calculated that they
weighed well over 5lb. He wondered how on earth it might be possible to smuggle something so large and bulky into a German prison
camp – which is probably what his French contacts were expecting
him to admit. However, on closer inspection, he thought it might
be possible to drive out the rivets which were holding the shears
together, and then send the various component parts in separate
parcels. The wooden handles could be dispensed with, as Gilbert
could no doubt find something suitable to replace them. So Jack
said that he would like to purchase them. The director generously

---

[*]   The German equivalent of the Home Guard or militia in the First World War, generally of fairly low quality.
[†]   This was not further explained, but it is possible that Gilbert was trying to encourage some attempt to
      make the neutral Dutch and Swiss more accommodating in their willingness to provide information which
      could be of use to prisoners wanting to escape, who were keen to know where the most suitable border
      crossing points might be located.
[‡]   Capable of acting or operating in two directions or with two motions.

insisted that no payment was necessary, for he would present them as a gift, and that they would be proud if the cutters proved capable of assisting a member of the Royal Flying Corps to escape from Germany.*

Jack took out all the rivets and bolts, reducing the parts to a more manageable size. He then bought three of the largest sized tins of Huntley & Palmers biscuits, the most suitable available, which were stocked in some Parisian shops. These contained four or five layers of biscuits, offering plenty of scope for concealment. He carefully removed the paper covers from the tins by wrapping them in hot wet towels so that they could be slipped off easily. Then he removed about half the biscuits, inserted the cutter parts, which had been carefully and tightly packaged, into the middle, repacked the tins with biscuits up to the top and replaced the paper cover. The tins showed no sign of having been interfered with. It was then necessary to remove the small label from the underside of the tin, which gave its weight, and replace it with another one, which he had printed, which gave the new, adjusted weight. All that remained was to send Gilbert a coded letter, giving him the serial number of those parcels being sent to him which contained the wire-cutter parts. Forewarned, Gilbert used one of the techniques mentioned earlier, creating some dummy (and innocent) parcels, which he arranged to be substituted for those containing the contraband. The parts arrived safely and were reassembled.† By then, Gilbert's planning had moved on, and he was engaged in excavating the tunnel instead, so didn't need the wire cutters. But they were used successfully by other prisoners on a number of occasions. The Germans found

---

* Perhaps not surprisingly, it has not been possible to find any record of this exchange with Peugeot.
† An additional bonus of this method of supply was that the paper which the Huntley & Palmers biscuits were wrapped in was very thin and made excellent tracing paper onto which maps could be copied.

and confiscated them more than once, but the ingenious prisoners found ways of stealing them back.

About a year later, after Gilbert's escape from Ströhen, Jack went back to meet the Peugeot director again and to tell him about the way in which his wire cutters had been used. He took Gilbert with him: it must have been quite a memorable occasion.[9]

In a further letter, Gilbert had specified that the maps he needed were for a different part of the border area than the Schaffhausen salient, which he already had.* These took quite some time to provide. As it happened, no great harm was done, because not long afterwards, Gilbert escaped from Heidelberg and on his recapture, was transferred to Crefeld, where the maps would have been of no use to him.[10] And furthermore, McWilliam had also managed to borrow another large map of the area between Heidelberg and the Swiss border. It measured six feet by eight inches, with a scale of 1:200,000. He copied it onto tracing paper, a process which took him about five weeks, working several hours a day.

The two of them spent much time assessing many different means of escape from Heidelberg. This also included trying to find any Germans who might be venal enough to provide them with assistance. It cost them plenty of money but got them nowhere. (It was, not surprisingly, a court-martial offence to attempt to bribe any of the guards, but such actions – and they certainly happened from time to time – were rarely reported, as most guards preferred to pocket the profit and keep quiet about it.) Eventually, Gilbert and McWilliam thought they had identified a possible opportunity

---

* After Ward and Champion jumped off a train from Vöhrenbach to Heidelberg in April 1916, the Schaffhausen salient would have been just about the nearest point on the Swiss border for them. (See Chapter 6.) Although no written confirmation exists, it is very possible that they would have provided the information about this border area, including some known sentry posts. Sidney Buckley and Johnny Evans, whose escape has been briefly mentioned already, later successfully crossed the border in this area in June 1917, though they had needed to walk considerably further.

for getting out through the wire. The location they identified was in a corner of the camp which was only patrolled by one sentry, with whom they had had some contact and whom they thought it might be possible to bribe.

But at this point, their planning was temporarily frustrated when Gilbert suddenly developed what appeared to be a very severe attack of appendicitis. There was no doctor in the camp, just one who sometimes came in on Saturday mornings. Gilbert's room-mates (there were eight of them, including McWilliam) informed the German medical orderly, who came up to see him. He judged that it was no more than an ordinary stomach ache and so gave Gilbert a strong laxative. By the next day, Gilbert was a lot worse, and his roommates asked for the doctor to visit. They were told that he might possibly be able to come the next day, but the orderly still considered the case to be trivial. By then, Gilbert was very ill indeed and in great pain, but no doctor appeared. The orderly said that he would telephone to request him to come. At lunch time, when McWilliam asked again, the orderly apologised and said that he had forgotten. When he telephoned, the hospital informed him that the doctor was too busy and would come the next day. So they asked to have Gilbert sent to hospital but were told that was not possible. Eventually, that evening, they convinced a more senior German officer that Gilbert would certainly be dead before morning if he was not seen at once. This man took the law into his own hands and ordered a car, in which Gilbert was immediately driven to hospital. He was operated on immediately, on arrival, and was also found to have peritonitis. It was a very near thing. The doctor admitted afterwards that if he had arrived half an hour later, Gilbert would have died.

In a letter written some weeks afterwards, Gilbert told his family about the incident and the operation. He added that it was performed without anaesthetic – he was informed that this was because of the scarcity of drugs in Germany, which precluded their use for prisoners. It was a month before he returned to the camp, and he was then still very weak, presumably because of some post-operative infection.

To undergo any major operation without an anaesthetic would be an extremely unpleasant experience for the hapless patient. In this case, it would have also required considerable manipulation and pulling of the tissues to get access to the appendix, which would have been very painful indeed. It would have taken at least half an hour and probably rather longer. Those circumstances, and the near certainty that he would have been sick and debilitated, would help to explain why Gilbert needed to stay in hospital for a month afterwards to recuperate. This would have been anything but a routine operation, and in many cases during that period, the patient would have been most unlikely to have survived.*

When Gilbert returned to the camp, he and McWilliam decided to abandon their project to get out through the wire. Gilbert needed longer to regain his health before they set out on a journey which might last as long as three weeks, the wire cutters had not yet arrived and the German guard who had shown interest in helping them suddenly developed cold feet. They reassessed their options and concluded that unless they simply waited in the hope of spotting some suitable random opportunity (as Gilbert was later to do at Crefeld) and wanted to be proactive, then tunnelling probably offered their best option.

---

* I am grateful to Kiko Rutter MB BChir FRCS for his explanation of what such an operation would have involved.

But it would not be straightforward. They could not start from the ground floor, because the barracks were full of cellars, which had concrete ceilings and floors and thick stone walls, presenting a formidable initial problem to overcome. Moreover, the cellars were mostly locked and forbidden to the prisoners, apart from a small number which some of them were permitted to use during the day, though those who did so were supervised by German guards. Additionally, there was a guardroom at the top of the stairs which provided access to one side of the barracks below – the stairs to which were blocked by a door whose proximity to the guardroom made it impossible to pick the lock. But since a tunnel from the ground floor was a non-starter, they worked out that they needed to find a way of getting into a suitable cellar which was not too great a distance from the wire.

Gilbert and McWilliam eventually settled on one cellar, which was located on the western side of the building. The cellars here were used for storing bread and vegetables or coal, with some only being used for depositing rubbish. This meant that the nearby stairs were always dirty, which might aid them in disguising surreptitious soil removal. These cellars were protected by a locked door, but it did not prove difficult to pick this lock and to make a skeleton key. Then they carefully watched the area to see who used the cellars, and when, and whether there were regular patterns of movement. They discovered that they were never visited, or even checked, at night. They tied a piece of thread across the door, to prove to their satisfaction that this was always the case. But to their dismay, they quite soon found it had been broken. Then they noticed that they themselves were being watched by two Frenchmen and, soon afterwards, heard noises from the room above the cellar in which they were intending to work! The thumps suggested the use of a muffled hammer and chisel. There followed a game of cat and mouse. Gilbert approached the Frenchmen, Lieutenants Lehmann and Perrot, whom he had seen carefully carrying what looked like contraband under their cloaks. He told them that they were making too much noise, adding exaggeratedly that they could be heard all over the building, specifying the room from which the noise had come. The Frenchmen denied this and suggested it was he who was up to something. Neither wanted to give the game away. It was only following another circuitous conversation, when Gilbert eventually decided to come clean and explain that he and McWilliam were planning something but had not yet started work – and offered to work together with the two Frenchmen – that they admitted what they were doing. It transpired that there were four of them, the others being Captain Mazeline and Lieutenant Petitjean: it was these two who had come up with the original idea for escaping and had found the most suitable site to work from. The timing of this discussion was fortuitous: they had just concluded that they needed extra help, so readily invited the British officers to participate.

The Frenchmen had chosen an adjacent cellar, a location which had some significant advantages. It was just about the nearest point to a gate on the southern side of the camp which was bracketed by two enormous stone pillars. If they could manage to emerge from their tunnel just beside one of the pillars, the escapers would have a better chance of avoiding being spotted by sentries who were patrolling in the area. Moreover, the Frenchmen had found an area in a corner which was not covered in concrete. This meant that establishing the first stage of the tunnel (which they had already begun) was going to be much easier. What's more, they had come up with a better solution to the problem of earth disposal than Gilbert and McWilliam had thought of. Their idea had simply been to conceal it under the pile of coal adjacent to their tunnel entrance. This would not have been nearly large enough. The Frenchmen were developing a different idea, involving storing the earth up in the roof, which was why they anticipated the need for some extra labour. The main problem they had to resolve was that since the cellar was used to store bread and vegetables, it was visited regularly during the day by the German cook and the gardener. They concluded that they would therefore only be able to work at night, and even then they would still need to be careful when crossing the room from the cellar door to the tunnel entrance. A sentry regularly walked past the window, and though he would not have found it easy to see much inside, it was quite possible that he could detect movement.

The trapdoor required careful construction. It needed to be made of sturdy wood, padded underneath so it would not sound hollow if walked on. Some wire loops were attached to the side, to facilitate its removal. And whenever it was put back to cover the hole, it needed to be covered with an inch or so of soil, to deaden further any potential hollow noise, and the cracks had to be carefully filled with mud, so that no outline was discernible. It proved to be so well designed that it not only survived unnoticed during regular daily visits by German staff over a five-month period from October 1916 to March 1917 but it also proved to be extremely difficult for their captors to find after the escape, once the tunnel exit itself had been discovered. The entrance to the tunnel measured sixty centimetres by forty centimetres, or two feet by just under one and a half. They then dug down a further seven feet, to take them to what they considered to be a safe depth. Since the cellar floor was some five feet below ground level, they were at that point about twelve feet underground.* They enlarged the bottom of the shaft to provide space for two men to pass each other and for an area where they could safely bag up and store the earth which they were going to need to dispose of. Thereafter, they reverted to the original – and very claustrophobic – dimensions, so as to limit as far as possible the volume of soil they would need to dispose of. The tunnel was then dug to the right, bypassing the foundations of the barracks and aiming for the gatepost. The soil, which was largely sandstone, was soft and easy to dig through. But it crumbled easily. (It was also yellow, very different from the earth outside, which would make it difficult to hide except in a concealed site.) Since the tunnel would also pass under a road on which heavy coal carts frequently passed, they decided it needed frames to reinforce it every couple of feet. They were initially able to use wood from some old deck chairs, but when that ran out, a French carpenter stole wood from a theatre stage, which had been discarded, and provided them with small planks carved with dovetailed ends to their specification, which they smuggled in and assembled underground.

At this point, McWilliam asked Gilbert and their French colleagues if they would mind his bringing in a friend, Captain Brendan Jolliffe of the Scots Guards,† who had been the only other escape-minded officer in the camp before Gilbert's arrival. McWilliam and Jolliffe had done plenty of planning together,

---

* It is not clear whether the tunnellers were aware of the risk that the Germans might be using listening devices to detect any signs of tunnelling. We know that geophones were sometimes used in British camps, but they do not appear to have been particularly effective, for some successful tunnels were not detected. No evidence has been discovered that they were used by the Germans during the First World War, and Gilbert and his colleagues were as confident as they could be that their captors did not suspect that the inmates were engaged in tunnelling. Things had changed by the Second World War. The Germans were known to be using seismographs, and Allied prisoners therefore dug their tunnels as deep as thirty feet below the surface in order to avoid detection.

† Jolliffe had been captured towards the end of the First Battle of Ypres, so had already been in captivity for two years.

though nothing came of it because they had lacked equipment and information. The Frenchmen initially had some reservations, but eventually they agreed to the idea. Since Jolliffe, as befitted a Scots Guardsman, was much taller than the others, they reckoned that he would not be able to work in such a small space. He was tasked with carrying the soil up to the eaves and hiding it there, though he was helped by whichever of the other two were not on duty digging down below.

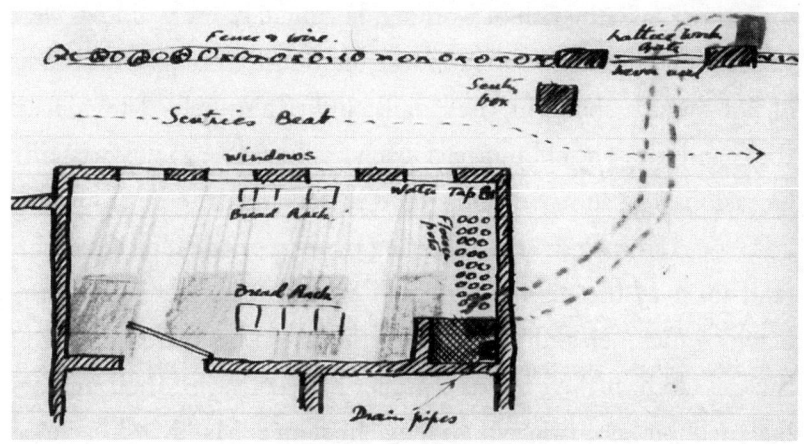

Sketch by Henry McWilliam showing the location of the tunnel entrance at Heidelberg and the route which it took towards the gate. Courtesy of the McWilliam family

So what was their tunnelling routine over the five months that it took them to complete the project? On every night when they were expecting to be working, they prepared carefully, dressing in warm, old and dark clothes. They would wear three pairs of socks, instead of shoes, so as to avoid making any noise. They also wore cloaks or coats, so that they would not look too suspicious in the event that they unexpectedly bumped into a German on the way.

When opening locked doors with a skeleton key, they also needed to exercise caution. These keys were made from melted-down aluminium spoons and were not robust. Frequent use risked making them more fragile still. It would not do to have one break in the lock. Sometimes, when they reached the cellar, they found that all four of the windows had been left open. In that case, they could not do anything on that night, for passing sentries could both see inside and also perhaps hear any noise which they might make. If only one window was open, then depending on which one it was, they could sometimes take the risk of working. Fortunately, the windows were very dusty, so provided they moved cautiously through the beams of light which shone in, their dark clothes also helped to conceal them and they should not have been easily visible to any passerby. Occasionally, a sentry would stop directly outside to light his pipe and would look directly in, requiring them to freeze. On cold nights (and most of the nights were cold because they were tunnelling between October and March), sentries could be heard coming as they would beat their hands together to keep warm. Their number included one eccentric, whom they christened 'Maddy'.[11] He would often run up and down his beat, either forwards or backwards, and even sometimes hop up and down on alternate legs!

When they reached the trapdoor concealing the tunnel, they sometimes had to remove flowerpots or other pieces of gardening equipment which had been deposited on or near it by the gardener. In that case, they would have to remember the exact position of each item, so that they could afterwards be put back exactly where they had come from. The process of carefully and silently opening the trapdoor would normally take them about twenty minutes. Next, they would remove the soil which had been dug out the previous night, put into bags fashioned from sheets, curtains or similar material and left at the foot of the shaft. There might be as many as thirty of these, carefully tied up with string and generally weighing about 30lb each. These would be carried over to the steps by the door and left for the carrying party, who would generally turn up at around midnight, once the first German patrol of the night had finished.

The group put together some braces, which they used to help them carry these bags, one on either side of their bodies at about waist height. They made a cumbersome and heavy load, but it was just about manageable – and this system left their hands free in case they were confronted by some problem, or an unwelcome surprise, on their way up to the attic. The passages and stairs were lit, so they also needed to be cautious when within sight of a window, in case a sentry was passing by. Since there was still a laborious journey to their hiding place, they decided it would be safer not to do it all at once. They would hide the bags of soil behind a large pile of sprung mattresses (which the Germans considered to be too comfortable to be used by prisoners) and then return the following day and complete the task in the murky daylight rather than in almost complete darkness, when they might have to negotiate a path through German washing in the attic, which was sometimes hanging up there to dry!

The tunnellers later calculated that they had probably removed as much as five tons of soil from their excavation, a remarkable figure.* Because of the significant weight involved, it may therefore seem extraordinary that the hiding place which they found for most of it was up in the eaves of their barracks. But since the fabric of these buildings was extremely solid – much of it was built of concrete

---

* This estimate was achieved by keeping a count of the bags which they had moved, and – since they had a good idea of their weight – they were able to calculate the approximate weight of the soil which had been excavated.

– this proved to be feasible, even though it was awkward to carry the heavy bags up there. It was well hidden behind several locked doors (for which, of course, they made skeleton keys) and in an area which they judged to be well beyond the sight of all but an extraordinarily diligent search. They gained access by climbing up into the attic and then lowering themselves down, carefully holding on to the joists and the ceiling of the attic and then crawling around a tight corner which brought them into a small cul-de-sac, which had been walled in and which looked as though it should provide sufficient space. McWilliam's sketch demonstrates how this was achieved.

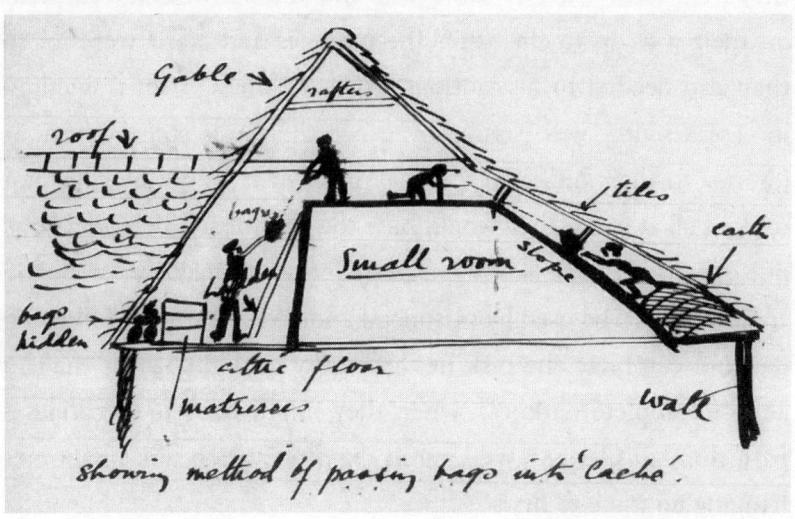

Sketch by McWilliam showing how earth was taken up into the attic and hidden there.
Five tons of earth were removed from the tunnel and much of it was secreted in the eaves.
Courtesy of the McWilliam family

Down in the tunnel, they faced some different problems. What would be the most suitable digging implement? They tried using small shovels, but their scraping made too much noise and they were anyway not the best instrument to break down the sandstone which they were working through. They settled instead for a screwdriver, driving the point into the sandstone and making enough of a hole to be able to crumble it into small pieces. Despite the strain which all this manipulation put on the screwdriver, it survived just about intact as they constructed forty-five yards of tunnel, though, as Jack observed, it looked more like a bradawl than a screwdriver by the time they had finished with it![12] The further they got away from the entrance, the greater the problem of ventilation became, as the air turned increasingly foul. The first sign of this would come when the candle used for ventilation would start guttering and then quickly go out. They were familiar enough with their work to be able to continue for a few more minutes in the dark – but then needed to withdraw for a while to allow a gradual restoration of the atmosphere. Even a digger's movement in and out would make a marginal improvement in air circulation. But this wasn't straightforward. Movement in either direction to get in or out of such a confined space was extremely difficult. There was no room to get up on their knees and crawl, so they had to dig in sufficiently with their toes and elbows to get a little purchase, sufficient to be able to inch backwards or forwards. And doing that was physically tiring, too. Eventually, McWilliam devised a basic ventilation system. He made a very simple fan, about 25 cm in diameter, from pieces of wood and tin, which could be turned by hand. Creating a pipe through which air might pass required even more ingenuity. Various means failed. A sausage-like shape made of wire, covered by cloth, which was painted to help make it airtight, worked for a while but was eventually crushed by the weight of shoulders and elbows rubbing against it. The best solution turned out to be some long rectangular wooden trunks: operating the fan for as little as a minute would usually provide enough clean air for an hour and a half.

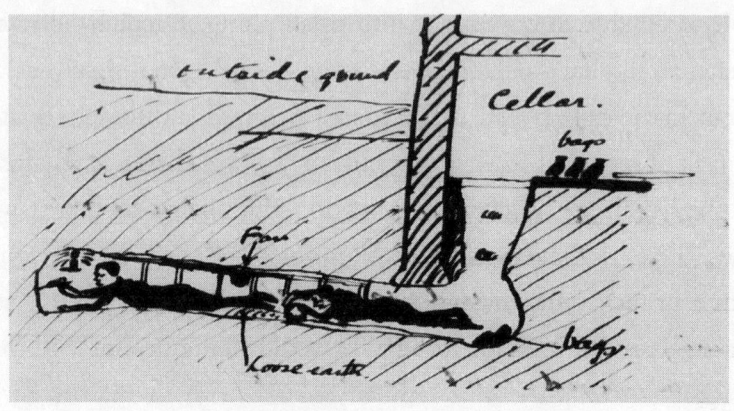

Sketch by McWilliam showing how the earth was removed from the tunnel. In such a confined space, it was an extremely awkward procedure to pass the soil back, past the digger's body, to the prisoner lying behind.
Courtesy of the McWilliam family

But that wasn't all. Moving and filling the bags was a complicated process, too. The digger could push the excavated earth down past his body to his feet, where his partner would be waiting, as the sketch above shows. But moving it any further by pushing it required great effort and used more precious air. So they made a sort of trolley out of a basket on runners to make the passage smoother as they dragged it back to the entrance where bags could be filled. There was only space to store two or three down below when they were working, so additional bags had to be taken out of the shaft and left by the entrance and then stored in it again when they finished their shift. More heavy work. Finally, every three days or so, it was necessary to add a new frame to strengthen the tunnel. This necessary precaution also slowed down their work further. They generally finished at about

5 a.m. and crashed into bed, exhausted but only able to sleep for a couple of hours before the first roll call of the day.

It can't have been easy for them to conceal what they were up to from their fellow prisoners throughout this period. Their room-mates would have seen them heading off, night after night, dressed in increasingly dirty old clothes, which they would have needed to conceal carefully against the possibility of German room searches. However discreet Gilbert and his tunnelling partners might have been, it would have been impossible for those sharing their rooms not to be curious, and the pattern of repeated activity must have made clear that it was most likely a tunnel which he and the others were involved in. There was always a risk of betrayal, and there were plenty of tunnels which were uncovered by the Germans because someone had given them away. They were fortunate that all those who had any inkling of what they might have been up to kept their speculation to themselves. They were also perhaps fortunate that no previous tunnel escape attempts had been made from Heidelberg, so the Germans had no reason to think that it might be a possi-bility. It is worth making a comparison with the rightly celebrated tunnel escape from Holzminden some fifteen months later. That tunnel was between sixty and eighty metres long (estimates vary), took eight months to build and of the twenty-nine officers who got out, ten successfully crossed to freedom over the Dutch border. James Bennett, one of those who succeeded, wrote that there were only about a dozen men (out of a total of 600 in the camp) really involved in working on the tunnel, for much of its existence. He was only brought in to assist because of the need to replace those tunnellers who had the misfortune to be transferred to other camps. Though the fact that they were able to tunnel during daylight hours

– even though their shifts were frequently cut short by the need to come back out for regular roll calls – meant that their absences would not have been so noticeable.*

The Germans had an unwelcome habit of removing prisoners from a camp and sending them to another with little or no warning and for no obvious reason. Not long after Jolliffe had been brought into the plan, this happened to their French colleagues Lehmann and Perrot, who were abruptly transferred. This reduced the group to five, so to spread the physically demanding work of tunnelling, they decided to see whether Jolliffe, despite his height, would be able to get into the tunnel and play a part in digging. He was suf- ficiently agile that this worked well. In the course of the next few days, they also agreed to bring in some further reinforcements from among those who had a shrewd idea of what they were up to. By this stage, they calculated that they had dug about halfway, so there would still be plenty more work to do. Two of them were British officers, Lieutenants McKeag and Newbold; the third was another French pilot, Lieutenant Mascolier. This group was later joined by another British officer, Lieutenant Toogood. They provided wel- come support but didn't participate in the actual escape.†

---

* Although the Holzminden tunnel was the longest built by the British during the war, there is evidence that the French managed to build something even longer. A French historian, Jean-Claude Auriol, recorded that the longest French tunnel was 191 metres long. It was built at Cüstrin camp in Brandenburg and was used for several escapes. It was only finally discovered as the result of an indiscretion. The Cüstrin tunnel was also much longer than the longest which was built by the French during the Second World War, measuring almost 140 metres, which was built by French officers imprisoned at Oflag II-D Gross Born, a German camp for prisoners of war near what is now Kłomino, in north-western Poland. It was also longer than 'Harry', the tunnel built by Allied prisoners in Stalag Luft 3 and used during the Great Escape, which measured approximately 111 metres. Auriol does not describe how the Cüstrin tunnel was equipped with ventilation, suitable boarding for support and all the other requirements of a durable escape route. (Jean- Claude Auriol, *Les Barbelés des Bannis: La Tragédie des Prisonniers de Guerre Français en Allemagne pendant la Grande Guerre* (Paris: Editions Tirésias, 2002), p. 245.)

† The reason for this was that after careful consideration, they concluded that it would not be possible for all nine of them to get out in one night with reasonable confidence that they could avoid detection. It was felt fair that those who had been involved the longest and worked the hardest should be given the best chance of having a clear run. It was therefore agreed that if the tunnel was not discovered (though this must surely have been a fairly forlorn hope), the four latecomers would make their own way out some ten days later.

The riskiest part of their work involved the movement of the soil from the cellar up to the roof and its concealment there. One day in December, they had a very nasty scare and a remarkably close shave. Several of the tunnelling gang were up in the eaves, emptying soil from sacks into their hiding place, when suddenly a German appeared. They later worked out that he had climbed up a ladder and got around behind the area where they were working, though they never worked out why. The three of them ran off in the other direction. Gilbert was guarding the door which they were using to get into the area. He locked it behind them. Rather than going quickly back the other way to cut them off, the German went to look for a guard. This gave them time to go back to their disposal area and hastily collect as much of their equipment as possible, though they had to leave some empty bags, as well as several full ones, behind. By the time the German came back with a guard, the four of them had disappeared.

Disheartened by this misfortune, they held a council of war. It seemed inevitable that the Germans would report their sighting of prisoners engaged in some nefarious activity. This was bound to lead to a very thorough search and the discovery of their tunnel. The immense amount of earth hidden up in the eaves could only point to the conclusion that active tunnelling was going on. But nothing happened. There was no reaction, no ransacking of the cellars or investigation either of the eaves or of anywhere else. It didn't seem possible that the discovery could be ignored. But it gradually became apparent that this must have been exactly what had happened. Nonetheless, they decided not to take a chance, just in case the tunnel had not been found and a trap was being laid, to catch them red-handed and find out where the entrance was. So to be on the safe side, they cautiously waited several more weeks. It was agreed that they would start again at the beginning of January, and once the tunnel was finished, they would not risk leaving in hostile winter conditions but would wait until the spring before attempting to make their getaway. And to avoid the risks of using the eaves again for soil disposal, they sensibly resolved that they should find somewhere else to dump it.

When they restarted, they found no evidence of any traps or potential difficulties in the cellar, other than some leaks. Gilbert was the first down into the tunnel, and everything was intact down there, too, though the air was not surprisingly very musty. But where – and how – to get rid of the soil? They flirted with the idea of trouser tubes, sausages of material containing sandy soil and open at one end, which they could put down their trouser legs and empty gradually by taking out handfuls and distributing them as they walked around outside the camp. (The idea was similar to that used by the so-called 'penguins' who later, in Stalag Luft 3 during the Second World War, walked in an odd way to hide the fact that they were disposing of sand dug out of their tunnel for the Great Escape.) They concluded that this wouldn't work – the earth was a different colour, anything more than a small quantity of sandy soil could be noticed and it would also stand out in those areas covered by snow. But they came up with several other more effective ideas. A huge quantity, estimated at as much as a ton, was deposited in the latrines; some was put in the stoves and burned, and following a heavy snowfall, some was worked into a very large ball of snow which they had rolled up and used as ammunition in a snowball fight! And they found one room in the barracks which had space in the ceiling and put a pile up there. Fortunately, they didn't overload it, and the ceiling remained intact and didn't collapse.

But they had still more problems to contend with. Not long after the tunnel was reopened, a badly leaking tap in the cellar soaked the floor – and all but the area of the trapdoor in the corner, for the water seeped down around the edges and left the trapdoor covering dry and of a different colour. So it stood out as obviously different. Moreover, the tunnel itself was half full of water. They worked hard to staunch the leakage and leave the cellar floor all the same colour. But they could not do anything to drain the tunnel, so had to wait until most of it had soaked away before they could start to dig again. It was around this time that all of the tunnellers became ill with some sort of debilitating flu, probably caused by working in such unhealthy, damp conditions in the same filthy clothes, which laid them up for a week or more.

Hard on the heels of the flood came another disaster. Some workmen were spotted just outside the camp fence, in the area where they planned for the tunnel to surface. They were taking measurements and marking out distances on the ground. It emerged that the Germans were planning to enlarge the camp by building some new barrack blocks in that section, with the fence being extended around the far side, so as to encompass the whole area. It would significantly lengthen the distance they needed to dig. Moreover, the work was planned to be completed by the end of February, long before the winter was finished and conditions for escaping improved. Happily, as McWilliam commented, 'some Belgian and French soldiers were entrusted with the labour, and they worked with such admirable and creditable indolence that having delayed its completion for at least a month, they were sent away in disgrace and their place was taken by Germans'.[13] That certainly helped the escapers' timetable: they discovered that the work would not be finished before the middle of April, by which time the weather – and travel conditions – should have improved. Though, unfortunately, the workmen covered the area with a sort of asphalt made of clinker and ashes, which would be very noisy to walk over when they were trying to sneak away after making their exit from the tunnel.

At last, in early March, one of the diggers struck stone, which they interpreted as meaning that they had reached one of the gateposts and the tunnel was nearly long enough. However, when Gilbert tested their calculation that night by putting up a stick with a couple of small mirrors on, which acted as a crude periscope, he discovered to his horror that they had miscalculated and come up in the wrong place. The stone which they had hit was the stone block which marked the middle of the gateway. Although McWilliam (who as a sailor was unanimously judged to have the best under-standing of navigation) had taken regular bearings to try to ensure that they dug in the right direction, it had not been easy to ensure that they were accurately keeping on track. They had missed their target by some eight to ten feet. They withdrew, shoring up the shaft very carefully, and then dug a few feet over to the right, to come up precisely by the far side of the post for which they had originally been aiming.

But then came a further very unwelcome development, causing consternation. They picked up a rumour, which came from what McWilliam described as a 'very reliable source',* that in about a week's time, all the British officers in the camp were going to be moved on to another camp.[14] This confronted the British partic-ipants in the scheme with a most unenviable choice. They could either break out of the tunnel almost straight away, at a time when the weather conditions remained quite unsuitable for the sort of journey they faced, or they could give up hope of using the tunnel

---

* There is no indication given as to who or what the source might have been, but the most likely explanation is that someone was bribing a guard in return for information and possibly assistance.

and leave it for exploitation by their French colleagues alone, who might bring in some others. (Something similar would happen to the French in Crefeld, as will be described in Chapter 9.) This was a most unattractive prospect for all of them after the hard work and effort which they had invested in the scheme for five long months. There was also a further difficulty for McWilliam, who was suffering from another nasty attack of flu and was in no fit state to make an escape attempt at that moment. Though sympathetic to his circumstances, the others decided that they could not afford to take the risk of waiting longer and determined to leave that very night.

They had already made all the necessary preparations, and their kit was ready. They had calculated that they would need to cover a distance of 250 kilometres to reach the Swiss border by the most direct route, and they planned to take with them sufficient food for a journey of twenty days, though they hoped to complete it in twelve. They had overcome some formidable logistical challenges in getting it all together. The food and equipment which they took with them makes an impressive list. Each man would take the following supplies:

- 4 x 1lb tins of bully beef
- 48 large square hard biscuits
- 6 tins of potted meat
- 1 large tin of cocoa
- 2 tins of Nestlé's milk
- 2lbs of dried fruit
- 4lbs of chocolate
- A Tommy cooker,* with a supply of spirit

---

* A Tommy cooker was a compact portable stove issued to British troops during both the First and Second World Wars.

They also took matches, Oxo cubes, sugar, a spoon, a large pocket knife, a housewife,* paper, bootlaces, two pairs of spare socks, thick gloves and a compass. In addition, Gilbert took a large goatskin for carrying water, though this did not prove very suitable. Each had a knapsack for their provisions. They also took a blanket each, cut to six feet by four feet, as well as a sheet of oiled tablecloth painted in a camouflage pattern. They rolled up their blankets in this sheet and tied them tightly around their haversacks. Jolliffe wore a converted naval uniform, while Gilbert wore a tweed coat and grey flannels. Both also planned to take a waterproof sheet, with tapes sewn on so that they could be tied together and, by using the blankets inside, make an adequate sleeping bag. Altogether, their kit weighed between forty and forty-five pounds.[15]

This was significantly more than Gilbert took with him when he escaped from Ströhen later in the year, but of course he made that attempt in late August, at the height of summer.

Gilbert also took with him what he imaginatively called his 'burglar's bag', containing all the items he might need while escaping or indeed at any other time! It included the following: a skeleton key, two metal files, a hacksaw blade, two small wood saw blades, a second compass and two torches with spare batteries. He also had a remarkably comprehensive collection of maps, a tribute to the supply system which his family had organised for him and the contacts which they had been able to tap. These comprised: four full-sized large scale Ordnance Survey maps of the route from Heidelberg to the border, all at least 1:100,000 scale if not larger, and a road map covering the same route; a detailed map of the Swiss

---

* This was a small holdall or pouch which contained everything that might be needed for someone to carry out repairs to their clothing or equipment. It would generally contain needles, a thimble, some darning wool for socks and plenty of thread.

frontier, 1:50,000; and two detailed maps (1:12,000 approximately) showing parts of the Swiss frontier where crossings had previously been made, which very usefully included the positions of sentry posts. It is a tribute to Gilbert's ingenuity that when he was recaptured, he managed to ensure that none of the items in his burglar's bag, or the maps, were discovered when he was thoroughly searched on arrest and then again on his return to the prison camp.

The weather was cold but clear and fine, so as good as it could be. Though, the lack of any wind meant any noise they made when removing the frozen layer of stones and clinker, which sat on top of the final layer of earth, from the tunnel entrance might carry to the ears of a sentry. That was an unavoidable risk. Although they had agreed with their French colleagues some time before that they would all leave on the same day, they were not planning to travel together. And they also concluded that it might improve their chances of avoiding detection if they did not all break out together, because the absence of a larger number was more likely to be noticed at the first roll call after their exit. It was decided that Mazeline and Petitjean would leave later that afternoon, timing their exit to coincide with the departure of the workmen from the camp site, so they could pretend to be part of the group. Their final preparations were quickly made. Gilbert and Jolliffe would leave later the same night.

And then, just at the point when Mazeline and Petitjean were actually starting to make their exit, the whole project had yet another extraordinarily close brush with disaster. The Frenchmen were already in the tunnel, soon to be followed by Gilbert, who would then do his best to close up their tunnel at its exit point, attempting to conceal it from external inspection until he and Jolliffe made their own way out a few hours later. After doing so, he would then return and also close up the hole in the cellar, removing all traces behind him. Unfortunately, an elaborate system they had organised to post their own sentries around the area of the cellar failed to provide anything but the briefest warning of the unexpected and very sudden arrival of a German cook, accompanied by several French orderlies. The cook unlocked the door and went down into the cellar. Those present in the surrounding area outside thought that discovery – and the frustration of their long and careful planning – was a certainty. Gilbert received warning about this danger when he was in the passage outside the cellar. He had about ten seconds to react. He dashed into the cellar, picked up all the remaining pieces of equipment, bags and pieces of timber and threw them into the entrance of the tunnel, jumping in afterwards and covering himself – and the outline of the tunnel entrance – with a black coat. As the cook collected the bread, Gilbert surreptitiously managed to attract the attention of one of the orderlies, who moved around to stand between the tunnel entrance and the cook, thereby doing his best to hide him, and the entrance, from sight. Loaves collected, the cook stood barely three yards away from the tunnel, handing out bread to the accompanying orderlies. This all took about ten minutes. The cook noticed nothing untoward, not even the trapdoor used to cover the tunnel entrance, which had been too heavy to move quickly. The fact that it was the same colour as the floor presumably explained why it didn't stand out as anything unusual.

And in the event, Mazeline and Petitjean had to abandon their attempt to get out anyway, because the process of cutting through the frozen soil which still blocked the entrance was taking them too long. They decided to leave the following night, instead, though this then had to be postponed by a further twenty-four hours because of the additional time needed to clear the exit. With a couple of extra days to recuperate, McWilliam judged that he was just about fit enough to go too, and they all finally left on 20 March. Mazeline and Petitjean successfully concealed themselves among the departing workmen, and Gilbert, Jolliffe and McWilliam got out after the final evening roll call. They had all left behind them some fairly realistic dummies in their beds, in the hope that this would satisfy inspection at the 11 p.m. *appell* and give them more time. They took their boots off and hung them round their necks, hoping that walking in stockinged feet would enable them to make less noise as they got across the area planned for the new camp. They had also smeared their socks with garlic, with the intention of discouraging any dogs from following them.

It was slow work going through the tunnel, pushing their rucksacks in front of them, as they were a very tight fit in the space which had been cleared, and they had to be careful to avoid causing a collapse of the roof. Eventually, after taking more than two hours to travel forty-five yards, Gilbert reached the exit. Though he climbed out very carefully, some stones and soil fell back into the hole with a fearfully loud noise. Fortunately, the sentry, who was on the other side of the pillar, heard nothing. He seemed to be distracted, probably by the cold, as he was humming a tune to himself and beating his hands together to keep them warm. He was also walking quite slowly, which meant that there were regular fairly long periods when his back was turned. This gave Gilbert an opportunity to work out the best moment to cross unnoticed across the floodlit area and over the ashes, to reach the shelter of buildings on the other side. He was followed by McWilliam and then by Jolliffe, neither of whom was noticed as they carefully made the hazardous trip through the disconcertingly bright lights. It had taken the three of them nearly an hour to navigate this obstacle. Before moving on, they took a moment to look back at the camp which they had just left and relish their first taste of freedom.

They were later informed that the day after their escape, it was announced that all the British officers would be leaving Heidelberg for an undisclosed destination twenty-four hours later. Moreover, the escapees were told that their departure had not been noticed at the first roll call the following morning, for the dummies had all done their job effectively. In fact, they were not missed for even longer. The absence of Jolliffe and the two Frenchmen was noticed at the midday *appell*, but since this happened just at the moment when the imminent departure of the British officers was announced, the Germans assumed that Jolliffe had gone into hiding to try to avoid being compelled to leave. They concluded that Mazeline and Petitjean had escaped, but they did not know how or when. Gilbert was missed at the next *appell*, at 5 p.m., and McWilliam at the following one, at 11 p.m. So the escapers had a start of nearly twenty-four hours. Even then, the Germans did not think that they had escaped: they did not suspect a tunnel and despite a thorough search throughout the camp, they assumed that all three were in hiding to avoid being moved the following day. The tunnel was only discovered by accident rather later, when a sentry who was walking around the perimeter fence looking for any evidence of the wire having been cut stumbled into it!

Sure enough, the next day, all the remaining British officers (bar a handful of badly wounded officers who remained to enable them to appear before a visiting Swiss medical commission) were transferred to Crefeld. The three of them had got out just in time.

They walked south for a couple of hours, and as it was starting to get light, they began looking for a suitable wood to lie up in during the day. And then they received their first experience of some of the unwelcome and unexpected surprises which they would have to negotiate on their journey. Jolliffe fell over some wire, and when he got up, he noticed that all of Gilbert's maps, which he had been carrying in his coat, had disappeared. A search of the area showed nothing, so they had to retrace their steps and fortunately discovered them all, intact, after less than half a mile. They had fallen out when the party had earlier made a brief stop at that spot. Then, shortly afterwards, when they were about to cross a road which was on the edge of a village, they heard voices – so they hid in some bushes and saw a steady stream of workmen heading off to work at a factory nearby. This presented them with a dilemma, for it was starting to get light and they could not remain there. They could not safely cross the road but neither could they retreat, for there was a canal just behind them. They had to withdraw cautiously and then negotiate – very carefully – a way through a gap between some of the houses in the village. Fortunately, at that relatively early hour, no one noticed them, and they were able to find shelter in a wood on the other side and burrow into some moss, which insulated their blankets and waterproof sheets and gave them a little warmth and protection while they slept and rested during their first day of freedom. They calculated that they had covered about twelve kilometres. When they awoke, they heard the sound of children playing nearby, the rhythmic chopping of a woodman's axe and the rumble of carts moving along a nearby road, but no one came near enough to discover them.

They left shortly after dark, aiming to cut across the railway line towards Karlsruhe, which ran parallel to the Rhine and would indicate the right direction. This not only saved time; it also enabled them to avoid the frequent use of a torch to consult their maps.

Wherever possible, they skirted villages. Unfortunately, one stretch took them through a large forest where many ditches had been dug for drainage purposes. Much of the land in between the ditches was wet and boggy and it was altogether impossible to avoid getting very wet. Their trousers became frozen stiff, forcing them to take an additional risk of walking along the raised embankment, which made them more visible. This route led them through a railway station, surrounded by water on both sides which was too deep to walk across. So they had no choice but to walk through the station itself and over or around all sorts of obstacles which were difficult and painful to navigate in the dark. Turning a corner, they found themselves in front of a well-lit signal box, but fortunately the occupant was busy preparing for the arrival of a train and too preoccupied to spot them. They eventually made their way off the embankment and onto what appeared to be some dry land which adjoined it. Unfortunately, it was not entirely safe. McWilliam slipped on some ice, badly damaging his knee in the process and falling into deep water up to his waist, which left his trousers frozen completely stiff for the rest of the night's journey. The terrain they covered during the rest of the night was similarly treacherous and difficult. Water was also difficult to obtain. The sides of Gilbert's skin gourd stuck frozen together every time it was empty and became almost impossible and cumbersome to fill, as he had to pull the sides apart with almost lifeless fingers and hold it under water until it was adequately filled. But despite the challenges which they had to negotiate, they walked nearly thirty kilometres before they found a suitable wood in which to spend the day. There was no moss this time but plenty of dead leaves and other undergrowth into which they could burrow and be reasonably comfortable, while they passed a fairly relaxing day.

They abandoned the railway at the beginning of the next night's journey and walked south down a long straight road through a wood, with no awkward villages to avoid. A couple of carts passed them, but since they were lit by lamps, they could see them approaching and duck into cover among the trees. But they took a wrong turning on the road and found themselves in a village. Again, they were lucky that no one noticed them, but this cost them time and effort before they were able to get back onto the right track. Then they were slowed up further because the terrain became swampy, crisscrossed with wide streams. Eventually, they despaired of this and decided to cross east over the railway line and walk due south, over the edge of the Black Forest mountains. This route would help to avoid getting too close to the large town of Karlsruhe. It would also enable them to give a wider berth to several military training areas which they knew were in front of them.

But by avoiding this risk, they created another, bigger problem for themselves. As they climbed up the valley, it became colder and windier. The woods were sparse and there was little vegetation, for the land had been ploughed up around whatever trees remained. They started looking for a hiding place at around 4 a.m. but found nothing which was remotely suitable. As it was starting to get light, they decided to gather together several piles of brushwood which had recently been chopped down and, because the ground was frozen too hard for them to be able to burrow into it, lay their shared sleeping bag in the middle and shelter themselves as best they could. They had, at least, covered thirty-five kilometres, their best day yet. But the brushwood provided no protection from the biting cold wind, and all of them found sleep impossible. And then, even worse, it started to snow.

As they huddled together, a woodcutter walked past. He did not see them, but they could hear him starting to chop wood nearby. Not long afterwards, they had become so cold that they decided they simply could not remain there any longer. They resolved to take the risk of bumping into other woodcutters and move downhill in the hope of finding another more suitable resting place. Their blankets and sheets were now sodden from the snow, which had blown inside their sleeping bag and then melted. As they crossed a road, they bumped into two other travellers who, fortunately, ignored them. When they came to the edge of the wood, they felt that they had to keep moving, out into the open, simply to keep warm. Eventually, they found a reasonably sheltered spot and were able to make a warm restorative drink and smoke a pipe. They knew exactly where they were and spirits rose sufficiently that they started to discuss what they might do when they reached the Swiss border. They also worked out a route which might give them a better chance of finding some shelter and a little warmth.

However, when they moved on, it started to snow more heavily. This covered the deeply ploughed fields through which they were walking, so that they could not distinguish the deep furrows in the earth and fell into them frequently. Their clothing became sodden and so heavy that it began to impede them. And then they found themselves on the edge of a village, by the side of a canal. They knew that the railway line they wished to follow was on the other side of the village, but the canal was too wide to jump and there was no bridge, so they felt they had no option but to take the risk of walking through the village, grunting a curt greeting to those whom they passed. But once they successfully reached the other side, they found that the heavy snow made the going even tougher and they were becoming badly fatigued. And their route had taken them higher again, so it was becoming even colder. The wood was bare of any shelter; the ground was too hard for them to dig into. But they eventually had to stop because they were on the verge of exhaustion. Searching around after a rest, they found a clump of small firs which provided minimal cover from a nearby road, and so they dragged piles of brushwood together to make what proved to be an inadequate shelter from the wind. And, after many fruitless attempts, they succeeded in lighting a fire. This was clearly a dangerous thing to do, but they felt that they could not otherwise survive. The fire did not provide much heat, but they took their boots and socks off in an attempt to dry them out a little. They could do nothing about their clothes, though, and so once again sleep was impossible.

At daybreak, they brewed themselves some beef cubes with bully beef and biscuits, and they felt a little better. Their situation was almost impossible, and they had a long discussion about what they should do, recognising that without shelter, they had very limited options. They eventually concluded that as long as the snow and freezing weather continued, their most sensible choice would be to continue walking during the day as well as the night and hope to make the most of whatever shelter they might find along the way.

In such dispiriting circumstances, it was hard to think of any-thing which might raise their morale. But Gilbert did his best with a novel idea. In order to give themselves energy, they had been munching a combination of chocolate and beef lozenges while they marched, with a handful of raisins or apricots occasionally instead, for variety's sake. Gilbert suggested that they try an apricot inside a handful of snow for a change, which they actually found refreshing as it was a more pleasant way to give themselves some liquid.

As they started walking again in the middle of the morning, the snow eased off. It was lying thickly everywhere, but one advantage at least of the extreme cold was that the surface was just about hard enough to hold their weight, and they did not fall through. Moreover, as they had left the road and were walking through fields, there was little chance of meeting anyone else. They made good progress but then came to a large valley, which had two villages nestling in it, as well as quite a few farms. They were tempted to wait until nightfall but acknowledged that if they did so, it would be impossible to keep warm. Following careful exploration, they were able to find a way down through a gully which shielded them from appearing above the skyline and gave them some respite at least from the wind. At the bottom, it was agreed that they would try to make a rudimentary shelter for a couple of hours and begin their journey again around nightfall. But by now, it was snowing heavily again, and their clothes once more became soaking wet. There were plenty of bundles of brushwood around, but after an experiment, they found that split faggots, or bundles of wood, proved to be more effective in providing protection from the wind. It was possible to use them to construct a little hut in which all three could huddle together. What was more, the shelter made enough of a windbreak that they could build a fire to give themselves something warm to eat and also to try to dry their boots. But they were still too wet and cold to be able to sleep – and it had now been two and a half days since any of them had managed more than a brief doze.

When they started walking again in the early evening, it was once more snowing heavily – and thickly enough that they could not even make out the lights of houses or telegraph poles which marked the major road which would be their next landmark. But since they were lower down the hill, it was a little less cold and the surface of the snow was no longer frozen, which meant that they were trudging up hills through knee-deep snow. Their situation was becoming desperate, not just because of their fatigue and the cold but from physical problems too. McWilliam's knee, injured in his earlier fall, was becoming almost impossible to walk on, one of Jolliffe's boots was badly damaged and leaking and Gilbert had a very painful blister on one heel. They decided that their only option was to look for an isolated farmhouse which had a barn or some outbuildings in which they might take shelter. They found nothing suitable and eventually approached a house which was protected by several loudly barking dogs. An elderly lady stuck her head out and asked what they wanted. Gilbert replied in fluent German that they were travelling to the next village but it was cut off by snow and so they needed a bed for the night. She gave him short shrift, replying tartly that she wasn't running an inn and they should just turn round and retrace their steps.

By this stage, their options were running out. Moreover, they were concerned that since the old lady had seen the three of them together and may have reported them, they might have a better chance of avoiding a possible search if they split into two groups and looked for shelter separately. There were two railway lines within reasonably easy reach: one, to the west, ran from Karlsruhe to Basle, while the other ran south. If they were lucky, it might be possible to jump onto a goods train and find some shelter that way. It was agreed that Gilbert and Jolliffe would go south and that McWilliam would go west. They insisted on escorting him to the outskirts of the village – which was about four kilometres north of Erzingen – an indication of their concern about the difficulty he was having in walking.

McWilliam walked into the village and tried to obtain a room for the night in the local inn. While he was negotiating this, a drunken German soldier approached him and, taking hold of him, accused him of being a Russian escaper. In his dishevelled state, with five days' growth of beard and filthy clothes, McWilliam certainly looked anything but a respectable traveller. Had he but known it (for he was carrying about 600 German marks with him), he might have been able to buy the man off. But he was in simply no condition to go any further. The local constabulary, who were also drinking there, were called out and said that he must go to the local jail. At that point, McWilliam gave in and revealed that he was a British officer. (He overcame their disbelief by opening his rucksack and showing them a tin of bully beef!) At least they gave him a decent glass of wine before he hobbled back into captivity. When he was woken the next morning, he was so stiff that he could barely walk but was nonetheless marched two miles to the nearest railway station. That must have been a very dispiriting journey for him. From there, he was taken back to Heidelberg.

Gilbert and Jolliffe did not remain at liberty for very much longer, either. They intended to see if they could catch a tram in Pforzheim the following evening and took refuge overnight in a woodcutter's cave in a nearby quarry, but they were picked up after they had lit a fire to try to get warm and dry out a little.[16]* This had attracted attention. They were brought back to Heidelberg the following day and put in the same (single) cell as McWilliam. McWilliam had been thoroughly searched on arrival and relieved of his escaping equipment and some of his clothes. It is not clear how Gilbert managed to fool the searching Germans and to retain all his gear. They were given no chance to clean up, and it was only after bribing one of the guards that they were permitted to have a cold shower. Their French allies Mazeline and Petitjean, who had endured similar privations,

---

* In a coded letter written later to his family, Gilbert calculated that he and Jolliffe had travelled ninety kilometres before they were recaptured, a significant achievement in such unpleasant weather conditions.

were caught on the same night in much the same area as the three of them, and they were also brought back to Heidelberg. But while the two Frenchmen remained there, the three British officers were told that they were going to be transferred on the following day to Crefeld, where they would serve fourteen days in solitary confinement, at that time the standard punishment for an escape attempt. On top of that, they were told that they would also serve a further five months in solitary as a reprisal.*

After five months of meticulous planning and plenty of careful, hard work, they were defeated by circumstances beyond their control, which obliged them to break out earlier than they would have wished, when the elements were against them. Notwithstanding that, they had persevered, and kept going far longer than might reasonably have been expected in the most extreme of weather conditions. The outcome must have been a bitter disappointment for them all – as indeed it would have been for any recaptured prisoner who had tasted freedom. But in the process, they had learned some valuable lessons about survival techniques and how to give themselves the best chance of avoiding being detected or drawing attention to themselves. This experience would stand Gilbert, at least, in good stead a few months later.

---

* Neither Brendan Jolliffe nor Henry McWilliam had any success with subsequent attempts to escape. Consequently, after nearly three years in captivity, Jolliffe was sent to Switzerland to be interned in November 1917, and McWilliam, who had been captured six months after Jolliffe, was interned in Holland in March 1918.

CHAPTER 8

SOLITARY CONFINEMENT
AND A BRIEF ESCAPE
FROM CREFELD

It is not clear why all the British officers were moved from Heidelberg all the way north to Crefeld. The camp was barely twenty
miles from the Dutch border, which would have been a very tempting prospect for those with an eye on escape. The optimists among
the inmates hoped that it was because the Germans were expecting
that they might all soon be repatriated and so were making some
preparations in advance. That was certainly not the case. Moreover,
Crefeld was not an easy camp to get out of.

The prison camp there had been built a few years before the war to
serve as a cavalry barracks for German Hussars.* It initially housed
around 350 prisoners. It was thought by many of them, particularly
during the first years of the war, to be among the best camps in Germany – it was well run, with good sanitary and medical conditions.
The American consul in Cologne first visited it in April 1915 and
gave it a positive report.¹ The commandant, Courth, was popular:

---

* It was also used again as a prison camp during the Second World War.

he was believed to have a British wife. Gilbert also commented that he was courteous and kind. However, Courth was obliged to follow orders and could not prevent conditions from deteriorating. Baron von Bissing, before he became Governor of Belgium,* commanded VII Army Corps, which had jurisdiction over Crefeld. He visited the camp in early 1915 and made a speech to the prisoners in which he told them that their conditions were too comfortable and that he would arrange for that to be changed. That duly happened, and things became worse. Lord Newton, then responsible for the Foreign Office Prisoners of War Department, criticised this outcome in a statement to the House of Lords but to no effect.[2] But it wasn't only stricter German treatment which caused problems. In 1917, after his repatriation back to the UK, Lieutenant J. E. P. Howey, RFC, criticised the extent of the gambling and drunkenness among prisoners in Crefeld, who were able to buy cheap wine from the canteen.[3] McWilliam also commented that because such large quantities were sometimes consumed, the Germans, while keen to profit from the sale of alcohol, were regularly compelled to ban it for periods of between three and ten days. It was not unknown for 1,200 bottles to be sold in a week, and the enforcement of discipline consequently became a problem.[4] This was later borne out by later reporting from Gilbert and his fellow escapers from Ströhen, Michael Harrison and Claude Templer, who commented that strong sherry had been substituted for cheap wine, so it was more potent.[5] The Foreign Office was concerned about the likely causes of this and drew it to the attention of the War Office – though, perhaps not surprisingly, the practice continued.

---

*   See Chapter 4.

The courtyard at Crefeld which served as an exercise yard.
Taken by Gilbert on a return visit after the war.

The journey to Crefeld which Gilbert made with Jolliffe and McWilliam was not a pleasant one. McWilliam's knee had become worse after his fall on the ice, and he was almost incapable of walking. Nonetheless, he was forced to march with the others and had to carry his possessions with him as best he could for some distance to the station. When they arrived, he was examined by the doctor and sent to the hospital. It would be some time before he was judged fit enough to undergo any punishment for his escape. Gilbert and Jolliffe were sentenced to fourteen days in solitary confinement, to be followed by a further five months. They were told that this was a reprisal for supposedly similar treatment given to German officers in England. However, they could not start their sentences straight away, because there were not enough cells to accommodate both the escapers who were being punished and also other prisoners who had been sentenced to a few days 'in jug' (as it was known), for minor infractions. When his sentence started, in late April 1917,

Gilbert wrote to his father to tell him of the conditions, describing them as cramped, dark and unpleasant. He made clear that he had been told to do so by his German captors because these were intended as a reprisal for the similar treatment of German prisoners in England.[6] In a more detailed and franker account given after his return to Britain, he stated that the cells, made of concrete, were miserable, dark, cramped places measuring not much longer than the length of the bed and about six feet wide. The window was covered with an iron flap, which largely shut out the light. They were allowed a lamp for a while in the evening, but it was impossible to read during the day unless the prisoner stood right next to the window. (A photograph of the exterior of the cell, taken by Gilbert after the war, is included in the plate section.) They were given two bowls of soup a day, and some coffee made of acorns, together with a lump of black bread weighing about 2lb which was to last seven days. They did sometimes receive food parcels, but these were often stopped for no reason. They were allowed half an hour's exercise a day. Pigs were kept in a cellar just underneath the area where they were confined, and Gilbert commented that in hot weather, the smells were terrible.[7]

Their initial sentence turned out to be twenty days, rather than fourteen, for reasons which were never explained. There were eight officers who were sentenced to this punishment in Crefeld, and apart from McWilliam, they were all locked up at the same time. Their number included Captain Gualter Somerville of the 2nd Royal Warwicks and Lieutenant Geoffrey Formilli, RFC, who had been caught as they attempted to escape from Crefeld in March 1917, when they were picked up at the final gate out of the camp.*

---

* Formilli was one of those who also escaped with Gilbert from Ströhen a few months later, though they split up just after getting away from the camp and his attempt was unsuccessful.

But the treatment which these two were given was made harsher than that meted out to the others, for despite their claim that they were already serving a long sentence for their attempted escape, they were also court-martialled and sentenced to a further three months' confinement in a fortress, an even more unpleasant punishment. Gilbert was temporarily released after serving his shorter period in solitary, until there was space available for him to serve his five-month term. In the event, this did not happen until after his arrival in his next camp, Ströhen, at the end of May.

While Gilbert was serving his first sentence, his family started to take action on his behalf. They continued to do this over the next few months. Gilbert senior wrote to the Foreign Office to tell them about the five-month sentence which his son, McWilliam and Jolliffe were going to have to serve. But he also went public. In order to keep the momentum going, he then wrote to *The Times* to publicise Gilbert's situation and to try to drum up support for some sort of campaign. He pointed out that 'a Commission is sitting in Holland, at The Hague, to deal with the different delicate questions concerning the treatment of prisoners of war. I am afraid they are not aware, however, of the scandalous treatment meted out to many of our officers and men in Germany.'

He continued:

This is the sort of thing our Minister in Holland has to contend with, when instructed to inquire into and protest against the measures adopted by the Germans towards some of our sons who have had the misfortune to fall into their hands. Without the slightest doubt his task would be materially facilitated were he strongly backed up by public opinion. The case of my son and his seven comrades is not an isolated one.

Will not the relatives of other prisoners having cognizance of similar so-called 'reprisals', join in strengthening the hands of those in charge of the interests of our officers and men in Germany, by letting it be clearly felt that the British public is whole-heartedly with them in whatever measures they may decide upon, and uninfluenced by the vapourings of those who, not having felt the sting of the war, object to reprisals?[8]

This had an immediate effect. *The Times* observed two days later that Gilbert senior's letter had inspired others and that this illustrated a widespread anxiety for the fate of British prisoners in Germany and a feeling that the government was deficient either in sympathy towards them or in determination to help them. One of the letters it also published was from A. E. Formilli, the father of Geoffrey Formilli, who was serving his sentence in a cell adjacent to Gilbert's and who was expecting to be worse off because of his additional punishment following his court martial.

Gilbert senior also wrote to Austin Lee, a counsellor in the British Embassy in Paris, about the five-month sentence in solitary which Gilbert junior and his fellow escapers from Heidelberg had not yet started. Lee wrote to Lord Newton, head of the Prisoners of War Department. Newton asked him to approach the French to see whether they had approached the Germans discreetly to discuss the treatment of prisoners of war. Lee replied that he knew that General Paul Pau (who had earlier served on the French Supreme War Council) had been in Switzerland recently for this purpose, and that he would explore further. Newton also asked the British Legation in The Hague to raise the subject.[9] Gilbert senior also wrote to MPs to try to get the matter raised in Parliament.[10] This encouraged others to do the same. And while we don't know quite how much effect all these initiatives might have had, very shortly afterwards, the government decided to negotiate with Germany over changes and improvements to the treatment of prisoners. These meetings resulted in the Hague Agreement of 2 July 1917, revised by a further agreement on 14 July, whereby extreme punishments for prisoners were discontinued. This was a very rare example of combatant countries negotiating with each other and reaching an important decision on a subject of substance while hostilities continued. The relevant clause stated: 'The duration of the punishment for a single attempt to escape on the part of a prisoner of war, even if repeated, shall not exceed military confinement for a period of fourteen days, and, if made in concert with other prisoners, a period of twenty-eight days.'[11]

But Gilbert's family didn't confine themselves to writing letters and trying to solicit assistance from the Foreign Office and prominent public figures to try to influence the sentence which he and the others had been given. They also took some further practical steps on their own initiative to find other ways of assisting him to escape. The one which was initially most productive was to develop contact with an officer working in the French intelligence service.*

The story of how, aided by a fortuitous coincidence, Jack eventually managed to track down this mysterious officer, and the benefits which both sides gained from the relationship of trust which they established with each other, would not be out of place in a decent espionage novel.

In one of his secret letters to the family, Gilbert informed them that he had heard of a French intelligence officer who was tasked with helping French prisoners to escape, and he requested that they

---

* Their contacts with GHQ₁b and MI₁c will be described in Chapter 9.

try to establish contact with him. But he was unable to give them any clues which could help to establish his identity or where he worked. Gilbert senior made some extensive but discreet enquiries, but he met with no success. He was given a series of brush-offs, all suggesting that he must have been misinformed and that no such person or office existed. When Jack recovered from his injury and started a new job in Paris at the end of 1916, he made similar enquiries among the military but had no luck either with any of his British contacts.

So with a mixture of daring and bravado (for he was a very junior officer), Jack then decided to call on the French War Office, without making any prior appointment. There, Jack asked to see their equivalent of the adjutant general. He was kept waiting for a while and then a staff officer came and conducted him into a very imposing office:

The General courteously motioned me to a chair as I announced myself, and laid aside some papers he was handling. It was all very cordial. I quickly explained why I had come to see him, and briefly outlined the manner in which I had been given to understand that a special section of his Intelligence Organisation existed to give assistance to would-be escapers.

He listened to me attentively, and I saw him glance momentarily at his aide. The latter stood at his side examining his fingernails, a deadpan expression on his face, and remained unmoved as the General shook his head and assured me that he knew of no such unit, or officer operating within the French military machine.

'You see, Monsieur,' he added, with a gesture of finality, 'we should be the first to know, here, should any such department exist, or be contemplated…'

There was only one thing I could do. I apologised to the best of my ability for having wasted the General's time by coming to him, thanked him for receiving me, saluted, and took my departure ... I went out into the street feeling thoroughly baffled and not a little worried, for one did not call at an Allied War Ministry and make a personal enquiry such as the one I had just made without some previous introduction – and nobody in my own service has authorised – or even knew of, the visit.[12]

Soon after that, Jack learned from Gilbert of his escape from Heidelberg, which encouraged him to continue his efforts to track down the French intelligence officer. He happened to hear of a British military intelligence officer, one Captain Hartington, working in the Mission Anglaise, which liaised closely with the French authorities, and arranged a meeting to see if he could help. He received a similarly apologetic and discouraging answer. On his way out, on the spur of the moment, he asked the French military policeman on duty at the door whether he had ever heard of a French officer who helped prisoners of war who wished to escape, explaining that he had a brother who was in a camp in Germany. The policeman smiled and interrupted him, using the splendid term '*les évadés*', and said, 'But yes! Monsieur means those of our combatants who seek to evade themselves?' Yes, he knew the officer and frequently helped those who had successfully escaped to make contact with him. He provided directions to his office, which was very close by, adding that Jack should ask the concierge for assistance, saying that he wanted to speak to '*le Capitaine* K'.

Jack could scarcely believe his good fortune, not least because it had come from such an unlikely source. He made his way over to the building and was directed by the concierge up a rickety flight of stairs at the back. He found himself in an austerely furnished room, which also had a cupboard containing what looked to be folded copies of maps. Looking down, he also noticed a thin bell-wire running down one of the legs of the small table in the room, which disappeared into the matting covering the floor. He didn't explore further but then, while he sat and waited, he noticed some knot-holes in the unpainted wood pine wall opposite him and had an un-comfortable feeling that he was being watched. Shortly afterwards, he was escorted into another room where he was introduced to Captain K.* Jack described him as being of an entirely nondescript appearance. He wore an old-style French uniform,

which had all the appearance of having been slept in. His hair was uncombed, and long walrus-type moustaches hung from the corners of his mouth. His eyes – well, they too were unremarka-ble, and if one noticed his hands at all, it would be to deplore the heavy tobacco-stain that tinted his fingers, and to dwell on the lack of attention to his fingernails. But, by Jove, his appearance belied his character![13]

Invited to explain the reason for his visit, Jack described the letter from Gilbert referring to a French officer who assisted escapers, the history of his captivity and his recent escape from Heidelberg. K's response must have taken Jack by surprise. Of Gilbert's escape, he said, 'Yes, we knew about that. It was an extraordinarily good tunnel. You have heard, of course, that he has been moved to Crefeld?' Then, remarkably, he went over to a filing cabinet and pulled out details of

---

* Jack does not identify Captain K or describe the nature of the organisation which he was working for. And despite some assiduous research in the French military archives in Vincennes and potentially relevant French literature, it has not proved possible to find any details of the service, its personnel or how it functioned during this period.

recent French escapers of which, he said, there had been some forty during the last month. 'They were chiefly soldiers who were work-ing on the land – not too difficult.' He picked out one concerning an officer who had been in Crefeld up to the time when all French prisoners were moved from there to other camps.

Drawing on this file, K then proceeded to provide Jack with de-tails of a cunningly constructed tunnel which the French had been working on at Crefeld, before they were moved, which was very close to completion. The French had built a tennis court, which was located not very far from the barbed wire inner fence of the camp. By the side of the court, there was a sort of box seat, in which some of the tennis equipment was stored. Several officers, wearing either voluminous greatcoats or cloaks, would sit on the seat watching the game. One of them would wriggle into the hollowed space under the box seat, where a tunnel had been started, which extended under the wall and the wire. By using this location as a starting point, they were much closer to the wire. They planned to tunnel up to an exit which would be hidden behind a rubbish heap outside the camp. By the time the French prisoners were removed and sent elsewhere, there remained barely ten feet which needed to be dug out.

Captain K provided Jack with full details of the tunnel, in the hope that Gilbert and his British fellow prisoners might be able to dig the final few yards and make their escape from it. The informa-tion which he provided included a drawing of the area, which had been made by one of the prisoners. He also provided two photo-graphs of the drawing, measuring about ten inches by five inches, which were printed onto sepia tissue paper, as well as photographs of a detailed map showing the few miles of German territory which the prisoners would need to cover between Crefeld and the safety of the Dutch frontier, as well as recommended crossing points. He had chosen to print them on tissue paper so that, if necessary, they could be rolled into cheroots for sending to Gilbert. He was sure that this method would defeat German censors if they decided to cut them up in a search for files or other escape equipment.

Since there were no French prisoners left in the camp, there was nothing to be gained from simply sitting on this information.* But it was nonetheless an extraordinarily generous act for Captain K to pass it on to a British officer whom he had only just met for the first time, and this vividly demonstrated the confidence which he had in Jack, who described it thus:

> The moment he had satisfied himself as to my good faith, there was nothing as far as I could see that he would not do to help us in our effort to provide my brother with all he asked for. I do not remember meeting a Frenchman so unbigoted and yet so unswayable when once he was convinced of the correctness of his course.[14]

Since the Germans quite often transferred all the prisoners of one nationality from one camp to another with little warning, it is not surprising that tunnels sometimes had to be abandoned when they were frustratingly close to completion. Such an experience befell the British contingent at Gütersloh, when they were given a day's notice of their move to Crefeld. They had been working on a tunnel there for nearly nine months. Despite various obstacles and inter-ruptions because of security concerns, they had dug for over 100

---

* As it happened, there was a British tunnel under construction at Crefeld during this period, but it was only half finished by the time that the British prisoners received a sudden instruction to prepare to move elsewhere. (Lewis-Stempel, p. 215.) Despite his tunnelling experience at Heidelberg, Gilbert was not involved in this project, which started some time before his arrival, though he was aware of it. Moreover, he only spent two months in the camp, quite a lot of it in solitary confinement.

days and the tunnel was thirty-five yards long. Those who had been working on it held a very stormy meeting to decide what they should do.* The Gütersloh tunnel was long enough and close enough to the surface (though uncomfortably close to the patrol beat of a sentry) that it was thought possible that they might be able to break it open and for a small number to get away. So they discussed whether it should be regarded as an entirely British enterprise (for all those who had been involved were British) and whether they would be justified in finishing it prematurely, so as to allow for a handful of British officers to escape, or whether it should be considered to be a contribution to the Allied cause and therefore handed over to another nationality who would thus be given the chance to finish it at greater leisure and so enable a larger number to make an escape. The parties supporting those two views were almost equally divided, and there was – unusually – a bitter argument which must have been very difficult for all those who had participated and who had contributed a great deal to the project. In the end, it was resolved that it should be handed over to the Allies, and the Russians were briefed about it.[†]

When Jack returned home, he and the family considered further the best way to send the prints which Captain K had provided to Gilbert. They concluded that they did not wish to put him to the trouble of arranging for the cheroots to be specially rolled to include them. They preferred instead to collect a range of items they could make up into a parcel. And they decided to cut up the drawing, maps and accompanying explanation into small pieces and hide these inside a set of dominoes. Cecil, unanimously judged the most

---

* One of the driving forces behind this project was Captain Frederick Moysey of the Suffolk Regiment, who was an inveterate escaper. He was wounded in the escape attempt from Schwarmstedt a few months later, in June 1917, when Captain William Morritt was shot and killed.
† Unfortunately, it is not known what the outcome was.

competent handyman by his family, was tasked to do this, and he set about it by separating the ivory top of several of the dominoes from their ebony bases.* He then gouged out a suitable trough in the base. Each map square was folded and ironed flat, then placed in the trough, and the domino weighted with a suitable piece of lead to ensure that the doctored pieces corresponded in weight to the undoctored pieces: this work required precision and took a long time.

With what was perhaps unnecessary elaboration, they arranged for this set and some other concealed items to be included in a parcel sent to Gilbert by a friend of the family, an American woman living in Paris. In advance of its despatch, she wrote to Gilbert to tell him she was doing this, including a coded message the family had concocted, telling him to examine certain domino numbers. Unfortunately, that letter never arrived,† so when the parcel containing the dominoes reached him, Gilbert didn't give them more than a cursory glance before setting the box aside, wondering why he had been sent dominoes, a game which the family never played at home even though it was at the time very popular in France. He wrote a letter back, asking the family to thank the American for her parcel but made no mention in code or invisible writing to the dominoes. The family only found out what had happened after his successful escape later that year.[16]

So Gilbert never learned of the nearly completed means of escape at Crefeld which was just under his feet. And the clever technique developed by those French prisoners to enable them to dig a much

---

* Plastics were not in use at that time.
† Gilbert and his family (in common with most prisoners) numbered the letters which they wrote to each other, so they would at least know whether a letter had gone missing, even if they did not know what message it had contained. But a letter written by someone else, as this was, would not have been numbered, so Gilbert would not have known that there was a letter which had gone astray.

shorter tunnel out of Crefeld was never exploited. It does not appear to have been written about after the First World War, either. That's just as well, for the Germans would almost certainly have read about it and so been in a position to thwart an equally imaginative and simple plan thought up by Lieutenant Michael Codner, Royal Artillery, Flight Lieutenant Eric Williams, RAF, and Flight Lieutenant Oliver Philpot, RAF, to dig a similarly short tunnel which enabled them to escape from Stalag Luft 3 in October 1943. In this case, they used a vaulting horse, which was carried out by prisoners every day and used quite intensively for gymnastics. The horse was designed to conceal men, tools and containers of soil. Each day, it was carried out to the same spot near the perimeter fence and while prisoners conducted gymnastic exercises above, a tunnel was dug. At the end of each day, a wooden board was placed over the tunnel entrance and covered with surface soil. The gymnastics disguised the real purpose of the vaulting horse and kept the sound of the digging from being detected by German seismographs. It took them three months to complete the tunnel. They worked in shifts of one or two diggers at a time, excavating over forty yards of tunnel, roughly the same length as the tunnel which Gilbert dug to get out of Heidelberg. They used bowls as shovels and metal rods to poke through the surface of the ground to create air holes. No shoring was used except near the entrance. Tunnellers were concealed inside the vaulting horse as it was carried to and fro. On return journeys, the excavated sand was taken away, too. All three escaped and successfully reached Sweden by stowing away on neutral ships.[*]

In the course of the relationship, Captain K provided Jack with

---

[*] There is no indication that any of them were aware of the earlier French attempt using the same technique. They thought it up based on the idea of the Trojan Horse used by the Greeks to get into the city of Troy. Williams described this story in *The Wooden Horse* (London: Collins, 1979).

more help and advice which was useful for the support which they were giving to Gilbert. For example, at their first meeting, K provided him with details of some other chemicals he might use when the regular ones had failed to work and they couldn't develop some of the messages which Gilbert had written on the inside of his envelopes.

The reader might wonder why K was willing to spend so much time in providing assistance to help one individual officer to escape, when he was presumably dealing with British intelligence services which were engaged in doing the same thing. The answer appears to be that – remarkably – he had no sort of liaison with any British service at this stage and that Jack was his only British contact. This subject – and what it led to – will be discussed further in the next chapter.

Gilbert only spent two months in Crefeld, between March and May 1917. He spent nearly half of that time in the cells, and he commented later that he was fortunate that his parcels arrived because it was impossible to eat the German food available to those in solitary confinement. While Gilbert was still in solitary, the Germans moved the French out to other camps. They left in some style, marching around the square with the band playing 'La Marseillaise', to the delight of the onlookers.* Not long after that, the atmosphere changed, and other troops were brought in and stationed in force around the perimeter of the prison. The reason was never established, though the prisoners picked up rumours that the German authorities were concerned about the threat of a mutiny among the inmates and so took active steps to discourage

---

* Military bands, and sometimes orchestras too, were formed in German prison camps during the First World War, though their choice of instruments was often restricted.

it. Perhaps this concern also resulted in their decision to close the camp and move all the prisoners elsewhere.

It was the preparations for this move which provided Gilbert with the opportunity to make a further attempt to escape.

The following is an account he wrote some years later of how he identified and exploited an opportunity to do this. It is worth reproducing in full because it conveys a sense of the restless energy shown by those who were inveterate escapers, always keeping their eyes open for possibilities, as well as their willingness to take chances, and also because of the vivid and detailed description which it provides of the imaginative – and uncomfortable – attempt which he made:

There were roughly 800 British officers in Crefeld camp at this time. After the mutiny scare the Germans decided to move us away from the frontier as soon as possible.* The guards were reinforced with a couple of companies of troops from the Russian front. They all wore *pickelhaubes*† and brought a couple of machine guns which they mounted on either side of the camp, commanding both stretches of barbed wire. We heard that there had been some friction between the *Landsturm* guard commander and the commander of the fresh troops. The latter intimated that the old guard could not guard us efficiently. The result was a double line of men – the inner circle *Landsturm* and the outer the regular troops. Outside this were the machine gun crews. With regard to these new men from the Russian front, I never saw a more unhealthy, ill-fed and browbeaten body of troops. Their faces were

---

* The camp was approximately thirty kilometres from the Dutch border.
† A spiked metal helmet.

haggard and emaciated and all seemed to bear some affliction or other – cross-eyed, or wearing glasses, and some quite lame.

I had been let out of cells after my first month of *Stubenarrest** to give place for others on the waiting list, and was on the watch for some chance to escape the five months' solitary confinement which still awaited me. The tunnel was still going forward but seemed very unlikely to finish in time before the evacuation.† I found a point of vantage to watch the merchant shippers leave the camp (the first batch) but as they were very carefully searched did not think there was much in it. I saw them all pass through the *Kommandantur*,‡ but never recognised Major Fox whom I later heard was disguised and with the party.§

A few days later we received orders to pack a box each for the move to other camps and to pack up the rest of our baggage to be stored in a warehouse somewhere – it was rumoured to be Hamburg. The next day we were kept hours on parade and divided up into about five parties. The subalterns were nearly all in two large parties and the more senior officers in three larger parties. These were given a number and I was in No. 3 party. One feature we noticed was that all friends were broken up and put in different parties. Some pals exchanged names in order to remain together, which created great complications on the final parade before leaving.

Two days before we were to be moved Morritt¶ and I were examining likely spots. We had noticed a small hut from the cells, in the middle of a grass plot, and had always been curious to

---

* Detention.
† This was not the French tunnel about which Captain K had briefed Jack but a British one, which evidently had rather further still to go.
‡ Headquarters office.
§ Major C. V. Fox, another inveterate escaper, whose escape was described in Chapter 6.
¶ William G. Morritt.

know what it was. We had an idea that it might lead to the sewers and possibly provide a means of exit. We set to work at an hour when the clerks in the offices overlooking the spot would not likely be present, and when the night sentry inside the camp had not been posted. A few skeleton keys soon opened the door and with a pal (Pinder, I believe*) on sentry duty for us, we entered. All was dark inside. I had an electric lamp and speedily switched on and examined all the floor and rubbish stacked up. Morritt dived down and scraped up the ring of a trapdoor on the floor. With our united efforts we pulled it right up and found a narrow steel ladder disappearing down into darkness. While I flashed the light Morritt went down and examined the vault below. There were some drains and pipes but all were of too small a gauge for a human body to pass through. We searched for any useful implements but only found a pair of dusty old field glasses, very probably concealed there by a Russian. They were useful in this camp for on a clear day, Holland and the intervening country could be seen from the roof of the highest building. We came out and got the door locked after some trouble with the key, just as the night sentry came strolling down on his beat. We sauntered away and he suspected nothing.

Early the next morning I was on the prowl again and met Morritt near the stables, where our kitboxes had been stacked. Large moving vans drawn by horses had been brought into the camp and were being packed by English orderlies. As we watched near the main gates a full one came out and after passing the first gate stopped a few minutes, and <u>was not searched by the guard</u>.† We

---

*   Lieutenant F. G. Pinder, RFC.
†   Underlined in the text.

both saw the chance and strolled to the other end of the camp where the carts were being loaded by the stables.

The boxes were being packed in at the back of the van and piled up by two orderlies. A German NCO directed operations and one or two German soldiers helped. We strolled round to the front of the cart, pretending to identify one of our own boxes and found that there was nothing doing there, as that end was being watched by two sentries outside the wire on their beat: one was watching the carts in a very suspicious manner.

We gave instructions to the orderlies to leave a space large enough to conceal two of us in the next cart, and then collected the necessary kit for the venture. We had prepared maps a long time before – and in fact had everything ready and conveniently concealed. It took us but a few minutes to fetch our coats and slip the necessary articles into the pockets. For a rapid chance like this, everything depended upon immediate mobilisation and continued preparedness. I am convinced that there are always chances for escape even in the best guarded camps, chances which are open for a few minutes or hours only and offering maximum chance of success with minimum risk. Don't think that I advocate a foolhardy seizing of any opportunity, far from it, but you must make up your mind quickly, weigh the chances and decide yes or no.

We decided 'yes' on this occasion when, in the afternoon, after several carts had been prepared without a successful opportunity, we saw the two men leave the back of the last cart but one. We had been sitting on a table nearby with overcoats beside us, reading some books which had been piled up there from the library. Previously we had been sitting on a grass plot in front of the stables with our coats as a ground sheet (hence the presence of our coats).

The two orderlies were standing by as we strode across to the cart putting on our coats. The NCO's back was turned and the *Landsturm* had gone to fetch something, so all was clear for perhaps forty seconds. We sprang in, I went first and went down the hole left between two piles of boxes and found that our men had manoeuvred the pile furthest in, leaving a kind of tunnel going towards the front of the cart. This was the shape of a right angle and very narrow, and consequently as I wriggled down it feet first my British warm* wrinkled up around me and jammed me in a sitting position on the bottom of the cart – giving minimal prospect of my being able to lever myself up again. Morritt sprang in after me and knelt on my head, which I put on one side allowing his knees to slip outside my shoulders. He whispered to me that he was not half covered and would I get down further. I replied that that was materially impossible and at this point we heard the Germans coming back, speaking to the orderlies. Then I heard another voice which I recognised to be the 'Crab'.† An orderly deftly placed a foot bath over Morritt's head and he pulled his Burberry coat around him and crouched low. The Crab was giving instructions for some articles to be taken out of the cart, saying that beds could not go. (The beds provided by the Huns‡ were made of planks and very uncomfortable at the best of times, and consequently many officers bought iron spring bedsteads from the canteen.) The orderlies climbed over us and removed some objects and then they left the cart, and we judged that they had finished loading it. I found that by turning my head slightly I could see through a crack between two of the side boards, and

---

* A thick woollen greatcoat.
† An ineffective German officer, so nicknamed because of his gait.
‡ A disparaging term for Germans, frequently used during the First World War.

that by putting my eye close to it I could get a tolerably good view of the outside world. We seemed to wait for ages, getting more and more cramped and every limb going to sleep, until I thought that I would not be able to move at all when I next needed to. The idea that the bath (most of them were very heavy) might shift when we got under way gave us a blue funk. German voices were heard and then I saw two Germans through the slot, one of them a civilian leading a horse. They came quite close, and I heard one of them say, 'Make sure that there is nobody in the cart.' The other laughed at the idea and harnessed the horse. They went around the back and fastened several chains and then we moved slowly forward with a jolt which set the boxes rocking.

I suppose that we went about twenty yards and then we stopped suddenly. The two men started chattering excitedly. I thought that all was lost, as I heard one of them climb up behind and crawl about. I don't know what they did but they were uncomfortably close and took about ten minutes to finish their job. I also knew that quite a number of people in the camp knew we were in the cart and might attract attention by showing too much interest in its progress. This was always a serious danger in all such attempts, especially when some 'Nosey Parker' got wind of it.

We moved on and got to the first gate. The ground sloped up to the gate, and as we started the climb I felt the boxes starting to slide. I gripped the middle one and whispered to Morritt to do the same – but it was too late, I could not hold it and some fell over into the back of the cart. We paused here while the sentry opened the gate and Morritt – who was now practically entirely exposed – pulled his Burberry over his head and simulated a bunch of clothes. The cart jerked forward and pulled up in front of the guardroom. I peered through the opening in the side and saw the NCO of the guard standing outside and scrutinising the cart. I was particularly bucked to recognise him, for he was the worst NCO of the whole guard. He used to do all he could to annoy us when we were in the cells. Responsibility for our escape would most probably fall on him. As I watched, he turned and ordered a soldier out. He called him to attention right in front of us and told him to load his rifle. As he did so, I could almost see down the barrel. My heart seemed to leap into my mouth as I thought that someone had spotted us and that this was going to be his way of dealing with us. But then, with great relief, I saw him put his rifle down and make towards the second gate. Then it struck me that he might be guarding the carts and would accompany us out to the town, an eventuality entirely unforeseen and exceedingly unwelcome. But we would have to take a chance on that.

The arrival of a couple of men with a box at the back of the cart diverted my attention. I heard one of them say to the driver, 'Three more boxes to go on, and your cart is indeed untidy, Karl.' 'That will be all right, we are only going to the town,' he replied. The two men threw the boxes in one after another. Fortunately, they did not fall on us, as there was just enough room for them in front of our own pile. Then we lurched forward again as the sentry opened the second gate. Everything looked rosy as I saw the sentries marching down their beat between the last two lines of barbed wire. The same man opened the third gate and we passed out into the road. We then trundled through the line of regular troops, all wearing spiked helmets, and turned down the road taking the first turning to the left. At the corner we passed one of the machine guns with the crew standing by at short distance, with one man by the gun.

The town* was barely a mile away, and we had decided to jump before we came to the crowded streets. Quite a number of the last line of sentries were watching the cart, and so we lay low and waited until the last minute. About 400 yards away from the camp, we put our heads up and crawled to the side and then rolled over into the ditch.[17]

It was broad daylight and there was no safe place to hide within easy reach. So Gilbert and Morritt walked openly through St Tönis, with Gilbert talking animatedly to Morritt in fluent German and Morritt (no German speaker) grunting occasionally in return. They managed to get several miles further on, away from the immediate vicinity of the camp but were still unable to find any suitable cover good enough to protect them from the searches which followed their escape. Consequently, they were detected several hours later, arrested and brought back to the cells.[†] Instead of losing his temper and raging at them, as frequently happened when captured prisoners were brought back, Commandant Courth justified his reputation for courtesy. He congratulated them on the cleverness of their escape and behaved very decently. He asked Gilbert and Morritt how they had managed it, and when he gave his word of honour that he would not punish those concerned, they told him. (He kept his word, and the orderlies were not punished.)

The fates of two of those mentioned in Gilbert's account were described in earlier chapters. Fox was recaptured a few days later and badly beaten up, causing him to lose the sight of one eye. He and Morritt were both transferred to a camp at Schwarmstedt. Fox

---

* This was St Tönis, which was amalgamated with a neighbouring principality in 1970 and is now known as Tönisvorst.
† Gilbert calculated that they had managed to travel some five miles before they were picked up.

escaped again a few weeks later, shortly after a fellow officer, John Caunter, had also got away on 19 June 1917, and they met again in the dark in the woods and successfully made their way to Holland. Separately, the unfortunate Morritt was shot dead without warning not long afterwards, as he was making his way out of the tunnel he had dug.

A few of the senior British officers in Crefeld were sent off to a range of other camps. Most of the rest ended up in either Schwarmstedt or Ströhen. No reason was given for the choice, though Gualter Somerville, Royal Warwicks, reckoned that those prisoners who had been in Crefeld longest and who had given no trouble ended up in Schwarmstedt, while those who had tried to escape, colonial officers (for there were some Indians among the inmates) and Royal Flying Corps officers and others who had annoyed the Germans running Crefeld ended up in the punishment camp at Ströhen. If Somerville was correct, then the Germans weren't entirely consistent, for both McWilliam and Morritt (who had form as escapers) went to Schwarmstedt.[18]

Gilbert did not spend long in the cells for this attempt, because shortly afterwards he was marched out of the camp in a group under a very strong escort and put on a train with a guard standing by each window. They were taken directly to Ströhen.

CHAPTER 9

WHAT DID INTELLIGENCE SERVICES DO TO HELP ESCAPERS?

There can't have been many families – if indeed there were any others at all – who, as they sought to help their relatives escape, were in contact with three different intelligence organisations during the First World War. The previous chapter provided some background on what the French were doing and how they helped Jack and his brother Gilbert. What about the British? And why were there two British organisations working on the same task, competing with each other and creating the risk of crossing wires?

These two organisations were MI1c and GHQ1b. MI1c had developed out of the Secret Service Bureau, set up in 1909 under Commander Mansfield Cumming and Captain Vernon Kell. The bureau was split into foreign and home sections, with Kell's home section looking after domestic security and eventually developing into MI5 (or the Security Service). Cumming was given responsibility for the foreign section, and the two sections soon found it necessary to operate from separate offices. After the outbreak of the First World War, the foreign section moved into Whitehall

Court, close to the War Office, and in 1916 adopted the cover of MIіc, appearing ostensibly to be a part of the War Office – though, even at this early stage, its remit was wider than just the collection and provision of military intelligence to the War Office and the Admiralty, for it was also providing political intelligence to the Foreign Office. During this period, the intelligence section of the general headquarters (GHQ) of the British Expeditionary Force, known as GHQіb and commanded by Brigadier General George Macdonogh, tried to take over the operations of the still fledgling organisation run by Cumming. The turf battles which ensued took up much time and effort, but Cumming's political skills enabled him to win sufficient support from the Foreign Office, and from some powerful backers in the War Office too, to be able to survive and to start to flourish. MIіc was able to grow significantly and to produce some extremely effective networks, particularly La Dame Blanche, which comprised nearly 800 agents in German-occupied Belgium and regularly provided valuable intelligence on German troop movements. GHQіb had its successes too, and while the squabbles and infighting between the organisations continued, they were able to develop a system of working together which generally allowed for different geographical areas of responsibility. But the solutions were not infallible. There was inevitably scope for crossed wires and misunderstandings – as well as occasional cooperation.

It was mentioned in Chapter 1 that very little is known about the organisation and work of officers working in the Intelligence Corps in the War Office, for most of them obeyed the post-war instruction to destroy their files. Similarly, information about the work of the Secret Intelligence Service (SIS), as it is now generally known – though, perhaps confusingly, it also came to be known as MI6 early in the Second World War[1] – has also been limited, for its files have not been released to the National Archives and remain closed. Keith Jeffery published an informative and officially sanctioned history about the first forty years of the service from 1909 to 1949. However, it contains just one brief reference about the work of MIɪc in support of British prisoners of war seeking to escape from German prison camps:

> In April 1917, Lieutenant H. Brickwood, a volunteer and officer whose family brewing business was based in Portsmouth and who had been working on coding, was put in charge of a new section formed 'to assist British Prisoners of War to escape from Germany by sending maps, compasses etc. to them by secret means'.[2]

Jeffery wrote that while the Service archive was rich, it was also in places patchy,* and that the SIS's attitude to archives was that they should only be kept if they served some clear operational purpose. So, since the First World War was thought to be the war to end all wars and therefore it was not expected that there would be another one, it would not be surprising if the service judged that there was no need to keep records about its work in supporting escaping activities – and this may therefore help to explain the dearth of information about MIɪc's activities in this respect.[3] It was probably for the same reason that a number of former prisoners concluded that they could write in some detail about their experiences of escaping, because they did not expect that such information would ever be of use to a future enemy – though, unfortunately, that turned out to be the case barely twenty years later.

In the course of research for this book, it has been possible to unearth some new material about the work of both MIɪc and GHQɪb

---

* For example, Jeffery commented that 'little raw intelligence from Cumming's agents during the first two years of the war has survived in the SIS archive'. (*MI6*, p. 73.)

in supporting the attempts of British prisoners to escape and to collate it with the extremely fragmentary details which were previously known. I have been able to extrapolate from this sufficiently to be able to add something useful to the picture of the work which both organisations did in this field, particularly as far as Gilbert and his colleagues were concerned.

For example, the section in MIıc supporting escape attempts by British prisoners was not formed in April 1917. It was in existence at least as early as January 1917, and it was headed by Major John Wansey Snepp. Snepp was an officer in the Royal Marines Light Infantry, who was severely wounded in action against the Turks in December 1914. His service record shows that he was posted to the Naval Intelligence Division in the Admiralty from April 1915 to July 1918. He may have been transferred to intelligence work from the outset, but the file is uninformative on that point. However, there is correspondence showing, from his detailed knowledge of the subject, that he must already have been at work in MIıc from the end of 1916, if not earlier. The range of commendations which he received for his work are a clear indication that he must have been remarkably successful. He was mentioned in a list issued in February 1917 by the Secretary of State for War of those who had performed valuable services in connection with the war, he received a Mention in Despatches in November 1917 and he was later awarded an OBE for valuable services during the war.* He

---

* Snepp's service record notes that he served on the *Empress of India* in the Black Sea in 1919–20, when the ship 'was in action against the Bolsheviks on several occasions'. It is also recorded that he spent time on special service with the 8th Battalion Royal Marines in Ireland between February and October 1921, but it is not clear whether or not this was linked to intelligence work. It is not impossible, for there were other officers who had escaped successfully during the war who subsequently became involved in intelligence activities in Ireland. One was Captain J. L. Hardy DSO MC, who worked in the Royal Ulster Constabulary and was targeted by the IRA in at least three assassination attempts. (See foreword by Nigel Cave in J. L. Hardy, *I Escape!* (Barnsley: Pen & Sword, 2014), pp. xii–xiii.) Sidney Buckley was another. After he returned to Oxford and completed his degree, there is evidence that the IRA gathered information about him because he was working in Ireland as a commercial traveller for Welch Margetson, which had factories in both London and Londonderry in 1921. They discovered that he had been a former officer in the RFC and an intelligence officer as well. (http://www.bloodysunday.co.uk/castle-intelligence/buckley/buckley.html)

left MIıc in July 1918, when he was judged to be fit enough to return to active duty. He concluded the war in command of a Royal Marine battery in Kyleakin, on the Isle of Skye, which must have seemed a rather tame end to his wartime career.[4]

The first traces of Snepp's activities are contained in a letter he wrote to Lieutenant W. H. (Bill) Bremner, RN.[*] It was dated 17 January 1917. Bremner was a family friend of Henry McWilliam, at that time busily digging the tunnel through which he and Gilbert planned to escape from Heidelberg. Snepp wrote a carefully phrased and discreet letter:

I have forwarded full details to our man in Berne, and he has replied as follows.

'I happen to know of an officer at Heidelberg whose arrangements for escape are made for the end of February. Could it be that they are known to each other? We have already sent various articles to him. I think I might possibly get a guide, but it is so difficult to get people on a flimsy excuse.[†] The officer I know is making a tunnel so there is no need for nippers.'[‡]

I did not mention names in my first letter, but he will have received the full details by now and I hope to hear from him soon.

Since Bremner was known to be a friend of McWilliam, and Jolliffe's name does not appear in this or any other correspondence which has been recovered, there is a good possibility that 'our man

---

[*] Bill Bremner's very informative family website https://www.bremnerroots.co.uk/bill/ reveals that he was a talented naval officer who spent the later part of the war and the period after it on coastal motor boats (CMBs). He was awarded a DSC for his part in a raid on Ostend and later a DSO after the Kronstadt raid against the Bolshevik Baltic fleet when Augustus Agar won a VC. From the mid-1930s onwards, Bremner spent the second half of his career in SIS. Given his earlier involvement with MIıc from 1917, when supporting attempts to help McWilliam to escape again, it is perhaps not surprising that he did so.

[†] The meaning of this is obscure.

[‡] Wire cutters.

in Berne' (i.e. the MI1c representative) was referring to Gilbert. Although there were also other tunnels being attempted from Heidelberg, the timing of late February fits reasonably closely with when Gilbert and McWilliam were hoping to get out. Perhaps slightly early, but tunnelling was suspended for some weeks in December after the unwelcome encounter with a German in the eaves, and Snepp may not by then have known about the delay. It is likely that the prisoner used by Gilbert to carry a letter on his behalf when he was repatriated to Switzerland would have informed 'our man' of the identities of those for whom he was carrying letters, because that would have provided a fair indication of those who were most escape conscious and therefore probably likely to benefit from assistance if they were not already getting it – which Gilbert, of course, certainly was.[5]

Surviving family papers provide scanty details of the nature of the contacts Jack or Gilbert later had with MI1c. However, we have a clear understanding of how Jack made contact with GHQ1b, and while not as remarkable as the way he managed to get in touch with '*le Capitaine* K', it is nonetheless really quite unusual. Jack had been continuing to have regular meetings with K during the spring and early summer and observed that in addition to assisting escaping activity, he was also becoming more interested in encouraging sabotage activities by French prisoners, particularly those working in munition factories and on the railways. (Not something which appears to have been encouraged by British organisations.)

But K also told Jack that a number of his correspondents in camps were expressing concerns about escaping materials which were being sent from Britain to British officers and men by what they considered to be dangerously risky means. They were worried that if the German authorities became aware of the extent of this activity, they would restrict or ban the delivery of parcels on a more permanent basis than the occasional restrictions which had been enforced in the past.

This put Jack in a quandary. He told K that he did not know of any sponsored activity of this kind, whoever might have been carrying it out. Moreover, he had not briefed any British authority about the contact he had been having with K, so it was not immediately obvious to him how he could take up the problem with the appropriate authority, since those whom he had initially approached had feigned ignorance and given him the brush off. After a thorough discussion, they agreed that Jack would send a full report on these developments to RFC headquarters, explaining how he had come to get in touch with K in the first place and asking for guidance and instructions about his future association with him. When he did so, he was also careful not to give any indication as to K's identity.

It took a while before there was a response, but then Jack was invited to visit the town commandant's office near Les Halles, where he was introduced to someone whom he called Major G. This abbreviation is rather easier to decode than that of 'le Capitaine K', for it was clearly Major George Bruce, responsible for running GHQ1b in Paris, who took Jack down to his office in the Rue St Roch, not far from the Tuileries. As they went there, Bruce explained that the timing of Jack's letter was fortuitous. Two RFC officers who had recently escaped from Germany by jumping off a train had learned of the activities of K while they were in captivity and also obtained some information about his work. Bruce said that they would therefore like to get in touch with him. He added that his headquarters in London were agreeable to Jack remaining in contact with K, but they very much hoped that in return he would be able to obtain K's consent to being introduced to one of the two RFC officers who had just come back from Germany. It seems a pleasing irony that they were asking for Jack's help to do this, given the problems which he had himself experienced when trying to make contact with K a few months earlier. When Jack put this proposal to him, K thought it an excellent idea, though preferred to meet unofficially outside the office of either party, so Jack fixed up for the pair to have their first meeting in the Tuileries Gardens and left them to it. K told him afterwards that the outcome had been quite satisfactory and that they had discovered means by which it should be possible to resolve some of the concerns which he had brought up several weeks earlier. Jack remained in contact with K, but it was little more than a couple of months later that he heard of Gilbert's successful escape from Ströhen, and their contact subsequently became infrequent.[6]

The officer whom Jack had arranged to meet was Sidney Buckley, who had reached Switzerland with Johnny Evans just a few weeks earlier. Lieutenant Colonel R. J. Drake (working on the General Staff of the British Expeditionary Force, BEF, with responsibility for intelligence) described much of what Buckley set out to do in a history of the intelligence work of the BEF in France, which he wrote in 1919. This is one of very few documents which survived the post-war cull, and his description of their work in supporting escape activities, even if occasionally partial, deserves to be reproduced in detail:

With regard to the Paris office, in addition to its work of endeavouring to establish a system in Luxembourg which would communicate through Switzerland,[*] Captain Bruce was given

---

[*] This is a reference to a remarkable operation which involved a very brave and intrepid Belgian officer, Albert-Ernest Baschwitz Meau, who had in April 1916 escaped from Magdeburg with J. L. Hardy. They were recaptured, but Baschwitz Meau later got away successfully and subsequently worked with GHQ1b, which sent him to Luxembourg by balloon. He used a very clever system to send back intelligence reporting on German rail movements through Luxembourg, which involved the use of coded messages which were included in apparently innocent newspaper articles, which after publication were available in Paris, where they were deciphered by GHQ1b. (See Janet Morgan, *The Secrets of the Rue St Roch*.)

the services of a Flying Corps Officer who had recently escaped from Germany – Lieutenant S. E. Buckley – with a view to organising the escape of our prisoners of war, in collaboration with the French, who had already had a very good system working for the escape of their own prisoners. This officer was put in touch with an officer of MI1c who had been taking some steps in this direction, but it is believed without very much success.[*]

As a result of their efforts, maps, compasses and other necessities were smuggled into prisoners of war in various camps in Germany as well as ciphers and codes by which they could communicate with the outside world. Lectures and instruction were also given to officers of units of the Expeditionary Force, and compasses, maps etc. were served out to them, attention being paid particularly to the officers of the RFC and the Tank Corps, who, from the nature of their employment, were more liable to capture than the average officer, and were, from their small numbers and the expense of their training, more desirable objects of attention than the average officer of a fighting unit.

It was felt undesirable that instruction in these matters should be given to these latter officers[†] on account of the possible effect on the 'morale' of the weaker members who might feel that as they had been given full instruction and means of escape, it was not so incumbent on them to fight to the last as might otherwise be the case.

---

[*] It is perhaps not surprising that Drake wanted to put a favourable gloss on what he was writing here, as indeed he also did in other parts of this history. But it is worth noting that he makes no mention of the fact that although there was plenty of close liaison and exchanges of sensitive material and intelligence between the British and the French in other areas earlier in the war, GHQ1b had no contact with its French counterparts before June 1917. And the limited evidence which is available suggests that MI1c was indeed having some respectable successes, though it is not possible to calculate how many. A more likely explanation for his final comment here, though, might be simply that MI1c kept quiet about its activities and did not share the details with him.

[†] I.e. infantry officers.

RESULTS OBTAINED

A considerable number of officers of the RFC especially were got in touch with, and a gratifying proportion of escapes were effected. Eventually, as was only to be expected, the Germans discovered the method of conveyance of maps, compasses, files etc. to our prisoners, and took such precautions as to render any further attempts most difficult. In addition, they threatened, at a conference on prisoners of war at The Hague, to forbid entirely the further despatch of parcels, should our efforts continue. The organisation, therefore, perforce, ceased then to perform any useful function, and Lieutenant Buckley's energies were directed to assist Captain Bruce in the general scheme of secret service, the field of which had by this time considerably developed.

A scheme put forward by Lieutenant Buckley by which he himself should again be taken prisoner with a view to conveying instruction in person as to the methods of escape to other prisoners of war, was negatived, as this officer had already suffered 18 months' incarceration in Germany, and had made five attempts to escape, escaping on the fifth. It was felt that he was already too well known to the German authorities to justify any such proposal being put into effect in fairness to him.

Another scheme put forward by him, by which we should attempt to obtain information with regard to the movement of constituted units by train in the interior of Germany, many of which passed along lines in the immediate vicinity of prisoner of war camps, was also negatived. It was felt that not only was it not fair to ask our prisoners of war to undertake the risks involved, but also that the information would deal with matters so far removed from our front as not to justify these risks.[7]

Drake's decision to concentrate on officers from the RFC and the Tank Corps, given their higher value and greater training, as well as smaller numbers, makes good sense. But his comments that a considerable number of RFC officers were contacted and a gratifying proportion of escapes were achieved may have been rather optimistic. Although all statistics from this period need to be treated with some caution, as discussed in Chapter 1, there is reliable evidence that altogether, at least thirty-five RFC, RNAS and RAF officers successfully escaped from Germany or German-occupied territory, out of a total of about fifty officers overall who succeeded in getting home. A significant proportion of those did so before either GHQ1b or MI1c began to be involved in providing material support, so it is not possible to calculate how much of a difference their work might subsequently have made. Not surprisingly, almost all the books written after the war by successful escapers made only the vaguest reference to the assistance which they had received from families or from an official source.* The only significant exception was H. A. Cartwright, in *Within Four Walls*. He described two occasions when parcels containing contraband arrived for him without warning. The first was at Magdeburg, when his wife's letter, telling him what was coming, arrived days if not weeks late. Fortunately, he had managed to remove the parcel without it being inspected. The second was at Küstrin, and again the warning letter arrived after a lazy censor had not bothered to inspect the parcel, which turned out to be full of escape equipment. 'The parcel was sent by some friends of Fox,† an officer in the Scots Guards who had escaped

---

* Only a handful of former RFC officers wrote books about their escaping activities after the war, and they did not go into detail – though there were others, such as Lawrence Wingfield, who were more specific in their private papers, which have ended up in archives.

† Major C. V. Fox, whose escape was described in Chapter 6.

some time before and made very thorough arrangements for the supply of necessaries to certain prisoners who were known to be trying to escape.' Cartwright continued:

> Fox's friends began to operate towards the end of 1917 or the beginning of 1918, and it was quite evident that they were in touch with our families and were thoroughly well informed in all matters of interest to escaping prisoners. I think that the first I heard from them was in a letter from one of them giving me a cypher in which they would communicate. The fact that the letter was from a stranger, and extraordinarily uninteresting, was quite enough to make me study it carefully and work out its hidden meaning.

Cartwright added that, sensibly enough, 'Fox's friends' were limiting the supply of these parcels to only one officer in three or four camps, so as to reduce the risks of discovery, and that each of these parcels contained sufficient equipment for distribution to several other prisoners. One of his later parcels included a near-perfect forgery of a workman's identity card, probably the first example of such a technique, though he never had a chance to use it.[8] Given that there is evidence that MI1c was working in this field in early 1917, if Cartwright had got the dates right, then his comment above suggests that Fox had more probably been in touch with GHQ1b, for it would have taken some time for the organisation Buckley was supporting to have become widely active.

Nonetheless, Drake's observation that it was only to be expected that the Germans would in time discover how escape equipment was disguised or concealed and sent to PoWs comes across as somewhat complacent. The systems which had been set up by the French and by families for supplying escape equipment had already worked perfectly well for a long time – either because the items were well hidden or because prisoners were warned in advance in a coded letter that an item of contraband was being sent to them and were given the parcel number and/or a description of the item. During that period, the number of parcels containing contraband which were discovered was not sufficiently large to trigger a German reaction. If they were forewarned, prisoners could either use a skeleton key to get into the parcel room or arrange to distract the German staff and either substitute an innocent parcel or discreetly smuggle out the item which contained the equipment they wanted. K's warning to Jack made clear that this was no longer always happening. It seems likely that once GHQ1b became active, the contraband parcel production of both services combined may have flooded the supply system. It may also be that the problem was exacerbated by too many late notifications of the arrival of contraband, and perhaps there were prisoners who were new to the game who were not careful enough to make appropriate arrangements for their reception.

In early 1918, the Germans made a series of complaints, through the Dutch government, that the British were using parcels as a means of supplying prisoners with prohibited items. They gave some specific examples. One described a box of biscuits which had been sent to an officer in a camp in the Harz mountains in Northern Germany. When the biscuits were removed, the box was found to contain a false bottom, and in the space between them, there were found seven excellent maps of both the Harz mountains and the Dutch frontier areas which an escaping prisoner might have been expected to make for. Others also contained maps, as well as luminous compasses, 'directions for the production of secret writings' and similar material. A letter written to Robert Vansittart, the deputy head of the Foreign Office Prisoners of War Department, described who was thought to be responsible:

> They are some of the things sent out by MI1c, 2 Whitehall Court, a department presided over by Major Snepp. One of Major Snepp's associates, Lieutenant Brickwood, is often here and has on several occasions taken away supplies of coupons for officers' parcels … These do not of course bear the Red Cross and we are very particular that our Red Cross labels should not be used for such purposes. We can, however, hardly refuse the coupons. I never liked this business much and of course as long as the Red Cross label is not abused, we have no *locus standi* to complain from. I think, however, that the time has come to consider whether more harm than good is being done by the operations of this MI1c department.[9]

But though the German complaints and restrictions limited the scope for sending escape equipment, causing Buckley to spend more time assisting the work of Bruce in other areas, it did not stop his escape-related work. There is correspondence from Drake himself in late February 1918 about the lectures which Buckley was continuing to give to RFC squadrons to help them be better prepared for capture and subsequent escape.[10]

After Buckley arrived in Paris, a circular message was sent to all the brigades and wings in the BEF, explaining that he would be visiting all of them to deliver a lecture on techniques which aircrew might employ to escape if they were unfortunate enough to be captured. The content of the lecture would cover a simple code for communicating with friends, details of the Dutch and Swiss frontiers, the best opportunities for escape and the use of maps, compasses and stars for navigation in the course of an escape attempt. It was actually much more extensive than that: the lecture notes (left behind for consultation by all aircrew and marked either 'Not to be taken out of the Squadron Office' or 'Not to be carried in aircraft') ran to six pages. It showed the extent to which lessons had been learned from those captured Allied airmen who had succeeded in escaping and returning home to recount their experiences and give their advice, and also how the British and French had exploited the results of their interrogations of captured German aircrew. A surviving version of Buckley's lecture, which was written in January 1918,[11] describes the different methods which the Germans might use to obtain information, starting with interrogation and also outlining what could be learned from personal documents, letters and diaries which might inadvertently be taken on board an aircraft. Given the significance of the subject, the briefing on the dangers of interrogation was quite thin, warning aircrew only to beware of kindness, to prepare to be confronted with statements allegedly made by brother officers and to be alert for microphones.

A slightly later and considerably more detailed document from the RAF Museum, which does not appear to have been given such widespread circulation, demonstrates that the information from the captured German pilot Hans Baldamus* (and no doubt others) had been absorbed and acted upon. The graphic nature of the warnings provided would have made it hard for aircrew to ignore:

If you are unfortunate enough to land behind enemy lines you may be agreeably surprised by the apparent warmth and generosity of your welcome there. The German officers will probably have you to stay with them as their guest for a few days at one of their

---

* See Chapter 4.

squadrons and will make you most comfortable. You will probably be extremely well entertained with the best of everything
which they can offer. An abundance of good champagne from
France will oil the wheels of conversation between officers of the
German Flying Corps and one whom they will probably term a
brother officer of the Royal Flying Corps. They will appear to be
very good fellows, straightforward, cheerful and keen on the sci-
entific side of flying, apart from their ordinary work, with which
they might say that they are quite fed up. They will probably lead
you to talk about the possibilities of aviation after the war and
profess little interest in aviation as actually applied to war. It may
not take much wine to gladden your heart and to induce you to
lay aside suspicion and reserve, and forget the guile which lies
behind their artless questions.

And so, unaccustomed as you are to this form of deceit, you
may fall victim to this clever combination of cunning and hospitality. But though they may succeed for the moment in making
a favourable impression, you will afterwards have every reason to
remember that during this war the Germans have proved themselves to be a cruel and unscrupulous enemy, but they are sound
financiers and have an eye to a good investment. It does not cost
them much to entertain you well, and even if it did, they expect
to get an adequate return for their money in the form of information unwittingly imparted by you.

That is why they will give you all the delights of the 'Carlton'
and the 'Savoy' with none of the regrets of an overdraft at Cox's*
and that is why you will be treated as a highly honoured guest,
instead of being half starved in one of their new notorious prison

---

* The bank normally used by RFC officers.

camps, a treatment that is in fact only postponed until they have squeezed every ounce of useful information out of you.

The work is done by experienced men. Quite unknown to yourself, one or more of the seemingly irresponsible flying men are highly trained intelligence officers who will sift little bits of information from your most brilliant '*bon mots*',* received with the keenest amusement – and gratification.[12]

Accompanying this briefing was a section on codes which could be used in correspondence home by officers in the event of their capture. This was also the next section in Buckley's lecture. Both set out clear instructions for all aircrew on codes and how they should write out full instructions for a code which they would intend to use if captured. This was to be placed in a sealed envelope and left in the squadron office. The envelope was to be addressed to a 'responsible person' at home, for forwarding once it was definitely established that they had been captured. Aircrew were told not to mention this to the person whom they had nominated, so as to prevent information about this arrangement from becoming too widely known. Examples were given of various simple codes which might be used and specific indicators which should be included in letters to show that a coded message had been written – for example, by writing the date as 12/12/1917, instead of 12 December 1917.

Both these briefings asked aircrew to request their 'responsible person' to decode the letter and send it to Major J. W. Snepp of the Royal Marines Light Infantry at MI1c, War Office. If it was not possible to decode the message, then the letter or postcard should be sent to Major Snepp for him to do so. Any letter containing an

---

* Clever remarks.

indicator that secret writing was being employed (for the briefing also covered this point) was also to be sent to Snepp. Advice was given on what invisible inks might be used and which testing agents they reacted to. It was also suggested that secret writing might be used on the insides of envelopes rather than on the letters themselves – perhaps it was Gilbert's effective use of this method which led to it being copied, but it is such a relatively obvious technique that it is hard to believe that it was not already being copied elsewhere too.

Though, in this connection, it is worth noting an interesting letter which Snepp wrote to Lieutenant Bremner in late January 1917. At this early stage, it's possible that he knew little about secret writing techniques and how they could be circumvented, because he expressed his concerns:

I see from the letter that Insall is using lemon juice or milk to write with. Will you please caution him if possible that these two 'secret' inks react to just about every known agent and are consequently most dangerous, as the merest attempt at skilled censorship would instantly reveal the subject. I am afraid that I cannot see how we could send any secret ink or method of writing out to him as he would not know where to look for it, and if his father wrote to him with lemon juice or milk, we would be practically certain to be bowled out by the German censor. If his father has used lemon juice or milk on the wrappings of parcels or by some other means, and is quite certain that the writing has not been in any way tampered with, I may be able to supply you with a method of writing which could be more or less safely used.[13]

Snepp didn't elaborate on the alternative method of writing. But it seems clear that he had not fully grasped the benefits of using the insides of envelopes for secret writing – and that over the next few months, he must have changed his mind!

In view of the focus of these lectures on setting up secure means of communication, it seems a reasonable conclusion both that Brickwood's section was established under Snepp to develop a range of suitable codes which could be used by captured prisoners, and also that Buckley's lectures showed that GHQıb was willing to cooperate with MIıc and avoid unnecessary duplication of resources by allowing MIıc to handle all coded correspondence received from prisoners in German captivity.

Buckley's lectures also covered the mechanics of preparing for escape by acquiring the necessary equipment and suitable clothing. He also discussed the methods which could be successfully used for getting away from captivity – including jumping off a train (for Buckley was one of a fair number who successfully achieved this), bluffing one's way out, concealing oneself in objects such as boxes or carts being removed from a camp, cutting the wire, tunnelling (which Buckley recommended only as a last resort, as it was very unsuccessful – Gilbert and the twenty-nine officers who got out through a tunnel from Holzminden might have disagreed with him, but this method was certainly very resource-intensive and vulnerable to betrayal) and bribery, which was not often successful and liable to incur severe punishment. He also highlighted methods of travel and possible routes to and over the Dutch and Swiss frontiers, as well as potential problems that would need to be addressed if travelling by train – for example, phrases to avoid when attempting to buy a ticket. He advised walkers to travel only by night and how and when to pass through villages or small towns, as well as discussing the importance of choosing before dawn a suitable hiding place in which to lie up in daylight.

The lecture included a great deal of valuable information, which would have drawn on the experiences of many escaping prisoners, both those who succeeded and those who did not. It is quite salutary to compare the advice which Buckley provided with that contained on cards which were given out to RAF aircrew by MI9 (and also marked 'Not to be carried in aircraft') during the Second World War. They were very similar.

With the benefit of more than a century of hindsight, and reflective of the sort of approach which we might expect to be taken now in similar circumstances, it is worth noting that there is one significant omission from the briefings provided by Buckley and others. Although they give plenty of information about the communications, equipment and different techniques which might be required by a successful escaper, they do not mention at all the psychological challenges which would have to be addressed. What was an escaper likely to experience when he was at large? What sort of problems might be encountered and how might he prepare to deal with them? How should a group discuss and resolve differences of opinion, particularly when strong feelings were likely to be easily aroused as a result of stress, lack of sleep, exhaustion and hunger?[14]

One of the main reasons why those who had a previous experience of escape had a better chance of success was because they had come across these and other problems already, and they had worked out ways of dealing with them. It is quite striking to read in different accounts of successful escapes how – before anyone broke out of their camps – these issues were thoroughly discussed by all who were going to be involved. For example, when starting their trek to Switzerland, Johnny Evans and Buckley himself agreed that, since they were escaping in summer, they would never start to walk before 9.30 p.m. in open country or 9.45 p.m. if there were villages close by – and Evans noted that they broke this rule twice and were nearly caught on both occasions. Even more importantly, they decided that in the event of a disagreement, they would always take the advice of the more cautious of the two of them at any moment.[15] Gilbert, Harrison and Templer had a similar discussion before they broke out of Ströhen and concluded that if they disagreed over any issue, they would abide by a majority decision, and that if all three disagreed with each other, then they would adopt the course of action which was least likely to lead to recapture. Harrison acknowledged also that most people who escaped in pairs had sometimes found difficulty in resolving differences of opinion, where to hesitate would almost certainly prove to be the worst solution.[16]

Samples of the surviving correspondence between Snepp, Bremner, Jack and Gilbert senior – and later Gilbert himself, after he regained his freedom – concentrate mainly on the mechanics of arranging to supply escape equipment and the exchange of information about the location of prisoners and what they were doing. (Since, as we have seen, prisoners' mail was often unreliable, it could take a long time to find out that they had been moved to another camp.) But occasionally, it covered other important subjects, for example relating to the lobbying which Gilbert senior was engaged in to try to persuade the British government to negotiate with the Germans to get them to discontinue the harsh five-month sentences in solitary confinement for prisoners who had escaped. Thus, in June 1917, Jack wrote to Bremner:

I have your letter of 14th instant for which many thanks. Yes, we sent Snepp the extracts you mention when we answered his letter.

Did not my brother accompany McW* on his jaunt at H† with another fellow? And is not his present situation the result of their joint efforts? You will have observed, I expect, that the affair is being looked into more or less seriously, and we hear that questions have been asked by our representative. Please let me have an answer to each of these questions as soon as you can, as for several reasons it is important that I should be certain on all the points.[17]

Jack wanted confirmation that it was Jolliffe who had accompanied Gilbert and McWilliam on their escape from Heidelberg, so as to be sure that Gilbert senior had his facts right before he launched his next salvo.

A few weeks later, in mid-July, Snepp wrote to Bremner to enquire about an attempted escape which McWilliam had made. At that stage, he did not know where McWilliam was and who else had been involved in the escape attempt. He also updated Bremner on Gilbert's circumstances:

Yours of 10th inst to hand. I should very much like to see the letter from Mrs McW about the attempted escape when you get it.

The last letter I got from Insall senior was dated 29 May 1917. In it he said that his son had everything he needed and was just waiting for the opportunity. Also that A. J. [Jack] Insall had supplied all the necessary information about the Dutch frontier. In fact, declining all help until he saw how his plan worked.

Do you know where McW is now? As you know, the Crefeld

---

* McWilliam.
† Heidelberg.

camp is no more. We should like to send Mrs McW the maps this week.

PS Insall accompanied McW on that jaunt at Heidelberg. Otherwise he would not now be undergoing a strafing.[18]

McWilliam had indeed made another escape attempt, this time on his own. Gilbert senior mentioned that in a letter to Austin Lee, at the embassy in Paris, on 10 June 1917, adding that McWilliam had damaged his knees again and was back in hospital.[19]

In fact, by then, McWilliam had been transferred to Schwarmstedt. He had informed Bremner of the move in a letter of 29 May, when he also asked for some ship's baccy* and a luminous watch to replace one which he said had been lost when he was captured. The latter was presumably a request for a compass and perhaps the baccy was a reference to maps. The letter was sent to Snepp, who told Bremner in July that it had tested negative for secret writing. He added that he was shortly going to send a parcel to McWilliam, which would be marked No. 20. He asked Bremner to inform Mrs McWilliam and request her to tell her son to examine it very carefully. Presumably, the maps he wanted were going to be concealed therein. It is not clear what happened to this, for McWilliam wrote to Bremner two months later in September to tell him that he 'had not received the cigarettes you promised as yet'.

It is a testament to the effectiveness of the system which Jack and Gilbert senior had developed to send Gilbert whatever materials he needed that they were able to turn down Snepp's offer of assistance from MI1c. Snepp wrote to Bremner again on the following day,

---

* Tobacco.

saying that he had just heard from Caunter of the Gloucesters, who had escaped, that Gilbert did not accompany McWilliam on his recent escape attempt, and he did not know when that occurred. He had also heard that Gilbert had made a separate attempt to get out during the period when the Crefeld camp was being broken up and that he had asked Gilbert senior for further details. Gilbert senior replied shortly afterwards and also confirmed that Gilbert had been moved to Ströhen.

After Gilbert's escape from Ströhen (which will be described in Chapter 10), he spent a very busy few weeks in London and then returned to Paris to stay with his family. There had been no time to meet Bremner, so he wrote to him instead. He commented that it had been a pity that they had not met, because he had something which he wanted to send to McWilliam as soon as possible. He was therefore going to do it from Paris. He added some advice, commenting: 'I shall write him a warning letter beforehand. If Mac's correspondence is inspected, as I believe it is, he had better get a quite harmless prisoner to write home for him to a friend or to the previous people where his letters could be collected.' For that reason, Gilbert intended to use the pen name of S. Lenoir, 22 Ave Louis de Grand, Paris, when writing to him. He added that he thought that he would be able to do more for McWilliam from Paris than he would be able to do in England. Tellingly, he explained that this was because 'parcels etc. are now being sent in a different way and I am rather afraid that a certain section of the WO* may overdo its job'. That strongly suggests that he was anxious that GHQ1b was likely to be overactive in its supply of parcels and therefore

---

* War Office.

concluded that a parcel sent from France would be less likely to attract the attention of German censors. He also provided an insight into how prisoners were able to communicate with each other when they were in different camps and summarised the limited equipment which McWilliam would be likely to need:

> I wrote to him from Ströhen, by forged letter which looked as if sent from England and the Germans redirected it. He answered verbally via a fellow who was sent from Schwarmstedt to Ströhen. They only need to have a luminous compass, good map, electric torch (bacon, biltong, solid spirit or Kampite*) to get clear of camp at night, live on vegetables in the field, and only walk at night,† and always know where they are and take great care on the frontier and their chances are fairly good. I will send Mac information. Does he need any of the other things? I know that his letters never came well when we were in Heidelberg.

Not long afterwards, Gilbert wrote again because he had heard that most of the prisoners at Schwarmstedt had been moved to Holzminden. (By then, as will be explained further in Chapter 10, Gilbert had been introduced to Jack's contact K and had a long conversation with him, so very probably received this update from him.) Since it was still possible for Gilbert to send parcels direct to PoWs from France, he was intending to send McWilliam a complete set of the equipment which he would need, but he would address it to another prisoner at Holzminden in case that was where he had ended up. This would have been to allow for the possibility

---

*   Solid fuel blocks which could be used with a Tommy trench cooker system.
†   Underlined in Gilbert's letter.

that the thorough German searches of prisoners being transferred might discover the contraband which McWilliam would have been carrying. However, Gilbert had also heard that Jolliffe had been sent back to Heidelberg, so asked Bremner to confirm as soon as possible where McWilliam had ended up, in case it was necessary for him to send him what he needed to another location. He also provided some very detailed guidance and directions on where McWilliam should cross the border if he was escaping from Holzminden:

> If you are writing, tell Mac to cross by Ahaus.* The road between Epe and Ottenstein is patrolled with dogs. Cross where the railway from Alstätte to Enschede crosses the frontier. One kilometre from the frontier leave the railway line and go north-west. It is a bit marshy here but there are no guards. The line itself is guarded on the frontier crossing. There is a small wood south of the line, just where you leave it to go north-west.[20]

It is not clear where this information came from. We now know that it could have been from one of three different organisations, but whoever provided it, this was an impressively detailed and valuable briefing. McWilliam had written to Bremner from Schwarmstedt a few weeks earlier, saying that with luck he hoped to be repatriated to Holland within a few weeks. In the event – as often seemed to occur – it took a further six months before this happened, but he would at least have been able to share this guidance with other prisoners who were also planning to escape.

---

* A town in Germany close to the Dutch border.

Those who were repatriated often received a warm welcome. Pictured here is Lieutenant J. W. Reynolds, who was imprisoned with Gilbert in Ingolstadt, being welcomed by a crowd when he was medically repatriated to Switzerland in June 1916. He would almost certainly have been smuggling out letters from prisoners which they would not have wanted to pass through the hands of German censors.

CHAPTER 10

SUCCESS AT LAST!

During the four years which the First World War lasted, there were quite a few German prison camps which could have competed for the title of the most unpleasant and difficult to be incarcerated in. For example, among those designated for officers, Fort IX at Ingolstadt was certainly a viable candidate. It was partially underground and it also had inadequate drainage, which meant that it was so damp that the walls oozed water for most of the year, creating a significant health hazard, which would have been exacerbated by freezing conditions and a lack of effective heating in winter. It was not the only camp where prisoners were forced to live or sleep underground: Fort Zorndorf was another, where prisoners lived in galleries which often lacked light in winter too.[1] There were many others where poor sanitation, cramped conditions and climatic problems in both summer and winter all caused problems.

But the worst camps were those which were designated *straflager*, or punishment camps, particularly Schwarmstedt and Ströhen. The physical conditions there were bad enough, but the treatment which prisoners received from their captors made it considerably worse. The following account of Ströhen provides a graphic description:

The camp was a sister camp to Schwarmstedt, but in addition to all the bad conditions of the latter, such as bad sanitation, bad food, leaking huts, lice and flea ridden beds, we ran up against some *Boche** officials who did their level best to make things more impossible than they were ... Cigarettes and potatoes from England were confiscated; and all windows had to be shut at night, although the weather was extremely hot and our overcrowded rooms unbearable at night. Having no ventilation, we broke all the windows; but the *Boche* refused to have them mended when winter came, so got their own back that way.[2]

The author might also have mentioned the bleakness of the moor on which Ströhen was situated, and the marshes which surrounded it, leading to infestations of midges, mosquitoes and flies in summer and chilling winds in the winter. Moreover, Michael Harrison, with whom Gilbert escaped, provided the following description of the commandant:

The Commandant was one of the most unpleasant individuals that I have ever come across. Mercifully his brutality was equalled by his inefficiency. So drastic was his treatment of prisoners who defied his authority in any way that I believe he was considered a most suitable Commandant for a reprisal camp.[3]

As will be discussed below, the commandant was responsible for the bayoneting (though fortunately not the deaths) of several of the prisoners during the next few months. His deputy, Karl Niemeyer, one of the most unpopular and callous of all the German officers

---

* A contemptuous term, initially used by the French, to refer to Germans, particularly soldiers, during the First World War.

charged with custody of prisoners during the war, also contributed to the harsh regime.* Niemeyer had lived in the United States before the war and spoke fragmentary and often inaccurate English, which was a source of considerable amusement to the inmates. He was later transferred to the camp at Holzminden, the site of the very successful tunnel breakout the following year. Prisoners were given three days' solitary confinement or 'jug' for the slightest offence. In June and the first half of July 1917, 125 prisoners were punished in this way.[4] (Gilbert similarly calculated that altogether more than 150 officers underwent solitary confinement in three months.[5]) This did at least have the advantage that those who were sentenced to five months in solitary for attempting to escape were often unable to start to serve their sentences, because there was insufficient space available. Prisoners tried various means of protesting, by writing to the Dutch Embassy as the 'protecting power'† or to the *Kriegsministerium*.‡ Their letters were not passed on and were sometimes later returned to them. If they described the camp conditions in their ordinary letters sent home to relatives, those were not passed on either. Eventually, they decided on a letter strike. No one wrote letters home, and this was noticed and became cause for widespread complaint at home.

Not long after Gilbert's arrival at Ströhen in May 1917, the camp was visited by the Dutch inspector Dr Römer. He reported that Ströhen contained over 400 British officers, a few from the merchant navy, and eight unfortunate Indian inmates who were housed together in a separate barrack. The latter received no letters or

---

* His brother Heinrich, at that time the commandant of Clausthal in the Harz mountains, was equally unpopular.
† The Dutch took over this responsibility when the United States declared war on Germany in April 1917.
‡ The German War Ministry.

parcels, had to cook for themselves, were badly homesick and could only hope to be repatriated.

Dr Römer also reported that the prisoners had made a long list of complaints to him. They included:

Bad sanitation, which he described in detail, adding, 'It will be seen from the foregoing that improvements should at once be made in this connection. The authorities agree.'

There were no resident medical staff. A German doctor made very infrequent visits. The lack of staff and medical care was considered to be the cause of death of a British officer in the camp.

There had been many complaints made against the commandant.

Officers were regularly sentenced without trial or knowledge of their offences. For example: Captain Baxter stated he was confined to the arrest barrack* for five days before [the] commandant visited him and that he was not notified of the reason for his punishment. It took four weeks before he was allowed to exercise in open air. Captain Batty-Smith, who had been similarly confined, said that he had written three letters to the Dutch embassy between 6 and 11 March, and that these were returned to him on 17 July with no reason being given. Lieutenant Clarke complained that his clothes were taken away for disinfection and were returned totally spoilt. Moreover, personal property (for example a watch) had been taken from him and not returned.

Lieutenant Insall made similar complaints to those of Clarke and Baxter. He added that confinement to barrack arrest, as far as food and treatment were concerned, too closely resembled solitary confinement.[6]

---

* A milder form of solitary confinement. Not long after the arrival of the main British contingent, the barrack was enlarged so as to accommodate a larger number of those judged to be minor miscreants.

Gilbert senior referred to the visit by Dr Römer in a letter which he wrote in June 1917 to Ian Malcolm MP* as a part of his campaign to raise awareness of what was happening in German camps and the harsh treatment which British prisoners were receiving. Gilbert senior commented that he trusted that Dr Römer's visit would have been of a serious nature and added that he hoped that 'the result will soon be forwarded to next of kin as promised in a note received last week from the Foreign Office'.† He also enclosed a letter from Gilbert, emphasising that it had been received secretly and noting:

It shows that my fears as to the conditions of this camp and the treatment of officers by the Commandant were only too well founded ... After reading this message from my son, being convinced that many of the Camp Commanders are of the same type and mentality, I trust that their camps will receive periodical and serious inspections from the Netherlands Legation.

It would not have been possible for Gilbert to have sent such a long and frank letter by ordinary prisoner of war mail, so it must have been carried out for him by a prisoner who was being repatriated. This would also explain why it appears to have taken some six weeks to arrive. The letter contains much graphic detail and is worth re-producing in full:

---

* Malcolm had held many diplomatic and political appointments. He had also worked as a Red Cross official in France, Switzerland and Russia. He was also close to the Foreign Secretary, Arthur Balfour, having served on the Balfour Mission earlier that year to promote closer cooperation between the US and Britain, and was later private secretary to Balfour during the Paris Peace Conference. So he would have had the ear of the Foreign Secretary, which Gilbert senior – who had very probably taken advice from his friend Austin Lee in the British Embassy in Paris – would have known.
† The Foreign Office Prisoners of War Department, to which Gilbert sent a copy of this letter, commented that it hoped it would be possible to provide him with very short particulars about the general conditions at Ströhen, but that did not happen.

There are about 300 British officers* here [few illegible words] cigarettes stopped, windows all shut at night. Food parcels stopped for certain periods. All people who have escaped shut in cells with only 2 bowls of soup a day and acorn coffee. Bread ration about 2lbs for 7 days. Parcels supposed to be allowed to all officers doing 5 months' reprisal for escaping. All get 5 months' solitary in small cell for attempt. Size of cell as long and broad as length of bed. No walks for people in camp, no ground for exercise other than space between huts. Water pump just by latrines. Water foul. About 8 wounded, still open wounds and bandages. All milk and everything else in parcels turned out and goes bad. Men in cells on bread and water only.

Letter to Dutch Ambassador returned. Jug for the slightest thing, all without trial. Letters repeatedly returned, so as last measure only method of protesting is a letter strike which starts now.

All parcels stopped in camp for several days on account of wire cutters being retrieved after confiscation.† Same again now, period unknown. People in cells get no baths and others 1 a week. Have all written often to the Commandant to be allowed to see terms of order under which we are punished, but to no avail.

About a week before we left, Crefeld was surrounded by a second line of guards and machine gun and then we were sent off to Camps II and III.‡ Senior officers to known camps and juniors to these reprisal camps. Guards on way of 1 per man per officer. Came to this camp and were shouted at by Camp Commander and *Feldwebels*.§ Set of huts in sand patch in marshes. Water very

---

* Dr Römer's figure of over 400 would have been more accurate, as he would have had access to German statistics.
† I.e. somehow reacquired by the prisoners.
‡ Schwarmstedt and Ströhen.
§ Sergeant majors.

bad, turns brown and thick when boiled. All were only allowed to take 1 box. Pounds' worth of food and stuff were left at Crefeld, which was immediately occupied by Rumanian officers. All who attempted escape – and there are lots of us now since 7 February, get 5 months' solitary confinement, besides our punishment, which often runs into months. One hour's walk in small closed courtyard, between cells. Bad air in cells, and 1 orderly for 12 only allowed to stay about 1 hour to work, 75 on waiting list for 3 days in jug for small offences, such as opening windows or refusing to read out German orders on parade. All Tommies* who escape get 3 months' reprisals without their parcels, which is hell. I was in a cell in Crefeld for 20 days, very small and dark; iron shutters over window excluding 2/3 of the light, which threw a beam only, across the cell. These are smaller here, but a bit lighter. Am doing 5 months. When we came in there was nothing except a few short planks nailed to the wall and supported by 2 legs. A small shelf and stool and can have been added since. No baths allowed in cell, only small bowl and can of cold water. Beds a sack of old bread cards and filthy paper, vermin of all kinds have been found and vermin powder was asked for, it came after delay and the officer was charged for it. All are known by numbers. All cigarettes are taken out of parcels and confiscated.

I escaped from Heidelberg and got 90km, but was taken in the snow. Day before leaving Crefeld got away again in a cart, but were taken before we could find cover, though got past St Tönis.

Officers on one occasion all woken up at 3 a.m. by being shaken by German officer. The Russians get absolute hell here, being packed into huts and locked in except for 2 hours a day, 250

---

* Soldiers and non-commissioned officers.

in a hut. We are under 100 in same huts. Cannot something be done now that we have more German officer prisoners than they have of us? People were jugged for several days for washing below the waist in the yard, as there were no baths. Senior officer also has 3 days. A small hole about 6 inches square was cut in the side of hut. There were 7 men in room, and windows all ordered to be shut. Some blew open* and [the] senior in the room at once got 3 days on the 2 soups and coffee ration. Soup made of preserved mangels,† it literally makes you sick to smell it. We are in no way treated like officers. Army Corps commander chiefly to blame, I think. (Army Corps No. X, i.e. 10.) Officers awaiting trial or doing any punishment other than 5 months' reprisal do not get their parcels, or any food but ration mentioned.

Got your Abdulla fags. Think I can manage pictures OK when they come.‡ Large Archie battery§ on Bruges Tower, seen by fellow shot down over it. At Zeebrugge or Ostend I forget which, aeroplane sheds hunted for on several occasions were found on both side of pier (under it) but fellow was shot down who found them.¶

Dr Römer's report and Gilbert senior's letter were both shown to Lord Newton, who commented that Ströhen was a very bad camp, although Dr Römer had tried to make the best of it.** Lord Newton judged that the situation was largely due to the commandant. He added that from Gilbert's letter, it would appear that a letter strike

---

* Presumably because of the draught caused by the hole which had been cut to provide some minimal ventilation.
† A coarse yellow or orange beet, grown as feed for cattle.
‡ The meaning of this reference is not clear.
§ Anti-aircraft battery.
¶ Here Gilbert was passing on information provided by recently captured fellow prisoners.
** There was often a feeling in the Foreign Office that those conducting inspections rather pulled their punches when describing conditions – and also, perhaps, that they showed a degree of over-confidence regarding the extent to which their inspections might provide a means of preventing abuses.

was on, which accounted for the absence of news which had been the subject of complaint by relatives. He asked for a letter to be sent to the Dutch, asking them to pay another visit shortly.[8]

The camp at Ströhen was unpleasant and had many disadvantages. However, it did have one quite significant attraction, which was its relative proximity to the border of neutral Holland. This facilitated the chance of making a successful escape attempt. And plenty of prisoners had a go. During the eight months that there were British inmates in Ströhen, there were more than 120 attempts to get out. Almost fifty individuals succeeded in getting away from the camp, and of those, eleven made a successful crossing of the border. There were frequent attempts at tunnelling, but the sandy soil and the high water table meant that they either collapsed or were flooded all too easily. Some got out by cutting the wire, others by simply bluffing their way through the gates.[9]

Occasionally, some of these attempts showed rather more enthusiasm than good judgement. On the first day after his arrival from Zorndorf, Lieutenant Duncan Grinnell-Milne, RFC, was asked whether he would like to join a 'battering-ram' party. The idea was that six men should make use of a heavy metal bar, which would be pinched from the gym, and use it to assault the lock of a door which opened towards the *Kommandantur*.* Those behind the scheme felt sure that the gate would give way and the group would be able to rush straight on and out of the camp, because for a large part of their route, they would be screened from sentries who might shoot at them, by two *Kommandantur* buildings. Thereafter, they would soon be among trees which would provide some additional protection. Since the willing participants outnumbered those needed to

---

* The main German administrative offices.

carry the bar, Grinnell-Milne (as it turned out, fortunately for him) was given a subordinate role, to stand watch, to give warning when the two sentries were at the end of their beats with their backs turned and to open a small inner gate to give the assault party a clear run at their target:

> From about thirty yards away there was a vague scuffling sound as the gang got into motion, and a few seconds later with much pounding of feet it came hurtling past complete with battering-ram ... There was a tremendous crash as the front man of the party hit the gate. In the darkness he missed the lock with the end of the ram and it was with his face that he charged the wooden framework. In spite of the five strong men behind him, however, his face was not strong enough to push down the obstruction, and he let out a yell that must have curdled the blood of all the sentries round the camp. The iron bar was immediately dropped with a loud clang, and the party having picked itself up, made off at top speed in the direction of the huts. Somewhat dazed by the rapidity of these happenings, I stood for a moment still holding the little gate open. A loud report close behind me brought me suddenly to my senses and I took to my heels as quickly as I could, much encouraged by the chorus of police whistles now being blown in every direction.[10]

As he ran, Grinnell-Milne heard someone behind him, screaming at him to stop. It turned out to be Niemeyer, who was brandishing two pistols. Grinnell-Milne was in no doubt that if he had obeyed Niemeyer's order, he would have been shot on the spot. All the escapers managed to regain the sanctuary of their huts, and a thorough German search the following morning found no escape equipment, only the iron bar which had been abandoned near the gate. Grinnell-Milne made another attempt several months later, which was much more carefully planned and organised. This time, dressed as a German sentry, he escorted two of his compatriots disguised as orderlies (one of them his brother, Douglas, who was also an officer in the RFC), and armed with a forged pass, he nearly managed to bluff his way out of the camp. Unfortunately, ill luck took a hand. A German sentry recognised that one of those whom Grinnell-Milne was accompanying was not an orderly but his brother.[11] However, Grinnell-Milne eventually escaped successfully from Aachen in April 1918.

During the summer of 1917, there were several incidents at Ströhen where prisoners were bayoneted, within the camp, when they were not trying to escape. In June, the Germans ordered some fifty newly captured infantry officers to give up their steel helmets at a specified roll call. This they mostly declined to do, instead hiding them or throwing them into ponds, so only eight were given up. This refusal to cooperate must have irritated the Germans, who dredged the ponds to recover many of those which had been abandoned. Lieutenant Gerald Featherstone Knight, RFC, wandered over to watch what was going on. He was ordered off by a tall, unshaven *Landsturmmann* who barred his way and shouted at him to go away. Knight replied, 'When you address me as a British officer, and not as a dog, then I will go back.' The sentry advanced slightly and shouted something further at Knight which he did not understand. So Knight turned towards a *feldwebel*, who was standing about twenty yards away. As he did so, the sentry attempted to slam his rifle butt down on Knight's foot, and made partial, painful, contact:

Things were certainly quite disturbing, for the next moment he stuck his bayonet almost through my right thigh. The proceeding was not particularly pleasant, feeling like a sharp burn. But I was almost too surprised to realise fully what had happened, so consequently remained standing where I was. Vaguely I realised that the sentry had withdrawn his bayonet for another thrust, this time evidently intended to enter my body. Glancing down, I saw that my trouser leg was saturated and streaming with blood, which was even welling out of my shoe onto the ground, showing that an artery had been severed ... I now decided that I could abandon my argument without loss of prestige.[12]

After waiting for four hours before the doctor arrived, Knight was taken to a hospital in Hanover. He spent a fortnight there and another fortnight in the camp hospital after his return. Not long after he came back, the commandant was removed, but the prisoners soon concluded that his replacement was from the same mould. Shortly after he had taken over, a group of prisoners were standing near the gate to watch the arrival of a group of new inmates being transferred from another camp. The commandant came out and told them to disperse, which, after an intervention from the interpreter, they slowly began to do. As they started to drift away, on the orders of the commandant (Knight heard him shouting '*los!*"), two sentries came running into the camp, with bayonets fixed, and one pricked Lieutenant Arthur Downes, South Staffs, in the stomach. To prevent the steady pressure from making the slight wound worse, Downes seized the end of the rifle and, jerking the point out, swung it to the side as he turned to walk quickly away. The sentry ran after him and

---

*   Meaning 'Come on!' or 'Charge!'

bayoneted him in the back, puncturing his lung. Downes collapsed and, after passing a very painful night in the camp medical centre, was taken to a hospital in Hanover the following morning, where he eventually recovered. Not content with one assault, the same sentry then tried to bayonet another prisoner, Captain Woodhouse, RFC. Woodhouse managed to jump out of the way and was only nicked. A large crowd started to gather and the atmosphere became tense. It was eventually diffused when the inmates spontaneously started to sing the national anthem. It helped that the tune was the same as that of a popular German patriotic song and so the guards, not realising quite what was happening, also stood still.[13] Another incident occurred a few days later when another RFC officer, Captain Wilson, managed to avoid an attempted bayoneting by jumping out of the way at the last moment. Claude Templer was also nearly bayoneted in this incident, and a *feldwebel* told Knight afterwards that the commandant had inspected the guards shortly afterwards and told them to have their bayonets sharpened.[14] After he had regained his freedom a few months later, Knight provided the details of the sentry who had attacked him as *Landsturmmann* Wilhelm Bornkamp, then living in Barenberg near Hanover.[15] As far as is known, none of those responsible for these actions were ever disciplined.*

In July 1917, the new Hague Agreement came into force, meaning that all those who were serving or who had been sentenced to lengthy terms of imprisonment for escaping offences committed before 4 August would be released. This affected quite a few prisoners in Ströhen, including Gilbert, as well as others serving sentences

---

* Not only Knight but also Gilbert and the two officers who escaped with him from Ströhen, Michael Harrison and Claude Templer, all provided detailed reports on these incidents as well as other examples of very bad conditions and treatment in the camp. Their reports helped to influence the Foreign Office to make sufficiently strong representations that the camp was closed later that year.

elsewhere who were transferred to Ströhen. (These included Lieutenant Geoffrey Formilli, RFC, another inveterate escaper who,
following a court martial, had been sent from Ströhen to Wesel
Fortress in June to serve a three-month term for an attempted
escape, in addition to the five-month reprisal term which he had
yet to undergo. He had been in Crefeld with Gilbert, where they
occupied adjacent cells as they served a preliminary sentence of
solitary confinement.)

So their fertile minds began to develop some embryonic plans for
escape. Gilbert was reunited with Claude Templer, whom he had
known when they were at school together in Paris, and together
with another inmate,* they came up with an idea to escape from the
parcel room. This was situated in a corner of the camp which they
judged was not particularly well guarded. At this stage, Michael
Harrison arrived in the camp. He had met Templer earlier in the
war when they were both imprisoned together in the camp at Burg,
from which Templer had made four unsuccessful escape attempts.[16]
Harrison naturally approached Templer to discuss the possibility of
making another escape, and Templer and Gilbert agreed to include
him in their planning. However, some practical problems arose
with the parcel room and so they started to look elsewhere. Since
Ströhen was intended to be a punishment camp, the space for exercise and recreation was very limited. This also meant that certain
other buildings and facilities such as the guardroom and even the
bathroom had to be located outside the camp – and were just next
to each other. Prisoners were generally only allowed access to a part
of it for an hour every day, from 8.30 a.m. to 9.30 a.m. If it was
possible to find a way of concealing themselves in the building after

---

* In the event, this prisoner did not participate in their escape, and his name is not known with certainty.

washing was completed, and to ensure that their absence would not be noticed, then an escape should be quite straightforward, because they would be outside the wire and beyond the guarding line of sentries. The Germans were aware of this risk and so ensured that a guard was stationed in each of the three rooms in the bathroom area (one containing about half a dozen showers, another the dressing room and the third some heating equipment) throughout the period when it was being used by the prisoners.

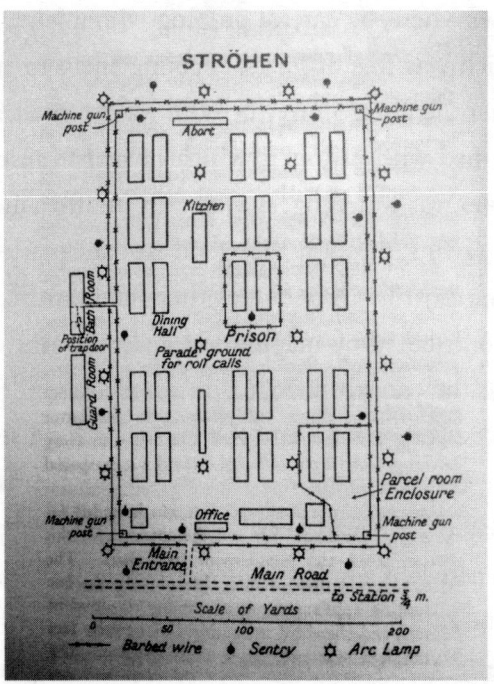

Diagram of the camp at Ströhen, showing the bathroom next to the German guardroom outside the perimeter of the camp on the left.
Courtesy of Nigel Cave.

After a careful and surreptitious survey of both the internal dimensions and those outside, they calculated that the bathroom floor was raised some six or eight inches above the ground. They reasoned that if they could get access to the area underneath and scoop out and shift sufficient earth without being noticed, there should be enough space for them to hide for the rest of the day. This would be no small undertaking and would require some meticulous choreography to obscure their preparatory work, which, because the sentry would never be far away, would necessarily involve the assistance of a large number of fellow prisoners. They selected the dressing room, a small area measuring about twelve by eight feet, and identified a corner where, by careful probing with a wire, they found a location which was free of joists, enabling them to gain access to the area under the floor. Since the room was so small, it was almost always crammed with prisoners which helped to restrict the view of anyone who was watching, as well as to muffle any sounds they made while sawing through the wood to gain entry to the space under the floorboards. Only one of them could work at a time, so the others contributed by helping to block what the sentry might see or hear, as they noisily changed or towelled themselves dry. This work had to be very precise and the trapdoor disguised after every visit, because the Germans were known to inspect the bathroom area every day once it had been used. They prudently carried out some experiments on similar wood in another building and established that the cut could be disguised by rubbing in a small amount of Seccotine (a type of refined liquid fish glue normally used to stick paper together) mixed together with dust.

It did not take too long for the work to be completed. Within four days, they had sawn through the two planks, which was all they needed to remove for the trapdoor. On the following two days, one of them stretched down into the hole to push or scoop away enough earth to enable someone to get down and carry on the excavation with the trapdoor shut above him. This was probably the most dangerous part of the whole project, because of the space required by both the open trapdoor and the digger who was lying on the floor alongside. But other prisoners successfully concealed all this activity from the sentry, and they got away with it. When there was room to work below, one of the group crawled down, completely naked, to carry on scraping the earth aside and compressing it as best he could, to make sufficient space for four of them. Remarkably, by mid-August and within a fortnight, they had already cleared enough room to accommodate three people.

At that stage, on 14 August, their planning was disrupted by three unexpected developments. First, the fourth of their party told the others that he wished to withdraw from the project. He had been advised by one of the senior British officers in the camp that it was not worth taking the risk of escaping. This officer considered that the chances of discovery were high, because the absence of the escapers would be noticed at the *appell* at 6 p.m. and there was a high chance that they would be discovered during the subsequent search. There had been further recent examples of German brutality, and he warned the intending escaper that it was quite possible that they would be bayoneted if they were found under the floorboards. So the man decided to withdraw. His colleagues all understood his reasoning and did not try to dissuade him. However, all three were seasoned escapers, not put off by these risks, and were quite ready to carry on themselves. But the man who had withdrawn offered to do anything he could to help them – and suggested that he could provide a distraction by cutting the wire on the other side of the camp, encouraging the searching Germans to think that the group had escaped by another means. The remaining three thought this an excellent idea and accepted it.[17]

On the same day, the group discovered that two other prisoners had been busy copying their idea to escape from the bathhouse! They were Geoffrey Formilli and Lieutenant L. D. Dalzell McLean, a pilot in the RNAS. The pair had already tried to make a trapdoor elsewhere in the dressing room. However, they had found some bricks which prevented access, so they had abandoned that area, intending to try again elsewhere. It seems extraordinary that they could have got as far as they did without Gilbert, Templer and Harrison becoming aware of what they were up to. The three of them speculated that they had copied the idea and were trying to get out first. Formilli and McLean were adamant that this was not the case.[18] Both of them had escaped before, so knew what they were doing. So it was agreed that the space which Gilbert and his colleagues had already made would be expanded further, necessarily taking a few days longer, and that all five of them would then escape together. And, fortunately, whatever traces may have remained of the first attempt by Formilli and McLean to cut through the floor were not discovered by German searches.

Then, just three days later, Gerald Featherstone Knight, who had sufficiently recovered from the ill-effects of his bayoneting just a few weeks previously, made a successful escape attempt on his own from the bathroom. The technique he used was remarkably imaginative. He was attracted by the bathroom for the same reason as Gilbert and his colleagues, because it was outside the wire. After a careful examination of the area, he worked out that it would be just possible, by standing upright, to fit himself into a small alcove in the shower room, which was about eleven-inches deep and a foot wide and which was set into an area created by a wall and the brickwork of a chimney which protruded into the room. This small space also offered an additional advantage because it was partially concealed behind an empty stove. So Knight concluded that if he was able to build a dummy wall, the decoration of which matched its surroundings, there was a reasonable chance that it would pass a close inspection and would serve to conceal him while he waited until the following night to get away. Those of his colleagues who were aware of what he intended made derisory comments, describing what he was planning as similar to building a doll's house. Their reactions were almost, but not quite, sufficient to discourage him. However, he eventually decided to persist with the idea and put it to the test, regardless of the consequences, if only to prove them wrong. He gained some assistance from an infantry officer who had done a camouflage course and was able to give him more than just moral support. He described the process of construction thus:

The wall was made from cardboard sewn tightly onto a light wooden frame, the whole being made in three sections which, when fitted together, reached the height of eight feet six inches. The top section was fitted with a leather hinge, which allowed the upper half of it to slope back at an angle of forty-five degrees, so that the hiding place should not appear to be hollow. When at last the doll's house was finished, it defied all efforts to whiten it, and seemed to have a rooted objection to being made to resemble the dirty whitewash of the bathroom. I tried melting old whitewash (scraped off the walls) with gum and hot water, but it either fell off when dry or showed the wet cardboard plainly through. Chloride of lime proved equally useless. Only a little white paint was procurable, but this was altogether too smooth and shiny. One day, when the three sections were drying outside on the sand, a German *feldwebel* came along, and enquired if I was making a model aeroplane. When I replied that his surmise was correct, he asked me, with a slow smile, if I intended flying away when the machine was completed. The wicked old creature departed, highly amused at my answer, 'Yes, I hope so.' Certainly many a true word is spoken in jest!

After a week's experimenting with useless colouring mixtures, I was almost in despair when the desired effect was produced by coating the cardboard with a thick cornflour paste, finally toning it down with a mixture of cobwebs and mud.[19]

When he was ready to go a few days later on 17 August, he walked into the bathroom, assisted by others who helped with carrying the cardboard section under their coats and trying to ensure that the flimsy cornflour camouflage did not drop off during their progress. His friends chose a suitable moment, when the sentry's attention was distracted, to fix the wall into place. After the others left, the sentry examined the room to make sure that nothing had been left behind. Knight could not resist the temptation to watch what was happening through a carefully crafted spy hole:

I saw a German standing only a few feet away, with his back to me, puffing a long pipe, his rifle slung over his shoulder. Almost immediately ... he turned and looked in my direction. I promptly shrivelled to nothing, and developed acute suspended animation. I simply dared not breathe, and felt as if my thoughts were becoming audible.[20]

Fortunately, the sentry then turned away, but Knight endured another unpleasant experience shortly afterwards when an NCO came in and searched for soap, which was for the Germans a precious commodity (and therefore often used by prisoners as a bribe).

While this was happening, the wall threatened to fall outwards, but Knight managed to hold on to it without making any noise. Having waited for a few hours until all was quiet,* he emerged from his hiding place and replaced the wall, so that someone else might have a chance to use it later. As he crept towards the window, he kicked over an overturned bucket which he had not seen in the dark, but somehow the noisy clatter did not attract the attention of Germans who were resting in the guardroom close by. Waiting until the sentries were at the furthest points of their beats, he climbed out of a window and, hampered by his pack, fell into a ditch. He still had to cross an area which was illuminated by the bright arc lights shining over the camp, but he negotiated this successfully and headed away over the moor, navigating by the stars because he did not have a compass. He travelled light, taking with him little more than chocolate and biscuits to subsist on.

Knight's journey to Holland lasted ten nights and was full of incident and some very close shaves. While still quite close to the camp, he detected the crouching shapes of guards whom he thought were looking for him, so slid into a deep stream up to his neck and waited for hours until he realised that the shapes were actually stacks of peat cuttings... He also slept (briefly) in a ditch where he intended to lie up during the day, until he was woken by the extremely painful bites of a multitude of wood ants, whose nest he was lying on. He was challenged on several occasions by farmers and labourers whom he met, but fortunately his minimal answers were sufficient to allay suspicion, and narrowly avoided discovery twice when he was hiding in a wood pile near an inhabited cottage

---

* Knight does not describe precisely how his roommates contrived to ensure that his absence was not noticed during the *appell*, but the alarm was not raised until the following morning, by which time he was well away.

and then lying in a stack of corn sheaves close to a further crop which was being cut. He swam two rivers and several canals, and just as his food supply had run out, found that he had crossed the Dutch border without realising it. Though exhausted and starving after his long journey, on the following day he persuaded two officers of the Dutch frontier guard to let him accompany them on a duck shooting expedition right on the border over which he had escaped the previous night. He cheekily asked a German sentry standing on the other side of the canal which marked the border whether they found many escaped prisoners in that area. The sentry was willing to admit that he was tired of the war but did not deign to answer the question about prisoners![21]

Gilbert and his colleagues had not known about Knight's escape plans until after he had left, even though there were others involved in helping to organise it, as there had been with the plan of Formilli and Dalzell McLean. This would have been a reflection of the care which inmates had developed over the years to avoid gossiping, for fear of plans being betrayed. It must have caused some a very unwelcome shock, for Gilbert's party would have been worried that if the Germans discovered how Knight got out, it could damage their prospects of escaping from the same location. This did not happen, and Knight's space was not used again, which suggests that Gilbert and his compatriots arranged to remove the cardboard walls before they were noticed, so that their own escape would not be prejudiced.

Gilbert's party did not wait long before they made their attempt. They chose to do so on 20 August, just three days after Knight.*

---

* This is the date given in Harrison's book. Gilbert's account of his escape in WO 161/96/24/3 gives the date of their departure as the night of 23 August. However, since Knight escaped on 17 August, his journey took ten days (and he wrote in 'Brother Bosch' that Gilbert and his companions arrived in the Dutch quarantine camp four days after he did) and the journey of Gilbert and his group also took ten days – though with an additional night in a hotel before they arrived in Enschede – Harrison's date seems more likely to be the correct one.

The five of them needed assistance so as to be able to bring in their equipment and stores without being observed. They were all installed, with the trapdoor closed above them, by 9 a.m. and were expecting to remain in their hiding place until early the following morning. Since it was the middle of the summer, the reader might imagine how stifling the atmosphere would become in the course of the day and, since there was only one small ventilation hole, how foetid the air would become. Gilbert was the unfortunate one who was the furthest away from the airhole providing this minor source of relief. Gilbert recalled years later that they were extremely cramped and had to lie absolutely flat, with almost no room to move at all.* He counted that Germans came into the room six times during the day, though more often in the search for soap than to examine the room.[22]

Since the guardroom was so close to the bathroom, the hiding prisoners were able to hear the German reaction once their absence was discovered during the *appell* at 6 p.m. Harrison, who was lying closest to the ventilation hole, found that it also served as a spy hole and he could watch as the guard was turned out less than ten yards away. The commandant was clearly and audibly incensed and tramped up and down bellowing orders to search parties – which also included instructions to examine the bathroom, so they could be heard starting to move around overhead. Though just as they did so, there was another roar from the commandant, who summoned all the guards back to the guardroom. Those in hiding assumed that this meant that a clue had been found, presumably the cut wire on the other side of the camp, because the search parties were then

---

* Gilbert visited RAF Wunstorf in Germany in August 1954 to watch the presentation of the Royal Standard to 11 Squadron. As he came in to land there, he recognised below him the outline of Ströhen camp, which had been converted into a rifle range. By an extraordinary coincidence, this was exactly thirty-seven years since he had made his escape. (RAF Museum, DC76/74/504.)

sent off into the surrounding countryside. The relieved feelings of the prisoners at this development can only be imagined...[23]

A small volley of shots was heard at one stage – perhaps two search parties had run into each other. However, things gradually quietened down, and at around 2 a.m., the five of them decided it was time to make their exit. However, to their consternation, they were not able to get out. On their departure, the searching Germans had left the door open, in a position across the trapdoor which made it impossible for the trap to be opened. Fortunately, Gilbert, who was lying just underneath, was able to use his pocket knife and poke it up between the floorboards, so as to prise the door loose and gradually move it away from the position where it was blocking their means of exit from the sardine tin-like surroundings where they had lain for seventeen hours.[24] They had taken the precaution of removing their boots, so as to minimise the possibility of making any noise, and headed off from the camp. Once they were a safe distance away, they put their boots back on and divided up into two parties, with Formilli and McLean making their journey separately. These two walked for seven days and had covered some seventy-five miles of their 85-mile journey before they were recaptured in the village of Sögel, by what McLean described as ill luck.[25]*

Gilbert's group decided to make for the Dutch border as far north as possible, before the River Ems became too wide to swim. They no doubt hoped that since the area was slightly more remote, it might also be less well guarded. Harrison calculated that it would

---

* Their experience after capture was unpleasant. The two were kept for a week in a civilian prison on bread and water and then taken to a military prison in Hanover where they received no food for some time before they were taken back to Ströhen. After spending ten days in the cells, they were informed on 16 September that they had been sentenced to fourteen days of solitary confinement as a punishment for escaping and that the sentence would be dated from the previous day, meaning that they would altogether spent nearly five weeks in solitary. This was a fairly common German practice, and although McLean protested stoutly and repeatedly, it availed him nothing. After more than two years as a prisoner, he was repatriated to Holland in December 1917, while Formilli, who was taken slightly later, spent the rest of the war in captivity.

involve a longer journey, of around 120 miles.* Since they completed it in ten days, this would have been quite an achievement, as they would have been limited by the number of hours when it would have been dark enough to travel and by the need to find a safe hiding place for the following day well before it became light, so they were generally walking only for four hours a night. Moreover, for the first few nights, they made only slow progress and as a result were nearly caught out on the fifth night when to try to make up time, they walked for longer than they should have done and didn't succeed in finding a hiding place until just before dawn. Once it became light, they discovered that they were uncomfortably close to a woodman's cottage, but by then it was too late to move. The occupants owned a dog, so they spent the day rubbing their legs and boots with garlic, to prevent the dog from following their scent if it picked up a trace of them and they had to leave in a hurry. Fortunately, that did not happen until the early evening, when the dog started barking, but they were then able to get away without being noticed.

The agreement which they had reached beforehand about how they would conduct themselves (for example, by arriving at the border in as fit a condition as possible and how they would resolve differences between them) was described in an earlier chapter: they were largely able to keep to it – though the incident with the dog described above shows how easy it could be to make an error of judgement which could prove to be their undoing. They were later to decide to revise the routine and methods which they were using. Because it was summer, they thought that they would not need

---

* Gilbert's figure for the distance they travelled was 130 kilometres or approximately eighty miles. Since they crossed the River Ems near Meppen, their rate of progress was slower than they had planned and they amended their planned route, perhaps Gilbert's figure is likely to be more accurate.

to carry heavy tinned food but would instead hope to forage for fresh vegetables during the night. They therefore just took with them a Tommy cooker, a small saucepan and a large supply of solid methylated spirits. For food, they carried chocolate, biltong, bacon, porridge and a few biscuits. This proved to be sufficient, and though they sometimes found the lack of bulk at meals left them feeling hungry, they were still quite fit and alert when they arrived at the Dutch border.

For the first three nights of their journey, they were struggling to get through the marshes, which hampered their progress. These wet and humid conditions also meant that they were bothered by swarms of mosquitoes. Harrison had prepared for this eventuality and brought with him a sack, instead of a rucksack, in which he could sleep in greater comfort during the day. He occasionally allowed Gilbert and Templer to use it, and so great was their need for sleep that they sometimes both used it at the same time! On the fourth night, there was a heavy thunderstorm, which also slowed them down, and since the rain continued well into the next day, it made for difficult walking conditions for the following night as well. The fifth night was slightly easier, although there were plenty of small rivers or streams to cross, but these did not offer any serious hindrances.

The seventh night was worse, because the terrain was extremely boggy and, eventually, they had to retrace their steps and take another route which went much further south. However, they thought that they had found an ideal location in which to conceal themselves during the following day, in a forest of pine trees which were quite densely packed, near Welte.[26] This proved to be an error, for the following morning, a woodman arrived to prune precisely the area in which they were hiding. They remained as still as possible, but after a few minutes, it became clear that he had spotted them. They decided to try to fool him by pretending that they were tramps and behave as though they had not seen him. Not surprisingly, he soon ran away, and once he had done so, the three got up and raced off in the opposite direction, liberally smearing themselves with garlic and spreading pepper behind them so as to obscure their scent and discourage any dogs from tracking them. They hid in another wood and took great care to conceal themselves, but if they were being pursued and search parties were looking for them, no one came close to where they were hidden.

Thereafter, they decided that they would only walk for four hours each night, from 11 p.m. to 3 a.m., and would then halt in the first suitable place which they found after that. Moreover, they would cut large lumps of turf and keep them to hand, so that they could lie under them and use them for more thorough concealment if there was any risk of discovery. Once that was done, they would sleep until the cold of the early morning woke them up and sleep again as best they could during the heat of the afternoon. After cooking and eating breakfast, they would prepare and cook a midday meal, using whatever vegetables they had foraged. These arrangements seemed to work well, and Harrison commented that their physical condition improved, despite the bad weather which had hampered them.

Their foraging didn't only provide them with vegetables. On one occasion, they found a can of milk left outside a farm. Harrison described the pleasure, as well as the nourishment, which it gave them, for none of them had tasted milk for two or three years. Inspired by their discovery, they looked out for more:

Failing to find any milk in cans, we decided to try our luck milking a cow, but unfortunately the first animal we accosted turned out to be a bull and very much resented the liberty we were taking. When he was fully awake, he made it quite clear that he wasn't going to tolerate our presence any longer, and we only escaped from his field with many torn clothes.[27]

When they later met Knight, he would have enjoyed hearing this story, for he would have told them that he had done much better than them with sourcing supplies of free milk. On his third night out, he had found himself in a field of Holstein cattle and decided to try his luck. However, the cow which he approached took fright and the whole herd started careering around the field, making a frighteningly loud noise and causing him to make off in great haste. Knight learned from his mistake. He found some ripe apples and presented them to the next cow he encountered. She accepted the bribe, and Knight helped himself to as much milk as he could drink. He found compliant and hungry cows on most of the remaining nights of his journey, and they provided a welcome supplement to his diet![28]

Heavy rain continued to cause problems for Gilbert and his companions, as they slowly negotiated their way through boggy country with further obstacles caused by flooded drains. But they persisted and reached the River Ems on the ninth night, at a spot roughly halfway between Meppen and Papenberg.[29] Since they were still in good physical condition, they were able to keep to their resolution not to cross this obstacle as soon as possible, for the border was only six miles away on the opposite side. Instead, they spent time on reconnaissance. During their rest period the following day, they worked out the best route and memorised the features which they would meet, so as to avoid the need to study their maps which would have required their using a torch.

In the evening, they made their way down to the Ems, which at that point was forty-five yards wide. They abandoned their surplus kit and hid it and then undressed. Gilbert and Templer wrapped their clothes in a waterproof sheet which they cut up and stored the bundles in their rucksacks. This gave them some buoyancy. Harrison put his clothes into his sack, which without waterproof protection became very heavy and an encumbrance on his crossing. They all kept their hats on their heads and stored their watches and compasses inside, which must have made an incongruous sight. They completed the crossing – Gilbert and Templer more easily than Harrison – by around midnight and, after dressing, discarded their sacks and rucksacks so as to carry no surplus weight.

Since it would not become light until nearly 5 a.m., they knew that they had plenty of time to cover the last six miles of their journey. Before they left Ströhen, they had been briefed that the ground which they would have to cover would not be patrolled or guarded until they reached the frontier itself. Nonetheless, they decided to take precautions, just in case. So they took turns for one of them to advance ahead of the other two and lie down every thirty yards to take a careful look at what lay in front of them. Harrison observed that since this was their tenth night out, their night vision was probably better than that of sentries, who were never on duty for more than two hours at a stretch. After two miles, their precautions proved justified, for they saw a sentry. Either the information they had been given about sentries was not reliable or the Germans had changed their dispositions. They resolved to continue and to pass as close to him as was reasonable, so as to minimise the chances of running into an unseen neighbour.

As they did so, the moon appeared from behind a cloud and the sky became quite clear and bright. They had no choice but to remain where they were and settle down beside a cabbage patch to wait until it was set, which would be at 2.30 a.m. During this period, they lay flat, with their hands and faces covered. While they were in these positions, with no cover to protect them, two groups of relief sentries (or patrols) walked along a track within five yards of where they lay. Fortunately, they were not observed.

After the moon had set, they resumed their journey. They soon had to climb over a series of wire fences. While they were crossing one of these (which had some rather stiffer wire than the others[30]) only several hundred yards further on from the sentry whom they had managed to avoid, they set off an alarm bell in a cottage close by. This was caused by their leader, and when it happened, the other two quickly crossed the fence as well and then they lay down again to watch the reaction it had caused. A sentry came out of the building and ran along a road about ten yards away from them, presumably to go and rouse the rest of the guards. Once he had passed, they got up and ran further away. They passed another field where horses were grazing, which galloped off making some noise, but fortunately that did not attract attention. At a safe distance, they stopped and saw a line of torches moving along the fence which they had just disturbed, but their lights did not change their direction and come towards them. The three then had to cross a series of quite deep drainage ditches, which were waist deep with water, with some wires strung over them. They could get past these by ducking under the water, so as not to touch the wires in case they were attached to further alarm bells. By this stage, they calculated that they had two more hours of darkness to cover the remaining four miles.

The ground over the next three miles was marshy, which gave some reassurance that it could not be regularly patrolled. Moreover, there was a slight head wind, which would reduce the chances that any sentries in front of them could hear their cautious movements. So they made steady progress, until they came to two sentry huts some sixty yards apart, next to some dry drainage ditches which they crawled carefully through without problem.

At this stage, they wondered whether they might already have crossed the border into Holland, for several of the ditches had banks which might have been dykes, which their maps showed were over the border. But they remained cautious, acknowledging the risk that they might not have travelled as quickly as they had thought, which was an error escapers sometimes made. There had been cases of prisoners who had given themselves up, believing that they had crossed the border while they were still in Germany. Then:

At 4.30 a.m. on 4 September 1917, while in this state of uncertain-ty, I saw what appeared to be a cloud in the west with a perfectly horizontal border. At first there was nothing particularly strange in this sight as it was so dim, but I could soon discern a perfectly cut V in it. For a moment I wondered if the strain had begun to tell on my nerves, then I realised that it was a bank about thirty feet high with a gap in it.

The dyke was in Holland without a shadow of a doubt.

As the reality dawned on me, I formed my idea of 'the finest view in Europe'. [31]

The area was not guarded, so they climbed the dyke, swam across the canal behind it and walked for a further two hours to put Germany as far behind them as possible. They reached the village of Terhaar, where they enjoyed what must have been the best breakfast of their lives. They also found a post office, from where they sent a postcard to the commandant at Ströhen to inform him of their safe arrival and to request that their mail be forwarded.[32] Given that the commandant was known to be prone to an easily aroused apoplexy, the reader may care to imagine how he would have reacted to receiving that message – assuming that his staff were brave enough to show it to him...

Harrison had been captured in October 1914, Templer in December 1914 and Gilbert in December 1915. Between them, the three of them had spent nearly eight years in German captivity. Also between them, they had made twenty attempts to escape before they succeeded – Templer held the record here with thirteen escapes.[*]

The Dutch then took them into custody, and because they had crossed the border by unorthodox means, sent them to the quarantine camp of Enschede, where they met Gerald Featherstone Knight again. That must have been quite a reunion.

The three successful escapers – Templer, Gilbert and Harrison – with Knight (who had arrived a few days earlier) sitting in front of them, in the Dutch quarantine camp at Enschede.

---

[*] Only Harold Medlicott, with fourteen attempts, had tried more often.

EPILOGUE

That should perhaps have been the end of the story. But it wasn't, quite.

Gilbert and his compatriots had little opportunity to enjoy their first taste of freedom that day. Since there was insufficient time to move them to the quarantine camp at Enschede, the Dutch authorities arranged for them to spend the night in the town of Coevorden. Once there, and despite their protests, they were taken to a police jail and locked into a cell which had minimal furnishings – a bucket and some straw as well as a couple of German deserters. After they had continued to complain vociferously for several hours, a Dutch officer arrived and agreed that they could spend the night in a hotel provided they gave their parole,* which they willingly provided. Thus, temporarily reprieved, they had a chance to do some shopping and buy new clothes and change out of the filthy garments they had worn during their journey out of Germany.

---

* Their word of honour not to escape.

Gilbert in the clothing he wore for his escape.

Perhaps because they were unaccustomed to exercising freedom of choice, they ended up buying ladies blouses instead of the shirts which they thought they were getting – these were too small in almost every respect, though they could just about be buttoned up. And this minor discomfort certainly did not prevent them from enjoying a champagne dinner that night.

But then they were taken to Enschede, which, apart from the pleasure of their reunion with Gerald Featherstone Knight, had little to offer and few comforts. Most of the other inmates were German deserters or Russian escapers. They were stuck there for eleven days before the Consul General in Rotterdam heard of their situation. He arranged for them to be released and taken to Rotterdam, where they were put straight onto a ship to await the departure of the next convoy to Britain. After a number of British vessels, some carrying diplomatic couriers or classified correspondence, had been intercepted and captured by the Germans, it became standard for all British shipping crossing the Channel to have naval escorts. So the ships needed to be ready to sail as soon as such escort vessels became available. Since this could happen with little warning, passengers were embarked immediately on their arrival in the port but then had to wait on board for several days or even longer before their departure.

It's worth trying to imagine what it must have been like for these young men. After years in German captivity, they had enjoyed one night of freedom, before being stuck in quarantine and then transferred to further confinement on a ship in circumstances which gave them no chance to celebrate or even let off a bit of steam and behave as normal human beings. A. J. Evans, who had successfully escaped with Buckley, wrote:

Escaped PoWs are usually most irresponsible people and should not be trusted as normal individuals till they have had time to settle down. I was no exception. Peter* was not pleased when I returned to visit him and borrowed (without asking) one of the squadron cars and went off to Paris for a couple of days.[1]

The three of them had no chance to do that. But – not surprisingly – they got bored, left the ship and went into Rotterdam for the day to amuse themselves, bringing back a few bottles of champagne they shared with some other equally frustrated fellow passengers. Ernest Maxse, the Consul General in Rotterdam, took a dim view of such

---

* Evans was returning to his old squadron, 16 Squadron, then commanded by Peter Portal, who was appointed Chief of the Air Staff in October 1940, remaining in the post until the end of the war, when he became Lord Portal of Hungerford.

disregard for regulations and complained to the Foreign Office. He wrote that they had left the ship without his permission, that the master of the ship had reported that they had purchased an unnecessarily large supply of liquor while on shore and that he had one or two minor difficulties on board. Subsequent reporting suggests that this was not entirely accurate, for they had not been informed that they had to remain on the ship – and moreover that they had told a member of the Consulate General staff what they intended to do and were not instructed that they should remain on board. The desk officer in the Prisoners of War Department in the Foreign Office accepted that Gilbert and his colleagues did not know that they were supposed to stay where they were. Robert Vansittart, the deputy head of the department, sensibly added: 'I don't think it is worth pursuing the correspondence. If we send this back to Maxse he will retort and the argument will go on. It will do no good and will do the officers harm – and my sympathies are entirely with them.'

However, Lord Newton disagreed and instructed that the War Office should be informed. Once they returned to Britain, the three miscreants were sternly told that they should submit statements explaining their actions. They may have been good conspirators when they were prisoners of war (when they needed to ensure that what they told the Germans was consistent), but in this case they were not, for their statements provided quite different and somewhat contradictory explanations of what had happened. But perhaps by then they were past caring about this sort of bureaucracy. At any rate, the War Office sensibly decided to take matters no further, passed the statements back to the Foreign Office and the matter was dropped.[2]

By that stage, too, they had better things to do. After their return to London in mid-September, Gilbert was awarded his VC by King

George V in a ceremony held outside Buckingham Palace less than a fortnight later on 26 September. (A photograph of this moment is included in the plate section.) All three of them then had separate audiences with the King.* Both Gilbert and Harrison were later awarded an MC for the courage which they had shown in escaping from German captivity. Had Templer survived the war, he would certainly have been awarded an MC as well, but the award could not be made posthumously. Gilbert was one of fourteen members of the Royal Air Force whose awards were gazetted in December 1919, 'in recognition of gallantry in escaping from captivity whilst Prisoners of War'.[3]

Photo of Gilbert (left) *lined up with all the others who received their VCs on 26 September, standing next to a widow whose husband had won it posthumously.*
Source: The Times History and Encyclopaedia of the War, *October 1917*

---

* There is a short film in the Imperial War Museum archives which includes a clip showing Gilbert being awarded his VC: https://www.iwm.org.uk/collections/item/object/1060005428. The film is rather misleadingly entitled 'War Office Official Topical Budget 318-2' and Gilbert is described as 'Lieutenant Install'. The segment showing the ceremony when eight VCs were conferred, including his investiture and subsequent discussion with some French officers, can be found after one minute and fifty seconds.

Escapes such as these certainly helped to boost the morale of the prisoners still incarcerated when word got back to them and to encourage more of them to believe that escape was feasible. But not everyone. A. J. Evans wrote about attitudes in general:

The older and senior inhabitants were convinced that escape was not possible and any thoughts of escape were strongly discouraged not only because escape would inevitably bring discomforts and restrictions on the rest of the camp, but particularly on those older members who were not fit to contemplate a march of some hundreds of miles through an alien land. It must be said that there was absolutely no official encouragement of attempting to escape such as MI9 propagated in the Second World War. The fact that many prisoners in the First World War gravely deteriorated mentally and physically as a result of four years behind barbed wire, while very few suffered from 'barbed wire' disease in the Second, is a convincing demonstration that attempts to escape should be encouraged in spite of any discomforts which they may entail.[4]

We now know that there was indeed some official encouragement and practical assistance provided from 1917 onwards, but it was never likely to be on a scale which would make a significant difference. Though its effects would have been incremental, through the encouragement which news of successful escapes also provided. For example, Lawrence Wingfield, who got out of Ströhen not long after Gilbert and made it across the border thanks to the helpful intervention of an Alsatian sentry, wrote: 'One of the prisoners at Ströhen was Lieutenant Gilbert Insall VC, and it was his successful escape in August of that year which really inspired me to have a go. I could not imagine that we were to meet again so soon.'[5]

On their return, all three officers, as well as Knight, were debriefed straight away about their experiences as prisoners of the Germans, by several departments in the War Office, including MI1a. All four of them went into some detail about the conditions at Ströhen, the bayoneting of Knight and Downes and other mistreatment, including the restrictions on correspondence.[6]* Harrison went further and wrote several additional letters to the Foreign Office about extra aspects of mistreatment, such as lengthy periods of detention without trial. He quoted one example involving Captain William Loder-Symonds, RFC, who had been detained for over six months while awaiting trial for offences supposedly committed in the course of an escape, without any date being given for his court martial. Harrison suggested the Foreign Office might consider reprisals as a means of helping to prevent recurrences of such treatment in future.[7]

Such specific and first-hand accounts which closely corroborated each other provided powerful evidence. The Foreign Office took them seriously, and Newton wrote to the Army Council recommending that they consider requesting the Germans to arrange the immediate transfer of all British officers from Ströhen to other camps, the transfer of the commandant and the punishment of the German sentries who had been involved in the bayoneting of Knight and Downes. To bolster his case, he also referred to recently received information about the detention in cells of around twenty British officers at Ströhen because the German authorities had

---

* A few weeks later, they were all also required to complete statements regarding the circumstances of their capture.

discovered that a tunnel had been dug but were unable to ascertain who had been responsible. Strong representations were made to the Germans, which achieved results, because Ströhen was closed not long afterwards. One is bound to wonder whether it might not have been so much the British protests, however well justified they may have been, which brought about this outcome, as the fact that a significant number of prisoners succeeded in escaping from Ströhen in the late summer and early autumn of 1917 and so the Germans might have decided that it would be better to transfer the rest of them elsewhere. But however the Germans reached their decision, it was a welcome one. The British prisoners were transferred to Holzminden, though they discovered to their chagrin that Niemeyer had also been transferred there as commandant.* But at least violent acts against these prisoners did not continue.

After the war, the Treaty of Versailles in 1919 had some harsh political and economic consequences for Germany, which was forced to accept guilt for having caused the war in the first place, to pay war reparations to all Allied countries which had fought against it, to surrender colonies in Africa, Asia and the Pacific, to cede territory to other nations like France and Poland and to reduce the size of its military. Given the climate which existed at that time, the reader might expect that there would also have been some significant judicial consequences for those who had been responsible for the mistreatment of those held captive in German prison camps.

However, this was not the case. There were several reasons for this. First, many of those who were thought to bear the greatest responsibility for these crimes could not be found and were never tracked down. The Niemeyer brothers, for example, just vanished.

---

* Though the prisoners did get their own back on him there too, by organising the tunnel escape the following year, when twenty-nine prisoners got out and ten avoided recapture and made it home.

Cecil Blain, who was one of those who escaped from Holzminden, went back to Germany to try to locate the brothers, but he did not succeed.[8] Another serious obstacle was that Articles 228–30 of the Treaty of Versailles, which allowed for the extradition and trial of suspected German war criminals, were not realistically enforceable. This meant that any war crimes trials which the Allies wished to bring to court would have to be held in Germany, which was tantamount to allowing the Germans to mark their own homework – with predictable results.

Initially, the Allies submitted a list of 853 people to the German government under Article 228. The number which the British finally brought to court at the Leipzig War Crimes Trials in 1921 was reduced to seven. The French did little better. It is worth considering two specific examples – concerning the typhus epidemics in Wittenberg (see Chapter 5) and Kassel-Niederzwehren, where there was ample compelling evidence of the number of fatalities caused by negligence and lack of care – in a little more detail to see how the judicial process was skewed. The British and French established a German commission of inquiry led by Dr Walther Schücking, a renowned international legal expert, to examine what happened and who was responsible. Despite the fact that the evidence of the chief German doctor at Wittenberg, Dr Aschenbach, largely corroborated the British accusations, the commission did not take any evidence from British prisoners who had been in the camp and found against the British case. The French, therefore, decided to go a stage further and brought the commandant of the Kassel-Niederzwehren camp, Major General Benno Kruska, and the chief of the guard, Lieutenant General Hans von Schack, to court. The outcome was the same: the key French witness, an Alsatian serving in the German Army, was accused of being a traitor and key evidence was ignored. The court concluded that the French had no evidence to support their case.[9]

There were some convictions at Leipzig but only of relatively minor cases, usually involving physical assault, which, in the three British cases that succeeded, led to sentences of between six and twelve months' imprisonment:

> Including the cases not related to the treatment of prisoners, the court heard six cases brought at the instigation of the British, which resulted in five convictions, five prosecutions brought by the French, which resulted in one conviction, and one case brought by the Belgians, which resulted in an acquittal.[10]

The Times correspondent described the trials as 'a scandalous failure of justice'.[11] Others agreed, too. Legal experts at the Inter-Allied Commission recommended that in view of the bias shown by the German court, the cases which remained should be heard elsewhere, and they suggested that Allied governments should themselves take over the responsibility for organising such a move. The British government did not accept this – at least, not publicly, for it wanted to put this phase behind it and to begin to work towards normalising relations with Germany. A motion in the House of Commons to debate the trials was defeated.[12] Perhaps the last word on this sorry tale should be given to Sir Eyre Crowe, the Permanent Under-Secretary in the Foreign Office, during a meeting with the German Ambassador a few months later in February 1922:

> The Ambassador thought that it was not his duty to discuss the alleged leniency of the sentences. He could not go behind the

judicial decision. The sentences were in accordance with German law, which had to be impartially applied.

I remarked that although this was not the point immediately at issue, I felt it impossible to refrain from observing what a mistake had apparently been made by the Allied Governments when agreeing to the trial of the culprits by a German court, and accepting the assurances of the German Government that they could absolutely rely on full justice being done. It was impossible, I thought, to convince opinion in this country that the sentences imposed by the court represented justice.[13]

After a busy few weeks in London being debriefed, Gilbert was given leave. In fact, because he had not fully recovered from the injury caused by the shell fragment, he was given three months' medical leave as respite and did not then report for duty until early in 1918. He returned to Paris to meet his family, and Jack took him to see K, who by then had been promoted to commandant. They had, not surprisingly, plenty to talk about. *Le Commandant* K, not for the first time, provided Jack with a slight surprise:

My brother fished out a small pocket diary to refresh his memory concerning the name of a certain Frenchman he had known in one of the camps he had been in. He was seated some five or six feet away from the Commandant, with K's paper-strewn desk between them. I was at the opposite corner, and all I could see, as Gilbert riffled over the pages of the little book, was a cluster of meaningless hieroglyphics.

'Oh yes,' said Gilbert, 'it was Captain So-and-So.' Did K know what became of him?

K thought for a moment and then, I believe, said that the Captain was still a prisoner, after one or two unsuccessful attempts. This was followed by a pause, broken by K.

'As to your two other queries, I can tell you—' and he switched to two other totally different subjects. My brother looked very puzzled.

'But I only mentioned the one about—'

'I know,' replied K with a sly smile, 'but I could not help seeing what you had written down there,' indicating the diary on Gilbert's knee. He turned to me and added: 'It is an accomplishment, if that is the word, that I frequently find rewarding.'

I had to agree, but could not help wondering how many times I had had occasion to consult my own scribbled notes when visiting K's little sanctum, and my own handwriting is so much easier to read than Gilbert's fearful scrawl.[14]

What of Gilbert's fellow escapers? Both Harrison and Templer rejoined their regiments. The authorities were not keen to allow escaped PoWs to return to the front where they had originally been captured, because of the likely unwelcome consequences if they were captured again. They would only do so if the officer concerned specifically requested it in writing. Both did that. As a result, Michael Harrison rejoined the Royal Irish Regiment on the Western Front in December 1917 and remained with them until the Armistice, though he was slightly wounded in the spring of 1918. After the creation of the Irish Free State, the regiment was disbanded and he transferred to the Royal Tank Corps. During the Second World War, he joined MI9 and ran training courses, where he lectured on escape and evasion. Claude Templer also rejoined his regiment, 1/Gloucesters, also on the Western Front, in March 1918. He was killed by a stray shell on 4 June 1918, when the company he com-manded was returning from a raid on the German trenches. He had been a war poet of some distinction and was twenty-three when he died. Gerald Featherstone Knight died of cancer in October 1919, shortly after the book describing his experiences as a prisoner had been published.

As for the close members of Gilbert's family who had supported him, his father, Gilbert senior, continued to practise as a dentist in Paris until his retirement, when he returned to England, where he died in 1946. Jack left the RAF and worked for the Imperial War Museum (IWM), setting up the Royal Air Force section of the museum, which was first located at the Crystal Palace and opened in 1920. He subsequently moved to the Air Historical Branch of the Air Ministry, making a major contribution to writing the history of the war in the air. Once this fairly massive enterprise was conclud-ed, he moved back to the IWM in the 1930s. Almost immediately after the outbreak of war in September 1939, he was seconded from the IWM to work for Section D of SIS, in a section creating black propaganda* for dissemination to neutral countries. A few months later, when the Special Operations Executive (SOE) was formed in the summer of 1940, the staff of Section D were transferred to it and Jack continued doing the same job in SO1, later moving to Electra House when the Political Warfare Executive took over most of SO1's responsibilities. He subsequently went to work for a section in the Admiralty dealing with boom defence, but he

---

* Black propaganda is intended to give the impression that it was created by those whom it is supposed to discredit, in contrast to grey propaganda, which does not identify its source, and white propaganda, which does not disguise its origins at all. So the process of spreading black propaganda was altogether more complicated, which explains why SOE continued to retain responsibility for disseminating it throughout the war, even after responsibility for creating it had been passed to the Political Warfare Executive.

remained on the IWM's payroll throughout the war, somewhat to their discomfiture.[15]

Jack in 1968.

After Cecil's demobilisation, he did a bewildering variety of jobs – from raising chickens to acting as an interpreter for the Foreign Office during conferences – as well as other diverse roles, none of which led to anything permanent. Then, in 1933, Jack, who was temporarily working for the Royal Air Force Ex-Officers' Employment Bureau, passed on to Cecil an advertisement from the Passport Control Office (a front for the Secret Intelligence Service), which was looking for mature ex-RAF officers with a knowledge of languages. Cecil, who was fluent in German and French, put his name forward, was offered a job and immediately posted to Berlin, where he found himself working for Frank Foley, head of the SIS station there. Much of Cecil's work involved examining the visa applications of those who wished to travel through or to British territory. Many were German Jews wishing to emigrate to Palestine or to Britain.* He was in the last group from the embassy to leave Berlin after war had been declared on 3 September 1939.

Visa for Lothar Auerbach, signed by Cecil in February 1939. Cecil arranged for the whole of his family to leave Germany.

The impact of some of what he did lives on. Some years ago, I received a letter from a German who was living in Britain. It came from Jurgen Schweining, who told me that his father-in-law Lothar Auerbach and his family, one of whom was now his wife, had received a visa in February 1939 for entry into Britain. He added that this visa, which had been signed by C. D. Insall, had probably saved their lives. He asked whether I was related to C. D. Insall, as he

---

* For further details of the work which Cecil and his colleagues were doing in Berlin, see Michael Smith, *Foley: The Spy Who Saved 10,000 Jews* (London: Biteback, 2016).

wished to contact the family to thank them for what Cecil had done for them.

I put him in touch with Cecil's son.

Gilbert began flying straight away on his return to duty in January 1918, though he took no further part in the war. He spent time as an instructor and was then posted to command 50 Squadron at Bekesbourne in Kent. The squadron had been stationed there for most of the war, with the task of defending London and south-eastern England against Zeppelin and later Gotha bombing raids. He was given a permanent commission in the RAF after the war, in August 1919, and remained in the RAF for the rest of his career.

Gilbert with VC medal ribbon and wound stripe, in early 1918.
Source: The Great War Aviation Society

Gilbert did have one further operational posting in a war zone, though on a rather smaller scale, when he was posted to Iraq to command 70 Squadron. During this period, he received a Mention in Despatches for 'distinguished services rendered in connection with operations against the Akhwan* in the Southern Desert, Iraq, between November 1927 and May 1928'.[16] He retired with the rank of group captain in 1945. During his flying career, he was one of the first to use aerial photography for archaeological purposes and discovered the Bronze Age site at Woodhenge in 1925. Later, during a posting to Egypt, he obtained pictures taken through clear water of what were then thought to be Cleopatra's baths near Aboukir Bay. He also traced the lost course of the Median Wall near Habbaniyah, in Iraq, which linked the Tigris and Euphrates rivers.[17] In October 1969, his house in Scrooby, in Yorkshire, was broken into and his medals were stolen. They were found and returned to him by the police in 1970. However, the incident affected his health, which gradually declined thereafter. He died in RAF Nocton Hall Hospital in February 1972. He was cremated, and his ashes were interred in the churchyard of All Saints Church in Nocton, where a headstone was placed. A funeral service for him took place at St Nicholas Church in Bawtry, near his home. It was held with full military honours – a fitting tribute, as it gave a chance for the Royal Air Force to say farewell to him and to acknowledge the extent of his achievements during thirty years in their service.

---

* The Akhwan, now known as the Ikhwan, raided southern Iraq from Saudi Arabia in November 1927. They raided Kuwait in early 1928, too, and 70 Squadron undertook a series of retaliatory operations against them.

ENDNOTES

CHAPTER 1: A MAD OLD BUGGER

1   A. J. Insall, *Observer: Memoirs of the RFC, 1915–18* (London: William Kimber, 1970), p. 185.
2   Oliver Wilkinson, *British Prisoners of War in First World War Germany* (Cambridge: Cambridge University Press, 2017), p. 104, quoting Carl. P. Dennett, an American Red Cross Commissioner, *Prisoners of the Great War: Authoritative Statement of Conditions in the Prison Camps of Germany* (Boston: Houghton Mifflin Company, 1919).
3   John Lewis-Stempel, *The War Behind the Wire: The Life, Death and Glory of British Prisoners of War, 1914–1918* (London: Weidenfeld & Nicolson, 2014), p. xx, quoting *Statistics of the Military Effort of the British Empire during the Great War, 1914–1920*, p. 329. Lewis-Stempel points out that this is the figure for British servicemen, including the Royal Navy and Royal Naval Division, who died in Germany and occupied France and Belgium. The figure for PoW fatalities for British and empire PoWs combined in Germany/France combined is 12,425. Of these, 447 were officers and 11,978 other ranks.
4   Janet Morgan, *The Secrets of the Rue St Roch: Intelligence Operations Behind Enemy Lines in the First World War* (London: Allen Lane, 2004), p. 366.
5   M. R. D. Foot and J. M. Langley, *MI9: Escape and Evasion 1939–1945* (London: Biteback, 2011), pp. 22–3, 26.
6   Ibid., p. 5.
7   Lewis-Stempel, p. xviii and p. 304.
8   Ibid., p. 195.
9   Peter Anderson, *I, That's Me: The Memoir of Officer-Escaper Major Peter Anderson DSO & Bar, 1914–1919* (Ottawa: CEF Books, 2009), p. 161.
10   A. J. Evans, *Heir to Adventure: Notes for an Autobiography* (unpublished), p. 108. Imperial War Museum (hereafter IWM), LBY 88/1271.
11   IWM, G. E. D. Greene, private papers, 20775.
12   IWM, L. A. Wingfield, private papers, 18776.
13   A. J. Evans, *The Escaping Club* (Stroud: Fonthill Media, 2012), p. 144.
14   The National Archives (hereafter TNA), WO339/68239. For comparison, Gilbert's certificate is on WO 339/53916.
15   *Observer*, pp. 11–12.
16   TNA, WO 339/53916.
17   Family papers.
18   Family papers.

CHAPTER 2: TAKING TO THE SKIES

1   A. J. Insall, 'Lighter than Air', a paper written for the Air Historical Branch, TNA, AIR 1/727/152/4.
2   David Henderson, *The Art of Reconnaissance* (London: John Murray, 1916), pp. 11–12.
3   S. W. Roskill (ed.), *Documents Relating to the Naval Air Service, Volume 1* (London: Navy Records Society, 1969), p. 14. John H. Morrow, *The Great War in the Air* (Washington: Smithsonian Institution Press, 1993), p. 21, quoted by Michael Sheil, 'Does the performance of the Royal Flying Corps at Cambrai in 1917 illustrate

that the demands for aerial observation had led to the development of air power?' (MA Thesis, University of Wolverhampton, 2018), p. 13.

4   Insall, quoting a letter by Lieutenant Cammell, TNA, AIR 1/727/152/4.
5   Sheil, p. 14.
6   Peter Dye, *The Bridge to Airpower: Logistics Support for Royal Flying Corps Operations on the Western Front, 1914–1918* (Annapolis: Naval Institute Press, 2015), p. 24. Dye's book provides an excellent description of how the remarkable growth of the RFC and the RAF was achieved.
7   Barker, p. 13.
8   Dye, p. 21.
9   *Observer*, pp. 13–14.
10 Arthur Gould Lee, *Open Cockpit* (London: Grub Street, 2013), p. 1.
11 Peter Dye, 'RFC Bombs and Bombing 1912–1918', *Royal Air Force Historical Society Journal*, No. 45, 2009, pp. 9–10.
12 Sheil, p. 19.
13 Lee, p. 2.
14 TNA, AIR 1/166/15/150/1.
15 Dye, p. 195.
16 *Observer*, p. 21.
17 Ibid., p. 24.
18 Ibid., p. 28.
19 Lee, pp. 23–4.
20 *Observer*, pp. 35–6.
21 Ibid., p. 37.
22 Correspondence held by 11 Squadron, RAF.

CHAPTER 3: EARLY DAYS ON THE FRENCH FRONT

1   Peter G. Cooksley, *The Royal Flying Corps 1914–1918* (Stroud: Spellmount, 2014), pp. 118–19, Sheil, p. 20.
2   Documents held by 11 Squadron, RAF.
3   Cooksley, pp. 24–5, Dye, p. 37.
4   Dye, p. 37.
5   E. Spears, *Liaison 1914: A Narrative of the Great Retreat* (London: Weidenfeld, 1999), p. 137, quoted by Sheil, p. 24.
6   Barker, p. 41.
7   *Observer*, p. 64.
8   Ibid., p. 47.
9   Barker, p. 39.
10 Cooksley, p. 122.
11 11 Squadron history. TNA, AIR 1/688/21/20/11.
12 *Observer*, p. 59.
13 11 Squadron documents.
14 See, for example, George Wilson, 'The Flight to the North, No. 2 Squadron – Farnborough to Montrose in 1913', *Royal Air Force Historical Society Journal*, No. 34.
15 Ibid.
16 *Observer*, p. 44.
17 Ibid., pp. 54–5.
18 Ibid., pp. 51–2.
19 11 Squadron documents.
20 Robert Hughes-Chamberlain, IWM interview 1971, 23153, quoted by Joshua Levine, *On a Wing and a Prayer* (London: Collins, 2008), pp. 163–4.
21 Barker, p. 58.
22 TNA, AIR 1/1219/205/4/2634/7.
23 TNA, AIR 1/166/15/150/1.
24 11 Squadron documents.
25 TNA, AIR 1/1219/205/4/2634/5.
26 *Observer*, pp. 89–99.
27 11 Squadron documents.
28 IWM, A. J. Insall private papers, documents 14685.
29 RAF Museum AC 72/20/15.

30 Ibid.
31 Note by Brancker, 6 September 1915. TNA, AIR 1/1209/204/5/2634/6.
32 IWM, A. J. Insall private papers, documents 14685.
33 TNA, WO 372/24/32607.
34 TNA, AIR 1/1209/205/5/2634/4.
35 *Observer*, pp. 74–5.
36 Willy Coppens, *Days on the Wing* (London: John Hamilton, 1932).
37 Ibid., p. 97.
38 IWM, HR/01/1940/024.

CHAPTER 4: WINNING A VC, CAPTURE – AND INTERROGATION

1   RAF Museum archive, AC72/20/15.
2   *Observer*, p. 100.
3   Family papers.
4   *Observer*, p. 102.
5   Fifth Supplement to the *London Gazette* of 21 December 1915, 23 December 1915, Number 29414, pp. 12,797–8.
6   Documents held by 11 Squadron, RAF.
7   Robert Hughes-Chamberlain, interview with the IWM, 1971, reference 23153, quoted by Roderick Bailey, *Forgotten Voices of the Victoria Cross* (London: Ebury Press, 2010), pp. 40–43.
8   Ibid., pp. 40–43.
9   Major Frederick Powell, interview with the IWM, 1973, reference 4523, quoted by Bailey, p. 43.
10 Ralph Barker, *The Royal Flying Corps in France: From Mons to the Somme* (London: Constable, 1994), p. 164.
11 Peter G. Cooksley and Peter F. Batchelor, *VCs of the First War: The Air VCs* (Stroud: History Press, 2014), pp. 82–3.
12 Ibid., p. 119.
13 Wilkinson, p. 30, quoting Alon Rachamimov, 'Arbiters of Allegiance: Austro-Hungarian Censors during World War I', in Pieter M. Judson and Marsha L. Rozenblit (eds), *Constructing Nationalities in East Central Europe* (New York: Berghahn Books, 2005), p. 167.
14 TNA, AIR 1/501/15/331/1.
15 Ibid.
16 Ibid.
17 Family papers.
18 IWM, Captain Herbert Ward papers, 22831.
19 German archives. GLAK, 456 F7/94.
20 TNA, WO 161/96/24.
21 Vincennes Historical Archives Centre, Paris, AI 1A 149.
22 'Intelligence Officer Fourth Army questionnaire, *Gefangenenvernehmung* (Prisoner interrogation)', January 1916, GLAK, 456 F6/229. This was a booklet printed by the German army's official printers E. S. Mittler & Sohn, suggesting that it had formal approval.
23 Bavarian Krigsarchiv (hereafter KA), Munich, KA 3 ID, Bd 79, *Nachrichtenwesen*, 2 April 1916, quoted by Christopher Duffy, *Through German Eyes: The British and the Somme 1916* (London: Phoenix, 2006), p. 43.
24 Duffy, quoting Walter Nicolai, *The German Secret Service* (London: Stanley Paul & Co., 1924), p. 185.
25 Nicolai, p. 185.
26 Bundesarchiv Militärarchiv, PH 3/554, folios 105–109.
27 Bennett family papers.
28 IWM, I I. T. Kemp, private papers, 14489.
29 Bundesarchiv Militärarchiv, PH 3/554, folios 105–109.
30 GLAK, 456 F7/94.
31 GLAK, 456 F7/107, folio 201–202.
32 GLAK, 456 F7/107, folio 198.
33 See, for example, Kemp's account in IWM, private papers, 14489.
34 *Observer*, p. 149.

CHAPTER 5: DEATH – AND LIFE – IN PRISON CAMPS

1   Wilkinson, p. 3, quoting Matthew Stibbe, *British Civilian Internees in Germany: The Ruhleben Camp, 1914–1918* (Manchester: Manchester University Press, 2008), p. 17.
2   Heather Jones, *Violence against Prisoners of War* (Cambridge: Cambridge University Press, 2011), pp. 19–27.

3 Ibid.
4 Matthew Stibbe, 'Prisoners of War During the First World War', *German Historical Institute London Bulletin*, Volume XXVIII, No. 2 (November 2006), p. 56.
5 Jones, p. 106.
6 Robert Fryson, 'The Douglas Camp Shootings of 1914', *Proceedings of the Isle of Man Natural History and Antiquarian Society*, Volume XI, No. 1 (2000), quoted by John Yarnall, *Barbed Wire Disease: British & German Prisoners of War, 1914–19* (Stroud: Spellmount, 2011), pp. 56–9.
7 *The Times*, 14 April 1915, p. 8.
8 *The Times*, 26 April 1915, p. 9.
9 See, for example, his speech in the House of Commons, Hansard, 27 April 1915, Column 573.
10 Yarnall, pp. 91–5.
11 Kenneth Steur, *Pursuit of an 'Unparalleled Opportunity': The American YMCA and Prisoner of War Diplomacy among the Central Power Nations during World War I, 1914–1923* (Columbia: Columbia University Press, Gutenberg-e Home), chapter 19, p. 3.
12 Yarnall, p. 103.
13 TNA, CAB 24/63/75.
14 Stibbe, pp. 49–50.
15 Wilkinson, p. 110, quoting TNA, FO 383/156, Comparison of diet in HM Prisons and that in Germany for PoWs.
16 Yarnall, p. 136, quoting Richard B. Speed III, *Prisoners, Diplomats and the Great War: A Study in the Diplomacy of Captivity* (Connecticut: Greenwood Press, 1990), p. 77.
17 Lewis-Stempel, p. 86.
18 Ibid., p. 86.
19 Wilkinson, p. 109.
20 Hansard, 15 March 1917, Volume 91, Column 1267.
21 Lewis-Stempel, pp. 89–94.
22 Jones, p. 96.
23 Yarnall, p. 68.
24 Lewis-Stempel, p. 79.
25 Jones, p. 97.
26 Yarnell, p. 69.
27 Ibid., p. 102.
28 Lewis-Stempel, pp. 82–3.
29 TNA, WO 161/96/11.
30 TNA, WO 161/96/20.
31 F. W. Harvey, *Comrades in Captivity: A Record of Life in Seven German Prison Camps* (Coleford: Douglas McLean, 2010).
32 TNA, 161/96/73.

CHAPTER 6: GETTING OUT – AND GETTING HOME
1 Lewis-Stempel, p. 3.
2 Ibid.
3 War Office, *Manual of Military Law* (London, 1907), pp. 269, 299.
4 Vincennes Historical Archives Centre, Paris, AI 1A 149 SHD GR7N 143.
5 TNA, CAB 24/53/15.
6 *Manual of Military Law*, p. 269.
7 Duncan Grinnell-Milne, *Wind in the Wires and an Escaper's Log* (Barnsley: Pen & Sword, 2016), pp. 206–7.
8 TNA, WO 161/96/12.
9 Lewis-Stempel, p. 190.
10 TNA, WO 161/95/66.
11 TNA, WO 161/96/102.
12 S. P. MacKenzie, 'The Ethics of Escape: British Officer PoWs in the First World War', *War in History*, Volume 15, No. 1 (January 2008), pp. 10–13.
13 M. C. C. Harrison and H. A. Cartwright, *Within Four Walls: A Classic of Escape* (Barnsley: Pen & Sword, 2016), p. 12, quoted by MacKenzie, p. 3.
14 Evans, *Heir to Adventure*, p. 100, IWM, LBY 88/1271.
15 A. J. Evans, *Escape and Liberation, 1940–1945* (London: Hodder & Stoughton, 1945), p. 11.
16 TNA, CAB 161/96/30 and WO 161/96/31.

17 TNA, AIR 1/726/129/1.
18 Evans, *Heir to Adventure*, p. 101.
19 Harrison and Cartwright, p. 148.
20 For a vivid and entertaining account of their escape, see Anselme Marchal, 'Hoodwinking the Germans', in Rachel Bilton (ed.), *Prisoners and Escape: Those Who Were There* (Barnsley: Pen & Sword, 2017), pp. 81–97.
21 Leeds University, Liddle Collection, diary of H. H. McWilliam, RN, p. 29. McWilliam wrote that he had tried several times to establish a code with home, but he had not succeeded.
22 *Observer*, p. 185.
23 Ibid., p. 195.
24 Ibid., pp. 149–50.
25 Lawrence Wingfield, in J. R. Ackerley (ed.), *Escapers All* (London: Bodley Head, 1932), p. 296, and Harrison and Cartwright, p. 152.
26 Harrison and Cartwright, p. 152.
27 IWM, Lamb documents, 11110.
28 Evans, *Heir to Adventure*, p. 108.
29 Bennett family papers.
30 Family papers.
31 J. A. L. Caunter, *13 Days: The Story of an Escape from a German Prison* (London: G. Bell & Sons, 1918), https://www.gutenberg.org/cache/epub/35724/pg35724-images.html
32 Lewis-Stempel pp. 52–3.
33 *Supplement to the Edinburgh Gazette*, 2 February 1920.
34 M. R. D. Foot, *MI9: Escape and Evasion 1939–1945* (London: Biteback, 2011), p. 279, quoting James's account, TNA, WO 208/3242, pp. 157–65.
35 Anderson, pp. 96–146.
36 TNA, 161/95/8.
37 IWM, Ward documents, 22831.
38 TNA, AIR 1/2395/297/1.
39 IWM, Ridley papers, 17954.
40 IWM, Blain papers, 20169.
41 Ibid.
42 Liddle Collection, McWilliam papers.
43 TNA, AIR 1/2251/209/54/29 and WO 161/96/4.
44 TNA, AIR 1/2251/209/54/29 and WO 161/96/11/1, though the latter states that the fine was twenty-five marks.
45 McWilliam papers.
46 Lewis-Stempel, pp. 190–91.
47 Foot, *MI9*, pp. 275–6.
48 E. H. Keeling, 'An Escape from Turkey in Asia', *Blackwoods Magazine*, Volume 203, No. 1231 (May 1918), and H. C. W. Bishop, *A Kut Prisoner* (London: Bodley Head, 1920), https://www.gutenberg.org/cache/epub/34069/pg34069-images.html
49 M. A. B. Johnston and K. D. Yearsley, *Four-fifty miles to Freedom: The Adventures of Eight British Officers in their Escape from the Turks* (London: Blackwood, 1919), https://www.gutenberg.org/files/50425/50425-h/50425-h.htm
50 TNA, CAB 24/28/12.
51 Ackerley, p. 269.
52 Gunther Plüschow, 'Escaping from England', in Ackerley, pp. 261–78. See also Anton Rippon, *Gunther Plüschow: Airman, Escaper and Explorer* (Barnsley: Pen & Sword, 2009).
53 TNA, CAB 23/4/1.
54 Hermann Tholens, 'Rendezvous with a Submarine', in Ackerley, pp. 281–8.

CHAPTER 7: TUNNELLING OUT OF HEIDELBERG

1 Lieutenant J. W. Reynolds, TNA, WO 161/85/53.
2 TNA, WO 161/96/24.
3 TNA, WO 161/96/24.
4 Captain C. Hutchinson, TNA, WO 161/95/53.
5 TNA, WO 383/268.
6 McWilliam papers.
7 *Observer*, p. 191.

8 IWM, Q 31452.
9 *Observer*, pp. 195–7.
10 Family papers.
11 Ibid.
12 *Observer*, p. 190.
13 McWilliam papers.
14 Ibid.
15 Ibid.
16 Family papers.

CHAPTER 8: SOLITARY CONFINEMENT AND A BRIEF ESCAPE FROM CREFELD

1 Miscellaneous No. 7 (1915) (Cd 7817), HMSO.
2 Hansard, Volume 18, speech by Lord Newton on 15 March 1915, Columns 747–8.
3 TNA, WO 161/96/3.
4 McWilliam papers.
5 TNA, FO 383/272, 1894084.
6 Letter from Gilbert to his father, 28 April 1917. TNA, FO 383/267/111938.
7 TNA, WO 161/96/24.
8 *The Times*, 3 July 1917.
9 TNA, FO 381/267.
10 TNA, FO 383/271.
11 US Naval War Department Digital Commons, 'Agreement between the British and German Governments concerning combatant prisoners of war and civilians' (The Hague, 14 July 1918).
12 *Observer*, pp. 186–7.
13 Ibid., p. 192.
14 Ibid., p. 192.
15 Harvey, pp. 133–6.
16 Family papers and *Observer*, pp. 192–3.
17 Family papers.
18 TNA, WO 161/96/33.

CHAPTER 9: WHAT DID INTELLIGENCE SERVICES DO TO HELP ESCAPERS?

1 Keith Jeffery, *MI6: The History of the Secret Intelligence Service 1909–1949* (London: Bloomsbury, 2010), p. 209.
2 Jeffery, p. 56. See also Michael Smith, *Six: The Real James Bonds 1909–1939* (London: Biteback, 2011), p. 64.
3 Jeffery, p. x.
4 TNA, ADM 196/63/100.
5 McWilliam papers.
6 *Observer*, pp. 198–201.
7 TNA, 'History of Intelligence (B)' by Colonel Drake, WO 106/45.
8 Harrison and Cartwright, *Within Four Walls*, pp. 159–61.
9 Smith, quoting German complaints in January and April 1918, and Agnew (position unknown) letter to Vansittart, June 1918, p. 65.
10 TNA, AIR 1/1976/204/273/48.
11 Ibid.
12 RAF Museum, X0004/1429/010/011.
13 McWilliam papers.
14 TNA, AIR 1/1976/204/273/48.
15 Evans, *The Escaping Club*, pp. 116–17.
16 Harrison and Cartwright, p. 235.
17 McWilliam papers, 25 June 1917.
18 McWilliam papers, 12 July 1917.
19 TNA, FO 383/268, 118291.
20 McWilliam papers, 30 October 1917.

CHAPTER 10: SUCCESS AT LAST!

1 Lewis-Stempel, p. 72.
2 Harvey, p. 207. The editor, Nigel Cave, believes that the chapter on Ströhen in this book was written by Captain George Holloway of the West Yorkshire Regiment, attached to the 8th Northumberland Fusiliers.

3   Harrison and Cartwright, *Within Four Walls*, p. 223.
4   Harvey, p. 207.
5   TNA, WO 161/96/24/3.
6   TNA, FO 383/271.
7   Ibid.
8   TNA, FO 381/271.
9   Harvey, p. 208.
10 Grinnell-Milne, pp. 323–4.
11 Ibid, pp. 329–40.
12 TNA, WO 161/96/25 and Gerald Featherstone Knight, *'Brother Bosch': An Airman's Escape from Germany* (London: Heinemann, 1919), p. 23.
13 Harrison and Cartwright, p. 224.
14 Knight, pp. 25–6.
15 TNA, WO 161/96/25.
16 Martin W. Bowman, *Voices in Flight: Escaping Soldiers and Airmen of World War 1* (Barnsley: Pen & Sword, 2017), p. 199.
17 Harrison and Cartwright, pp. 225–30, Claude Templer, *Poems and Imaginings* (London: Forgotten Books, 2018), p. 18.
18 TNA, WO 161/96/47/3.
19 Knight, pp. 29–30.
20 Ibid., p. 30.
21 Knight, pp. 29–44.
22 TNA, WO 161/96/24/3.
23 Harrison and Cartwright, pp. 224–33.
24 *Observer*, p. 201.
25 TNA, WO 161/96/47/3.
26 TNA, WO 161/96/27.
27 Harrison and Cartwright, pp. 242–3.
28 Knight, pp. 31–2.
29 TNA, WO 161/96/27.
30 Ibid.
31 Harrison and Cartwright, p. 248.
32 Templer, p. 20 and Lewis-Stempel, pp. 243–4.

EPILOGUE

1   Evans, *Heir to Adventure*.
2   TNA, FO 383/310.
3   *London Gazette*, 16 December 1919, www.thegazette.co.uk/London/issue/31691/supplement/15615.
4   IWM, LBY 88/1271, A. J. Evans.
5   IWM, Wingfield papers, 18776.
6   Their main reports are all in TNA, WO 161/96/23-27. See also AIR 1/501/15/331/1, which contains MI1a extracts from additional reports by both Gilbert and Knight, as well as other RFC officers such as Buckley and Formilli.
7   TNA, FO 383/310.
8   Lewis-Stempel, p. 272, quoting Max Arthur, *We Will Remember Them: Voices from the Aftermath of the Great War* (London: Orion, 2009), p. 43.
9   Jones, pp. 107–9 and 219–21.
10 Yarnall, p. 194.
11 *The Times*, 27 May 1921, p. 11.
12 Lewis-Stempel, p. 287.
13 Yarnell, p. 196, quoting *Documents on British Foreign Policy 1919–1929, Series I, Volume 20* (London: HMSO, 1976), p. 375.
14 *Observer*, p. 202.
15 IWM, HR/01/1940/024.
16 TNA, WO 339/53916. This appeared in the *London Gazette* on 15 March 1929.
17 RAF Museum, DC76/74/504.

ACKNOWLEDGEMENTS

Although this book is dedicated to my grandfather Jack, other members of my family have also contributed to my research – not least Gilbert and Cecil, who have left papers describing many of the activities which I have been able to write about. They were three remarkable brothers.

I am also grateful to Nick and Kat Insall (Gilbert's grandchildren) and to Lynn Insall (Cecil's daughter-in-law), who have provided me with a wealth of documentary material as well as some truly historic photographs.

I have had much valuable support from the Gerry Holdsworth Special Forces Charity and also from the Department of War Studies at King's College London.

But there are many others who have helped me as well. Laurie Vaughan and James Vaughan, daughter and grandson of James Bennett, one of those who successfully escaped from Holzminden, guided me through the treasure trove of the papers and recordings which James left. Veronika, Giles and Simon McWilliam gave me some helpful information, as well as permission to draw on Henry's papers which described and vividly illustrated his part in the escape with Gilbert from Heidelberg. Sarah Paterson, a curator at the Imperial War Museum, gave me much useful guidance and pointed me towards some of Jack's personal correspondence which I would otherwise have probably missed. Dr Alastair Noble, a historian at the RAF Air Historical Branch, has given me plenty of assistance throughout my research and sourced some valuable documents. Dr Tony Cowan, a significant military historian of the First World War, tracked down in an archive in Karlsruhe the records of the German interrogations of Gilbert and Thomas Donald, his observer, which were among the relatively few military records that survived the Second World War. David Anderson has provided much expert advice and help on aviation-related matters.

Jean-Philippe Miller-Tremblay spent much time helping me in the search to identify the mysterious (and clearly very effective) *Capitaine* K. We didn't succeed, but he unearthed some interesting consolations instead.

Antony McCord, Sarah Mahaffy, Nick Carrick and Mick Smith all painstakingly read my drafts and provided some very sensible advice and insights: the final result has benefited from their help.

There are others who have contributed in all sorts of different ways, whether by informing me of medical matters or aviation techniques of which I was ignorant, pointing me towards obvious things which I had overlooked or coming up with some very helpful suggestions. They include Kiko Rutter, Chris Puddle, Roderick Bailey, Patrick Baty, Jim Beach, Charles Bland, Jonathan Boff, Jock Bruce, Michael Dobbs, Stuart Hadaway, Gavin Hood, Heather Jones, Janet Morgan, Spencer Stevens and Jack's great-grandson Ali Insall.

There have been many staff in various archives who have done much to help me over the past couple of years. They include Jane

Rosen and some of her colleagues at the Imperial War Museum, Qona Wright at the University of Leeds Special Collections, Lucia Wallbank at the RAF Museum and the staff at the National Archives.

Mark Graham and Emma Webber, of XI(F) Squadron, RAF Coningsby, kindly arranged for me to visit the squadron and to explore the wealth of the material they hold in their history room.

It's been a pleasure to be working again with James Stephens at Biteback and with his editors Olivia Beattie and Ella Boardman. The finished text is the better for their careful and thorough attentions.

And finally, I wish to express my thanks to my wife Nonie for the patience and forbearance she has shown throughout the time I have taken to research and write this book. It isn't easy living with a preoccupied author, and I am truly grateful to her for her support and encouragement.

SELECT BIBLIOGRAPHY

There has been a considerable number of books written about these subjects or important aspects of them. I have only included here those books which I have cited in the text or which I consider to be especially relevant.

Ackerley, J. R., *Escapers All* (London: Bodley Head, 1932)

Anderson, Peter, *I, That's Me: The Memoir of Officer-Escaper Major Peter Anderson DSO & Bar, 1914–1919* (Ottawa: CEF Books, 2009)

Ashcroft, Michael, *Heroes of the Skies: Amazing True Stories of Courage in the Air* (London: Headline, 2012)

Bailey, Roderick, *Forgotten Voices of the Victoria Cross* (London: Ebury, 2010)

Barker, Ralph, *The Royal Flying Corps in France: From Bloody April 1917 to Final Victory* (London: Constable, 1995)

Barker, Ralph, *The Royal Flying Corps in France: From Mons to the Somme* (London: Constable, 1994)

Bascomb, Neal, *The Escape Artists: A Band of Daredevil Pilots and the Greatest Prison Breakout of WW1* (London: John Murray, 2019)

Bilton, Rachel (ed.), *Prisoners and Escape: Those Who Were There* (Barnsley: Pen & Sword, 2017)

Bowyer, Chaz, *Airmen of World War I: Men of the British and Empire Air Forces in Old Photographs* (London: Arms & Armour, 1975)

Bowyer, Chaz, *For Valour: The Air VCs* (London: Grub Street, 1992)

Caunter, J. A. L., *13 Days: The Chronicle of an Escape from a German Prison* (London: G. Bell & Sons, 1918). See also https://www.gutenberg.org/cache/epub/35724/pg35724-images.html

Cooksley, Peter G., *The Royal Flying Corps, 1914–1918* (Stroud: Spellmount, 2014)

Cooksley, Peter G. and Batchelor, Peter F., *VCs of the First World War: The Air VCs* (Stroud: History Press, 2014)

Coppens, Willy, *Days on the Wing* (London: John Hamilton, 1932)

Cowan, Tony, *Holding Out: The Germany Army and Operational Command in 1917* (Cambridge: Cambridge University Press, 2023)

Duffy, Christopher, *Through German Eyes: The British and the Somme 1916* (London: Phoenix, 2007)

Durnford, Hugh, *The Tunnellers of Holzminden* (Cambridge: Cambridge University Press, 1920)

Durnford, Hugh, *Tunnelling to Freedom and Other Escape Narratives from World War 1* (Mineola, NY: Dover Publications, 2004)

Dye, Peter, *The Bridge to Airpower: Logistics Support for Royal Flying Corps Operations on the Western Front, 1914–1918* (Annapolis: Naval Institute Press, 2015)

Evans, Alfred J., *Escape and Liberation, 1940–1945* (London: Hodder & Stoughton, 1945)

Evans, Alfred J., *The Escaping Club* (Stroud: Fonthill Media, 2012)

Foot, M. R. D. and Langley, J. M., *MI9: Escape and Evasion 1939–1945* (London: Biteback, 2011)

Fry, Helen, *MI9: A History of the Secret Service for Escape and Evasion in World War Two* (London: Yale University Press, 2020)

Gudgin, Peter, *Military Intelligence: The British Story* (London: Arms & Armour, 1989)

Hanson, Neil, *Escape from Germany: The Greatest PoW Break-Out of the First World War* (London: Doubleday, 2011)

Harding, Geoffrey, *Escape Fever* (London: John Hamilton, 1935)

Hardy, Jocelyn L., *I Escape! The Great War's Most Remarkable PoW* (Barnsley: Pen & Sword, 2014)

Harrison, M. C. C. and Cartwright, H. A., *Within Four Walls: A Classic of Escape* (Barnsley: Pen & Sword, 2016)

Harvey, Frederick W., *Comrades in Captivity: A Record of Life in Seven German Prison Camps* (Coleford: Douglas McLean, 2010)

Harvey, Frederick W., *Gloucestershire Friends: Poems from a German Prison Camp* (London: Sidgwick & Jackson, 1917). See also https://www.gutenberg.org/files/66362/66362-h/66362-h.htm

IWM, *Most Secret: MI9 Escape and Evasion Devices* (London: Imperial War Museum, 2023)

Insall, A. J. (Jack), *Observer: Memoirs of the RFC, 1915–18* (London: William Kimber, 1970)

Insall, A. J. (Jack) and others, *The Western Front: Then and Now* (London: George Newnes, 1938)

Jackson, Robert, *The Prisoners, 1914–1918* (London: Routledge, 1989)

Jones, Heather, *Violence against Prisoners of War in the First World War: Britain, France and Germany, 1914–1920* (Cambridge: Cambridge University Press, 2011)

Knight, Gerald Featherstone, *'Brother Bosch': An Airman's Escape from Germany* (London: Heinemann, 1919). See also https://www.gutenberg.org/files/27229/27229-h/27229-h.htm

Langley, J. M., *Fight Another Day: The True Story of the World War II Escape Networks Operated by MI6* (London: Collins, 1974)

Lee, Arthur Gould, *Open Cockpit: A Pilot of the Royal Flying Corps* (London: Grub Street, 2013)

Levine, Joshua, *On a Wing and a Prayer* (London: Collins, 2008)

Lewis, Cecil, *Sagittarius Rising* (London: Greenhill Books, 2003)

Lewis-Stempel, John, *The War Behind the Wire: The Life, Death and Glory of British Prisoners of War, 1914–18* (London: Weidenfeld & Nicolson, 2014)

Mackersey, Ian, *No Empty Chairs: The Short and Heroic Lives of the Young Aviators Who Fought and Died in the First World War* (London: Weidenfeld & Nicolson, 2013)

Morgan, Janet, *The Secrets of the Rue St Roch: Intelligence Operations Behind Enemy Lines in the First World War* (London: Allen Lane, 2004)

Moynihan, Michael (ed.), *Black Bread and Barbed Wire: Prisoners in the First World War* (London: Leo Cooper, 1978)

Neave, Airey, *Saturday at MI9: The Classic Account of the WW2 Escape Organisation* (Barnsley: Pen & Sword, 2010)

Nicolai, Walter, *The German Secret Service* (London: Stanley Paul and Co., 1924)

Paterson, Sarah, *Tracing Your Prisoner of War Ancestors: The First World War: A Guide for Family Historians* (Barnsley: Pen & Sword, 2012)

Phillimore, Lord Godfrey, *Recollections of a Prisoner of War* (London: Edward Arnold, 1930)

Rippon, Anton, *Gunther Plüschow: Airman, Escaper and Explorer* (Barnsley: Pen & Sword, 2009)

Roe, F. Gordon, *The Bronze Cross* (London: P. R. Gawthorn, 1945)

Ryan, Mark, *The Hornet's Sting: The Amazing Untold Story of Britain's Second World War Spy Thomas Sneum* (London: Piatkus, 2009)

Smith, Michael, *Six: The Real James Bonds 1909–1939* (London: Biteback, 2011)

Sweetman, John, *Cavalry of the Clouds: Air War Over Europe 1914–1918* (Stroud: Spellmount, 2010)

Templer, Claude, *Poems and Imaginings* (London: Forgotten Books, 2018)

Tredrey, F. D., *Pioneer Pilot: The Great Smith Barry Who Taught the World to Fly* (London: Peter Davies, 1976)

Van Emden, Richard, *Prisoners of the Kaiser: The Last PoWs of the Great War* (Barnsley: Pen & Sword, 2000)

Wilkinson, Oliver, *British Prisoners of War in First World War Germany* (Cambridge: Cambridge University Press, 2017)

Williams, Eric, *The Wooden Horse* (London: Collins, 1979)

Williams, W. Alister, *Against the Odds: The Life of Group Captain Lionel Rees VC* (Wrexham: Bridge Books, 1989)

Yarnall, John, *Barbed Wire Disease: British & German Prisoners of War, 1914–1919* (Stroud: Spellmount, 2011)

INDEX